DAILY LIFE IN

THE INDUSTRIAL UNITED STATES, 1870–1900

The Greenwood Press "Daily Life Through History" Series

The Age of Charlemagne
John J. Butt

The Age of Sail
Dorothy Denneen Volo and James M. Volo

The American Revolution
Dorothy Denneen Volo and James M. Volo

The Ancient Egyptians
Bob Brier and Hoyt Hobbs

The Ancient Greeks
Robert Garland

Ancient Mesopotamia
Karen Rhea Nemet-Nejat

The Ancient Romans
David Matz

The Aztecs: People of the Sun and Earth
David Carrasco with Scott Sessions

Chaucer's England
Jeffrey L. Singman and Will McLean

Civil War America
Dorothy Denneen Volo and James M. Volo

Colonial New England
Claudia Durst Johnson

Early Modern Japan
Louis G. Perez

18th-Century England
Kirstin Olsen

Elizabeth England
Jeffrey L. Singman

The Holocaust
Eve Nussbaum Soumerai and Carol D. Schulz

The Inca Empire
Michael A. Malpass

Maya Civilization
Robert J. Sharer

Medieval Europe
Jeffrey L. Singman

The Nineteenth Century American Frontier
Mary Ellen Jones

The Nubians
Robert S. Bianchi

The Old Colonial Frontier
James M. Volo and Dorothy Denneen Volo

Renaissance Italy
Elizabeth S. Cohen and Thomas V. Cohen

The Soviet Union
Katherine B. Eaton

The Spanish Inquisition
James M. Anderson

Traditional China: The Tang Dynasty
Charles Benn

The United States, 1920–1939: Decades of Promise and Pain
David E. Kyvig

The United States, 1940–1959: Shifting Worlds
Eugenia Kaledin

The United States, 1960–1990: Decades of Discord
Myron A. Marty

Victorian England
Sally Mitchell

World War I
Neil M. Heyman

DAILY LIFE IN

THE INDUSTRIAL UNITED STATES, 1870–1900

JULIE HUSBAND AND JIM O' LOUGHLIN

The Greenwood Press "Daily Life Through History" Series

GREENWOOD PRESS
Westport, Connecticut • London

Library of Congress Cataloging-in-Publication Data

Husband, Julie.
    Daily life in the industrial United States, 1870–1900 / Julie Husband and Jim O'Loughlin.
        p. cm. — (The Greenwood Press "Daily life through history" series, ISSN 1080–4749)
    Includes bibliographical references and index.
    ISBN 0–313–32302–X
    1. United States—Social life and customs—1865–1918. 2. United States—Social conditions—1865–1918. 3. Industrialization—Social aspects—United States—History—19th century. 4. United States—Biography. I. O'Loughlin, Jim. II. Title. III. Series.
    E168.H965   2004
    973.8—dc22   2004012697

British Library Cataloguing in Publication Data is available.

Copyright © 2004 by Julie Husband and Jim O'Loughlin

All rights reserved. No portion of this book may be reproduced, by any process or technique, without the express written consent of the publisher.

Library of Congress Catalog Card Number: 2004012697
ISBN: 0–313–32302-X
ISSN: 1080–4749

First published in 2004

Greenwood Press, 88 Post Road West, Westport, CT 06881
An imprint of Greenwood Publishing Group, Inc.
www.greenwood.com

Printed in the United States of America

The paper used in this book complies with the Permanent Paper Standard issued by the National Information Standards Organization (Z39.48–1984).

10   9   8   7   6   5   4   3   2   1

Contents

Acknowledgments   vii

Chronology   ix

Introduction: "I Felt Everything Get Bigger
and Go Quicker Every Day"   1

1. The City   19

2. The Railroad   47

3. The Factory and Organized Labor Responses   71

4. Housework, Houses, and Women at Home   99

5. Childhood and Family Life   121

6. Consumer Culture   151

7. Leisure and Entertainment   177

8. Education and Health Care   201

9. Religious and Civic Life   223

Conclusion: Not the Gilded Age   243

Glossary   245

Works Cited   249

Index   263

Acknowledgments

We would like to thank our colleagues at the University of Northern Iowa who offered support in many ways. Trudy Eden, Suzy Freedman, and John Smith all shared their expertise at crucial moments. UNI's Graduate College supported our research with a summer fellowship and the College of Humanities and Fine Arts enabled us to travel to archives in Rochester, NY, and Hartford, CT. UNI's Department of English Language and Literature and its chairperson, Jeffrey Copeland, have provided us with a supportive environment in which to work. Two graduate research assistants, Olga Cherchesova and Maria Goltsova, were tremendously helpful and likely learned more about the American industrial era than they ever thought they would when they traveled from St. Petersburg, Russia.

Several curators gave us invaluable assistance in locating specialized studies and materials. Christopher Bensch from the Strong Museum in Rochester, New York; Gordon C. Beeton from the Slater Mill Historic Site in Pawtucket, Rhode Island; Clare Sheridan at the American Textile History Museum in Lowell, Massachusetts, and several librarians at the Harriet Beecher Stowe Center in Hartford, Connecticut, helped us to navigate their extensive archives.

We were fortunate to have both Kevin Ohe and Michael Hermann of Greenwood Publishing Group work with us as editors on this project. Elizabeth Kincaid's expertise in navigating the photo archives of the Library of Congress also helped smooth out the production process.

Finally, we want to thank our families: Thomas Connolly, who was our most enthusiastic reader and who shared his memories of New Hampshire's textile factories; our parents, Bert Husband, Kathleen Husband, Jim O'Loughlin, and Joan O'Loughlin, who pitched in with babysitting, encouragement, and unfailing confidence in us; our son Nicky, who has prodded us with questions about "that time you write about," and our daughter Devin, whose birth coincided with the beginning of this project and whose own joy continuously reminds us of the pleasures of daily life.

Chronology

1862   Congress passes the Homestead Act and the Transcontinental Railroad Acts.

1865   The Confederacy surrenders, ending the Civil War.

1869   The first transcontinental railroad is completed.

1871   Approximately one-third of Chicago is destroyed by the Great Chicago Fire. Rebuilding efforts lead to extensive urban planning and attention to infrastructure.

1873   Panic of 1873 leads to a four-year depression.

Comstock law passes, outlawing the dissemination of drugs, medicines, instruments, or information regarding contraception or abortion through the mail.

1874   Women's Christian Temperance Union founded.

Massachusetts limits work days to 10 hours for women.

The Chautauqua Movement begins at Lake Chautauqua, New York.

1877   End of Congressional Reconstruction in the South. Through intimidation, most African Americans are prohibited from voting and new, oppressive laws are passed.

U.S. Army defeats Sioux rebellion, crushing last substantial Native American resistance to white settlement of the West.

A railroad strike develops into a nationwide action known at "The Great Uprising."

1878   The American Cereal Co. begins to sell Quaker Oats, the first mass-marketed breakfast food.

1879   Thomas Edison invents the Incandescent Electric Lamp, the first indoor electric lighting.

1881   Booker T. Washington establishes Tuskegee Institute.

Joel Chandler Harris publishes *Uncle Remus: His Songs and Sayings*.

1882   John D. Rockefeller organizes the Standard Oil Trust.

The Chinese Exclusion Act restricts the immigration of Chinese laborers and makes Chinese residents ineligible for U.S. citizenship.

1883   Clocks across the United States set to uniform railroad time.

1884   Mark Twain publishes *Adventures of Huckleberry Finn*.

1886   Sears, Roebuck & Company begins their mail-order business.

The last remaining non-standard railroad ties shift to standard gauge.

1887   The "safety bicycle," with equal-sized wheels, is developed in England.

1889   Jane Addams opens Hull-House in Chicago.

Congress passes the Sherman Anti-Trust Act.

1890   Jacob Riis publishes *How the Other Half Lives*.

1891   *The Ladies Home Journal* says it will no longer accept patent medicine advertising.

1892   Strike at Carnegie Steel Company in Homestead ends when Pennsylvania militia intervenes. Strike breakers reopen plant and the union is crushed.

1893   World's Columbian Exhibition in Chicago attracts one-third of the U.S. population.

Frederick Jackson Turner delivers the paper "The Significance of the Frontier in American History," declaring the frontier closed and predicting more frequent labor unrest.

Financial panic of 1893 leads to severe depression.

Milk stations in New York City open, offering affordable, pasteurized milk for babies.

Stephen Crane publishes *Maggie: A Girl of the Streets.*

1894 Pullman strike in Chicago leads to national strike among railroad workers. U.S. troops are called out to defeat the strikers.

Boston begins systematic medical inspections of school children.

First kinetoscope, or motion picture, show opens in New York.

1896 The Monarch Bicycle Company sells 50,000 bicycles, compared with 1,200 sold in 1893.

Abraham Cahan publishes *Yekl: A Tale of the New York Ghetto.*

1897 The Supreme Court reverses course and declares that the Sherman Anti-Trust Act applies to the railroads.

1898 When the U.S. battleship *Maine* explodes in a Havana port, U.S. newspapers accuse the Spanish colonial government of attacking U.S. interests and the U.S. goes to war.

1899 Kate Chopin publishes *The Awakening.*

1900 The U.S. population reaches 76 million, nearly double its population in 1870.

Eastman Kodak introduces the Brownie Camera, which is so affordable and easy to use that it is marketed to middle-class children.

Theodore Dreiser publishes *Sister Carrie.*

Introduction:
"I Felt Everything Get Bigger and Go Quicker Every Day"

For many, such as the Lithuanian immigrant quoted above, the industrial era meant a movement from farm to factory; it also meant faster transportation, bigger buildings, more crowded cities, and more fluid populations. American cities grew at unprecedented rates as immigrants and rural Americans alike came in search of new opportunities. Chicago, the nation's railroad hub and fastest growing city, grew from a town of 100,000 in 1860 to a city of 1,000,000 by 1890 (Lichtenstein et al. 29). Mechanization and the division of labor transformed artisan laborers into factory operatives. The same forces took many forms of production out of the home and made shopping for mass-produced items a crucial part of women's work. An unprecedented boom in railroad construction provided cheap transportation for people and products throughout the nation. New forms of leisure became an important part of Americans' lives. This book examines the daily lives of a wide variety of Americans directly impacted by industrialization between 1870 and 1900.

In order to give readers a rich sense of the experiences of those most directly affected by industrialization, we reproduce the firsthand accounts of urban newsboys, upper-middle-class professionals, Jewish journalists, Irish domestic workers, German philanthropists, street children, housewives, newlyweds, steel workers, textile operatives, railroad brakemen, and a host of other "ordinary" Americans living in extraordinary times. Because our focus is on the urban and industrializing United States, the lives of agricultural people during the period are given little attention. Although New England farmers, western pioneers and southern sharecroppers experienced changing living conditions, their compelling stories are largely outside the scope of this book.

When writing of a time when there were so many technological innovations, there is a temptation to focus on the latest devices that changed the ways in which people lived. However, to do so would be misleading because it would misrepresent the experiences of the majority of Americans who were working class. The average annual salary of non–farm workers between 1870 and 1900 never exceeded $500, which was considered the minimum earnings a family needed to survive. Fully 40 percent of industrial workers lived below the poverty line and another 45 percent lived just above it in the 1880s (Trachtenberg in Giamo 14). Consequently, the average nonfarm household had to have one or more children earning wages or had to have at least one boarder. For such families, many of the day's new inventions—from indoor toilets to electric lights—were out of reach. Our purpose is to describe a wide range of experiences while recognizing that the majority of Americans were working class.

The first three chapters following this introduction—"The City," "The Railroad," and "The Factory and Organized Labor Responses"—describe large-scale developments that had an unprecedented impact on the ways in which people lived their daily lives. Chapters 4 through 6—"Housework, Houses, and Women at Home," "Childhood and Family Life," and "Consumer Culture"—focus primarily on changes and continuities in the home life of Americans. Chapters 7 through 9 examine how Americans lived their public lives during the industrial era. "Entertainment and Leisure, "Education and Health Care," and "Religious and Civic Life" follow daily life in industrial America's communities and neighborhoods.

This introductory chapter, however, takes a different approach by outlining some of the major national and international issues of this period. Daily life did not take place apart from these developments, and seemingly distant happenings often had a huge impact on the individual choices people made. This introduction briefly explores some of the most significant aspects of industrial era American history: the role of the United States in the world, the effects of immigration, controversies between capital and labor, and federal government policies.

THE UNITED STATES IN THE WORLD

The United States had one of the fastest growing economies in the world in the 1870–1900 period. No other country of the same size grew more rapidly in terms of population or capital. Other countries, notably Britain and France, had experienced industrialization earlier, but in the late nineteenth century, the United States had the most dynamic economy in the world. In world affairs, the United States grew increasingly difficult to challenge and increasingly willing to intervene in international affairs.

Introduction: "I Felt Everything Get Bigger and Go Quicker Every Day"

For many, such as the Lithuanian immigrant quoted above, the industrial era meant a movement from farm to factory; it also meant faster transportation, bigger buildings, more crowded cities, and more fluid populations. American cities grew at unprecedented rates as immigrants and rural Americans alike came in search of new opportunities. Chicago, the nation's railroad hub and fastest growing city, grew from a town of 100,000 in 1860 to a city of 1,000,000 by 1890 (Lichtenstein et al. 29). Mechanization and the division of labor transformed artisan laborers into factory operatives. The same forces took many forms of production out of the home and made shopping for mass-produced items a crucial part of women's work. An unprecedented boom in railroad construction provided cheap transportation for people and products throughout the nation. New forms of leisure became an important part of Americans' lives. This book examines the daily lives of a wide variety of Americans directly impacted by industrialization between 1870 and 1900.

In order to give readers a rich sense of the experiences of those most directly affected by industrialization, we reproduce the firsthand accounts of urban newsboys, upper-middle-class professionals, Jewish journalists, Irish domestic workers, German philanthropists, street children, housewives, newlyweds, steel workers, textile operatives, railroad brakemen, and a host of other "ordinary" Americans living in extraordinary times. Because our focus is on the urban and industrializing United States, the lives of agricultural people during the period are given little attention. Although New England farmers, western pioneers and southern sharecroppers experienced changing living conditions, their compelling stories are largely outside the scope of this book.

When writing of a time when there were so many technological innovations, there is a temptation to focus on the latest devices that changed the ways in which people lived. However, to do so would be misleading because it would misrepresent the experiences of the majority of Americans who were working class. The average annual salary of non–farm workers between 1870 and 1900 never exceeded $500, which was considered the minimum earnings a family needed to survive. Fully 40 percent of industrial workers lived below the poverty line and another 45 percent lived just above it in the 1880s (Trachtenberg in Giamo 14). Consequently, the average nonfarm household had to have one or more children earning wages or had to have at least one boarder. For such families, many of the day's new inventions—from indoor toilets to electric lights—were out of reach. Our purpose is to describe a wide range of experiences while recognizing that the majority of Americans were working class.

The first three chapters following this introduction—"The City," "The Railroad," and "The Factory and Organized Labor Responses"—describe large-scale developments that had an unprecedented impact on the ways in which people lived their daily lives. Chapters 4 through 6—"Housework, Houses, and Women at Home," "Childhood and Family Life," and "Consumer Culture"—focus primarily on changes and continuities in the home life of Americans. Chapters 7 through 9 examine how Americans lived their public lives during the industrial era. "Entertainment and Leisure, "Education and Health Care," and "Religious and Civic Life" follow daily life in industrial America's communities and neighborhoods.

This introductory chapter, however, takes a different approach by outlining some of the major national and international issues of this period. Daily life did not take place apart from these developments, and seemingly distant happenings often had a huge impact on the individual choices people made. This introduction briefly explores some of the most significant aspects of industrial era American history: the role of the United States in the world, the effects of immigration, controversies between capital and labor, and federal government policies.

THE UNITED STATES IN THE WORLD

The United States had one of the fastest growing economies in the world in the 1870–1900 period. No other country of the same size grew more rapidly in terms of population or capital. Other countries, notably Britain and France, had experienced industrialization earlier, but in the late nineteenth century, the United States had the most dynamic economy in the world. In world affairs, the United States grew increasingly difficult to challenge and increasingly willing to intervene in international affairs.

Even as western expansion had brought many Native Americans unwillingly under the American flag, Americans defined themselves against European imperialists. They generally understood western territories, which were contiguous with the United States, to be fundamentally different from European overseas possessions. By 1870, all of the contiguous 48 states were either states or territories, and by 1900 only Arizona, New Mexico, and Oklahoma remained territories. Rapid white settlement of western territories had enhanced an American sense of Manifest Destiny, by which many understood it to be the nation's divine mission to clear western lands and Christianize Native Americans.

After the North put down the southern rebellion in 1865, U.S. foreign policy advisors briefly turned their attention to the Caribbean and to Canada. Both regions had proven to be avenues through which aggressors could attack the Union. Consequently, Secretary of State William Seward made several attempts to expand into the Caribbean. First Seward proposed buying the Danish Virgin Islands and then ports in Haiti and the Dominican Republic. In both cases, Congress opposed acquiring colonies as antidemocratic. At roughly the same time, Seward and many Americans argued that Canada represented an avenue through which Britain, which many Americans believed had favored the Confederacy, could attack the United States. With the call to "squeeze England out of the continent," Senator Charles Sumner and other American expansionists urged the annexation of Canada (qtd. in Deconde 249).

Most Americans, however, wanted little to do with new military actions immediately after the Civil War. As the country turned to domestic commitments—administering southern Reconstruction and building railroads—appeals to Manifest Destiny were less persuasive.

In this context, the Spanish-American War of 1898 represents a new phase of overt imperialism in American foreign policy. The war began when Cuban nationals rebelled against their Spanish rulers. Portrayed in the American press as freedom fighters throwing off a repressive colonial government, the Cuban revolutionaries garnered much popular sympathy. The penny press achieved huge circulations with their low prices and sensational news reporting. Two newspapers led the pack: Joseph Pulitzer's *The World* and William Randolph Hearst's *New York Morning Journal* with circulations of 743,024 and 430,410 respectively on the eve of the Spanish-American War (Wisan 298–99). In an effort to win the circulation battle, both papers began carrying lurid accounts of Spanish atrocities in Cuba, whipping up a frenzy of anti-Catholic and anti-Spanish sentiment. Though President McKinley's administration and the business community had generally opposed war, McKinley was eventually pressured by public opinion to attack Spanish forces in Cuba.

Alleging that the Spanish had attacked a U.S. war vessel in a Cuban harbor, the United States declared war against Spain. European countries generally sympathized with the beleaguered Spanish empire and viewed the Americans as aggressors, but they refused to intervene out of fear of damaging trade relations and facing a formidable military power. To quickly and decisively beat the Spanish, the United States attacked Spanish naval bases in the Philippines. When the United States defeated the Spanish it demanded Cuba, Puerto Rico, Guam, and the Philippines. A war that had begun as a war of liberation had become an imperialistic war. Business interests, seeing the advantage of Pacific stations on the trade route to Asia, favored the occupation of the Philippines. Whereas Cuban plantation owners generally saw trade advantages in becoming an American protectorate, the Filipinos resisted. Over the next four years, the United States fought Filipino rebels, killing approximately 18,000 in battle and contributing to the deaths of hundreds of thousands due to war-related famine (Lichtenstein et al. 152). The United States then ruled for nearly fifty years as an occupying, colonial government. Mark Twain compared the United States to a pirate ship, suggesting the flag be changed so that "the white stripes [were] painted black and the stars [were] replaced by the skull and cross bones" (qtd. in Deconde 323). Many Americans protested the American occupation.

As historian David Ryan points out, this episode in American foreign relations should not be viewed as an anomaly:

Traditional interpretations characterize the United States as an imperial power between 1898 and 1946, the period of colonial government of the Philippines. The more informal methods of control were downplayed. Such constructions best suited the US identity and were often reflected in the historiography as an aberration, the worst chapter in US history.... Far from being an aberration, US expansionism has been a consistent feature of its history and this has always involved power over others. (56)

Ryan argues that rule of the Philippines by the United States should be viewed as an extension of American westward expansion rather than as a break with national policy. In fact, following the Spanish-American War, Native Americans often played the role of Puerto Ricans in reenactments of the Battle of San Juan Hill. These "Wild West" shows dramatize the continuity in the minds of Americans between their mission to civilize and Christianize Native Americans and their mission in the former Spanish colonies.

THE MESSIANIC NATIONALISM OF MANIFEST DESTINY

The following is an excerpt of the "March of the Flag" speech delivered by Senator Albert J. Beveridge (R) of Indiana in 1898:

It is a glorious history our God has bestowed upon his chosen people: a history whose keynote was struck by Liberty Bell [sic]; a history heroic with faith in our mission and our future; a history of statesmen who flung the boundaries of the Republic out into unexplored lands and savage deserts and through the ranks of hostile mountains, even to the gates of sunset; a history of a multiplying people who overran a continent in half a century; a history of prophets who saw the consequences of evils inherited from the past and of martyrs who died to save us from them; a history divinely logical, in the process of whose tremendous reasoning we find ourselves today.

[…] Have we no mission to perform, no duty to discharge to our fellowman? Has the Almighty Father endowed us with gifts beyond our desserts and marked us as the people of his peculiar favor, merely to rot in our own selfishness, as men and nations must, who take cowardice for their companion and self for their Deity—as China has, as India has, as Egypt has?

Shall we be as the man who had one talent and hid it, or as he who had ten talents and used them until they grew to riches? And shall we reap the reward that waits on our discharge of our high duty as the sovereign power of earth; shall we occupy new markets for what our farmers raise, new markets for what our factories make, new markets for what our merchants sell—aye, and, please God, new markets for what our ships shall carry?

—From *Major Problems in American Diplomatic History*, ed. Daniel M. Smith, 288

One example of the more subtle policies of imperialism is the U.S. annexation of Hawaii in 1898. The Hawaiian Islands had become wealthy through the export of sugar, largely to the United States. American missionaries in Hawaii had acquired large tracts of land from the native Hawaiians, developed sugar plantations, and encouraged immigration from China and Japan to accommodate the expansion of these plantations. Favorable trade treaties with the United States kept these American landowners wealthy, but when tariff reforms threatened trade relations, these American missionaries advocated the annexation of independent Hawaii. They organized a coup and, despite the resistance of many Americans, orchestrated the peaceful annexation of Hawaii in 1898. American military operations in the Pacific during the Spanish-American War helped to convince Americans of the strategic importance of Hawaii and to ignore the resistance of both native Hawaiians and the substantial Chinese and Japanese populations to annexation.

IMMIGRATION: POWERING THE ERA'S INDUSTRIAL GROWTH

One reason the Chinese and Japanese immigrants to Hawaii resisted American annexation was because of American immigration policy in the United States. While there were no limitations on the number of European immigrants **Immigration Policy** in the period, the United States all but shut off Chinese immigration in 1882. After the period of intense railroad construction ended, a glut of laborers in the West led to violent, racist attacks against Chinese immigrants. In 1882 Congress passed the Chinese Exclusion Act prohibiting Chinese laborers from immigrating to the United States. Ironically, the Preamble of the Act assigned responsibility for these attacks to the Chinese, "[I]n the opinion of the Government of the United States the coming of Chinese laborers to this country endangers the good order of certain localities within the territory thereof..." The Act had its desired effect and immigration from China dropped off dramatically.

Even as Chinese immigration was severely limited, immigration from Europe reached unprecedented levels by the 1880s. However, what makes immigration to the United States unique compared with immigration to other "New World" destinations is not the volume of immigration; for example, proportionate to native population, Argentina's rate of immigration was higher. What makes the United States unique is the spectrum of places from which immigrants came. In addition to the traditional origins of American immigrants—Britain, Germany, and Scandinavia—large inflows of immigrants came from southern and eastern Europe by the late 1800s. Moreover, Irish emigration overtook emigration from England and Wales. Proportionate to native population, Irish emigration was the highest by far compared with other donor countries. Among immigrants from all nations between 1870 and 1900, approximately half came to purchase farms and approximately half came to earn wages in industry (Nugent 150–52).

IMMIGRANTS TO THE UNITED STATES BY COUNTRY

	1870	1880	1890	1900
Germany	118,225	84,638	92,427	18,507
Great Britain	103,677	73,273	69,730	12,509
Ireland	56,996	71,603	53,024	35,730
Canada*	40,414	99,744	183	396
Scandinavia	30,742	65,657	50,638	31,151
China	15,740	5,802	1,716	1,247
Austria-Hungary	4,425	17,267	56,199	114,847
Italy	2,891	12,354	52,003	100,135
Russia and Baltic States	907	5,014	35,598	90,787
Poland **	223	2,177	11,073	——
Japan	48	4	691	12,635
All immigrants	387,203	457,257	455,302	448,572
Total U.S. pop.	39,818,449	50,155,783	62,947,714	75,994,575

* Figures are adjusted to account for repatriation. As a bordering country, Canada attracted large numbers of return migrants by 1890 as the U.S. economy slowed.

** Figures for 1900 included with Austria-Hungary, Germany and Russia.

Historical Statistics of the United States: Colonial Times to 1970. Part 1. Washington, D.C.: Government Printing Office, 1975. Series A1-8 and C89-101; I: 8 and 105.

There were both push and pull factors carrying people from Europe to the United States. The same pull factors applied to all of the European countries. By 1870, steamships took passengers across the Atlantic, and steamship travel **Motives of Immigrants** was considerably faster and safer compared to traveling on sailboats. There were very few fatalities and trans-Atlantic voyages generally took less than two weeks from Britain and about three from Italy. In addition, steamship fares were relatively low. Even a female Irish domestic servant could save her 2 £ and 10 passage in little more than half a year. During the boom years of 1879–1893, wages were comparatively high in the United States and employment relatively easy to find. Skilled laborers could earn two to four times the wages available in European cities. The American government offered free homesteads and railroads offered attractive incentives for farm families willing to settle permanently. Thus, it was relatively inexpensive to travel to the United States; land was cheap and wages were comparatively high (Nugent 52, 153).

There were also a number of "push" factors driving emigrants to leave their European homes. Most of these were economic in nature. Population growth and a shortage of new farmland left many without viable sources of income. Rural emigrants from Ireland and Scandinavia, in particular, often spent some time working in cities as domestic servants or factory laborers before journeying across the Atlantic to the United States.

While a shortage of economic opportunities in their home countries pushed most immigrants, religious persecution pushed others. Jewish emigrants from Eastern Europe, Russian Mennonites, Danish Mormons, and Baptists under German rule all suffered some form of religious oppression. The assassination of Czar Alexander II in 1881, blamed on Russian Jews, led to violent attacks and new restrictive legislation. These pogroms turned the steady flow of emigrants from the Pale of Settlement, where most Jews were required to live, into a flood. In early 1881, 1,200 Russian Jews per week left Hamburg, Germany, the nearest port for most, for the United States. Jewish emigrants of the 1870–1900 period were the most likely of any ethnic group to migrate as a family and among the least likely to return to their native countries. Restrictions on owning land in the Austro-Hungarian and Russian empires meant that the majority of Jewish emigrants were skilled craftsmen such as tailors or retailers. Immigration historian Walter Nugent comments, "The Jewish migration was decidedly labor-seeking rather than land-seeking, but at once more highly skilled, more organized in families, and more permanent than any other labor-seeking group" (93–94).

While immigrants from Great Britain continued to come in large numbers to the United States, they were also the most likely to return to their home countries. Inexpensive **British and Irish Immigration** steamship tickets and the lack of a language or cultural barrier encouraged frequent crossings between Britain and the United States.

The number of Irish-born Americans overtook the number of British-born Americans by 1870 for several reasons. Unlike British immigrants, few Irish immigrants returned to their native country. Not only did the Irish emigrate at a much higher rate than other Europeans but they were also disproportionately female, urban, and permanent. Several factors explain these trends.

The potato blight of 1845–1850 in Ireland had touched off a famine that ultimately reduced the population of Ireland from 8 million to less than 3 million by 1895. Even as a fungus wiped out the potato crops that sustained the Irish peasantry, British landlords evicted their tenants and exported crops grown in Ireland. The British sent no food aid during the first three years of the famine, but they did send soldiers to guard the cartloads of food leaving Irish ports. Approximately one million people died of either starvation or the diseases that prey upon weak and homeless people—typhus, dysentery, edema, and scurvy. Millions more emigrated over the next fifty years, leaving for industrial towns in England or, if they could find money from family or charity organizations, to the United States and Australia. Those staying behind held "American wakes" for their departing loved ones whom they expected would never return (Diner, *Erin's Daughters* 2; Moran 87, 91).

Unlike other immigrant groups, Irish women frequently came to the United States in advance of the rest of their families. Women accounted for 52.9 percent of Irish immigrants as compared with 41 percent of German, 21 percent of southern Italian, and a miniscule 4 percent of Greek immigrants (Diner, *Erin's Daughters* 31). The majority of these women were young and single. One reason single women came in such large numbers was that the famine had dramatically altered family patterns. Irish men and women often refused to marry and when they did marry, they married later in life compared with European and American families. The famine had taught them the risks of large families; they had seen too many mothers and fathers watch in horror as they lost child after child to malnutrition and disease. Moreover, in rural Ireland only one son could inherit a farm, and without a farm or any other source of capital sons could not marry. With few eligible men to marry and still fewer sources of income in Ireland, Irish women saw opportunities in America they could not hope for in Ireland. They emigrated primarily in search of economic security for themselves and their families. Moreover, while women in other European countries suffered under comparable patriarchal systems, the lack of a language barrier in the United States and cultural traditions in which Irish women produced for the cash economy, made it much easier for Irish women to leave their families for American employment.

German and Eastern European Immigration   Eastern European immigrants to the United States became far more common after the opening of railroads from inland areas to Hamburg and Bremen, Germany. Even as the railroads made emigration increasingly profitable, they made technologically backward farms increasingly unprofitable. Many of these Eastern European immigrants came to the United States for a short period of time, sent their wages home, and returned to larger and better capitalized farms. These "birds of passage" were usually men who came without their families.

The exception to this pattern was among German and Czech immigrants. They tended to come as families from rural areas and to buy homesteads in the United States. Many settled in Kansas and Nebraska during the 1870s and 1880s and few returned to their native countries. When the U.S. Census declared the frontier closed in 1893, German and Czech immigration fell off. Though recent scholarship has cast some doubt on the claim that new farmland was unavailable, farm families ceased to immigrate in large numbers after 1893 (Nugent 71).

Italians, who made up a small number of American immigrants in 1870, began coming in larger numbers in the late 1880s. Better opportunities in the United States for industrial laborers initially drew northern Italians. By the mid-1890s, far more Italians came from the South as a result of an agricultural depression there and especially oppressive conditions for tenant farmers. Still, until the twentieth century, most Italian immigrants who came to the United States were men coming for seasonal employment opportunities. They generally returned to their families in Italy for the winter. Recent scholarship has compared southern Italian immigration to French Canadian immigration. Bruno Ramirez argues that commercial farms squeezed out technologically underdeveloped family farms in both regions, turning small farmers into tenant farmers or day laborers, many of whom left in search of better employment opportunities in the United States (Nugent 95, 99).

Italian and French Canadian Immigration

While there are many exceptions to the generalizations above—many German immigrants flocked to the slaughterhouses of Chicago, some Italian immigrants came as families during the period, and, of course, some immigrants did settle in the American South—immigrants tended to follow the paths of countrymen who had immigrated before them, leading to pronounced differences among the migration patterns of different ethnic groups.

THE LABOR QUESTION

The rapid growth of a wage-earning population in the United States alarmed American social commentators. In the American cotton textile industry alone, the wage-earning population grew from 1,000 in 1800 to 135,000 in 1870 (*Historical Statistics* D 175). Many feared the great social upheavals such developments continued to cause in European countries industrializing before the United States. The outbreak of civil war in 1871 between the radicals of Paris, who called for the common ownership of property, and the conservative French government caused American George Templeton Strong to comment, "The old Red Devil of Paris is unchained again at last" (348). Contemporary accounts of the thousands killed in the uprising turned many wealthy Americans, like Strong, against working-class efforts to organize. Questions about the rights of the working class and the role of the government in regulating labor relations came to be known as the "labor question" or, to the more pessimistic, the "labor problem."

Following the logic of President Thomas Jefferson, some believed the growth of a wage-dependent class threatened American democracy. They argued that the wage laborer lived at the mercy of the capitalist who could either give the laborer work or let the laborer starve. To this group, the wage laborer could not be an independent citizen capable of voting in the interests of the community as a whole, because he would vote in the interests of his class, industry, or ethnic group. Moreover, some working-class men of the era allowed themselves to be bought off with liquor and cash; these men were then herded from polling place to polling place to repeatedly vote for the same candidate. Alternatively, such social critics argued, property owners had a greater interest in the long-term health of the nation and community because they were stakeholders. For this group, industrialization itself was a problem and only the return to a more agrarian economy could preserve democracy.

Others defined the labor problem as essentially a problem with the effectiveness of the wage-earning population. Capitalists and managers complained that workers were insufficiently disciplined, that they failed to come to work, drank too much, or were simply not sufficiently skilled. Their habits were preindustrial, holdovers from the days when time was measured by the sun and the seasons rather than the clock. Frequently, this complaint was coupled with nativist sentiment, as capitalists and managers argued that the new immigrants were less intelligent and less trained compared with native-born workers. The Chinese and Irish, in particular, were frequently caricatured in the magazines and newspapers of the day. New York social critic George Templeton Strong reflected the sentiment of many native-born Americans when he described Bret Harte's "Ballad of the Heathen Chinee" as "very funny" and said it was "in everybody's mouth" (326). The poem plays upon common stereotypes of Chinese immigrant workers as duplicitous, effeminate, and threatening to the living standards of white workers. As the railroads came to rely more on Chinese labor to lay tracks in the west, and as eastern manufacturers came to rely increasingly on low paid Irish workers, better paid American-born workers and capitalists increasingly caricatured the new immigrants as lazy, irrational, and intemperate.

Finally, the labor problem was defined by many through the clashes between capitalists and workers rebelling against poor pay and dangerous working conditions. Workers complained that employers were "doing

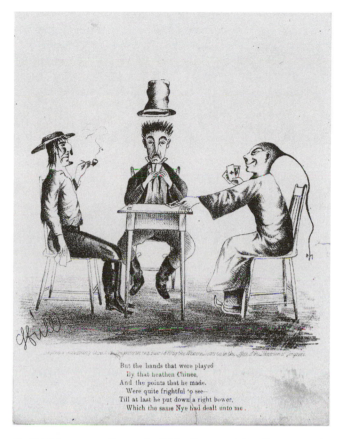

But the hands that were played
By that heathen Chinee,
And the points that he made,
Were quite frightful to see—
Till at last he put down a right bower,
Which the same Nye had dealt unto me.

Anti-Chinese sentiment built in the west, leading to anti-Chinese riots, and, eventually, to the Chinese Exclusion Act in 1882. (Courtesy Library of Congress)

everything [...] they possibly can to crush down the poor people" (O'Donnell 36). Samuel Gompers, who was to become the first president of the American Federation of Labor, described the feelings between employees and employers in this way:

It is a truth so self-evident that there is no hiding it at all, that as a rule the employed can never get an advance in wages without either entering upon a strike, of longer or shorter duration, or at least threatening a strike. That I believe would be the universal testimony of all who have ever been connected with labor organizations. We have known the employers to go on prospering, to grow richer and richer, to live in larger residences and travel more extensively, with their family expenditures constantly increasing, yet all the time, when approached for an increase of wages, they would declare that they were making nothing. (7)

IRISH INDUSTRIES.

This 1881 cartoon suggested that the "labor problem" was the result of Irish immigration. (Courtesy Library of Congress)

Employers, on the other hand, viewed the clashes between capitalists and laborers in different terms. Jay Gould, who was to become infamous for his manipulation of the stock market, blamed workers' poverty on their own bad habits. Like many, he claimed workers drank too much and wasted their money on luxuries like cigarettes. When a Congressional committee asked him about the inability of hardworking men to find stable employment, Gould testified, "I have noticed...that generally if men are temperate and industrious they are pretty sure of success. In cases such as the one you describe I could almost always go back behind the scenes and find a cause for such a person's 'misfortunes'" (48). As for the causes behind recent tensions between wage laborers and capitalists, Gould said, "I think that if left alone they would mutually regulate their relations. I think there is no disagreement between the great mass of the employees and their employers. These societies that are gotten up magnify these things and create evils which do not exist—create trouble which ought not to exist" (48). Many of the wealthy found comfort in sociologists' adaptation of Charles Darwin's evolutionary theory. They believed that intense competition among workers would weed out the weakest individuals and improve American society as a whole.

SOCIAL DARWINISM

Searching for a way to explain vast income disparities and rising labor unrest, nineteenth-century sociologists seized upon Charles Darwin's theories of evolution. Applying Darwin's theory of "survival of the fittest" to human society, they claimed that laissez-faire (roughly translated as "leave it alone") economic policies ultimately strengthened the nation by eliminating the weakest workers and increasing the power of the most successful. These Social Darwinists acted as apologists for the growing disparity between the power and wealth of the trusts and the poverty of the working-class masses. By labeling monopoly capitalism "natural," the Social Darwinists suggested any attempts to ensure worker safety, to provide a minimum standard of living, and to curb monopolies were futile or perhaps even destructive to the efficient operation of the social organization.

In the following excerpt, Yale sociologist William Graham Sumner, a leading Social Darwinist, ridicules efforts by social reformers to change the legal and social environment for industrial development.

[Industrial development] has been attended all the way by lamentations about the good old times; about the decline of small industries; about the lost spirit of comradeship between employer and employee; about the narrowing of the interests of the workman; about his conversion into a machine or into a "ware," and about industrial war. These lamentations have all had reference to unquestionable phenomena attendant on advancing organization. [...] I must expect to be told here, according to the current fashions of thinking, that we ought to control the development of the organization. The first instinct of the modern man is to get a law passed to forbid or prevent what, in his wisdom, he disapproves. A thing which is inevitable, however, is one which we cannot control. We have to make up our minds to it, adjust ourselves to it, and sit down to live with it. Its inevitableness may be disputed, in which case we must re-examine it; but if our analysis is correct, when we reach what is inevitable we reach the end, and our regulations must apply to ourselves, not to the social facts.

—From William Graham Sumner, "The Absurd Effort to Make the World Over"

A large wage-dependent population created labor unrest that had been associated with Britain and France but had been virtually unheard of in the United States. With its vast natural resources and relatively small population, the United States seemed to many immune to France's proletarian revolutions and Britain's vast labor strikes. Americans dissatisfied with wages could move west to free or cheap land, establish a homestead and become independent farmers. When questioned about why he did not go west, Thomas O'Donnell, a mill worker, responded, "How could I go, walk it?...I can't see how I could get out West. I have got nothing to go with." The interviewer pressed further, claiming it would not cost more than $1,500. O'Donnell rebutted, "Well, I never saw over a $20 bill, and that is when I have been getting a month's pay at once. If someone would give me $1,500 I will go" (34).

Even as workers felt increasingly exploited, they saw their employers accumulate a previously unimaginable amount of wealth. They built palatial estates. U.S. Steel titan Andrew Carnegie, notable among New York's millionaires for his rejection of conspicuous consumption, nevertheless

Andrew Carnegie's sumptuous residence in New York City reflected the conspicuous consumption of major industrialists. (Courtesy Library of Congress)

lived in a mansion that occupied an entire city block in New York City. Its 64 rooms housed an impressive collection of art and required two tons of coal per day in the winter for heating ("Andrew Carnegie"). Railroad and steamship tycoon Cornelius Vanderbilt built a 70-room Italian Renaissance–style palazzo, which eclipsed the other sumptuous mansions in Newport, Rhode Island. In Newport, the "robber barons" of the day sailed yachts and held balls that were widely publicized in the new "society pages," fueling resentment among some. To many workers, the lavish lifestyles of these manufacturers made their calls for self-denial and discipline among workers sound hypocritical and self-serving.

FEDERAL POLICIES SHAPING SOCIAL AND ECONOMIC LIFE

The Homestead Act of 1862 and Federal Subsidies to Railroads
As part of an effort to establish trade between the east coast and newly acquired territory in the west, the federal government subsidized the building of railroads and made free land available to western settlers. Huge subsidies of government land and low-interest loans spurred an unprecedented boom in railroad building between 1867 and

1873. Meanwhile the federal government offered 160 acres of unclaimed land to anyone over 21 willing to pay a nominal $12 filing fee. If after five years the settler could verify that he had built a homestead and begun to use the land productively, he or she could pay $6 and establish a permanent claim. The federal government transferred 270 million acres—10 percent of the area of the United States—to private individuals under this act ("Homestead Act").

The Homestead Act and railroad subsidies had far-reaching consequences during the industrial era. Ideally, framers hoped they would transform the sparsely populated West to a land of small farmers and ranchers. In practice, these government actions opened the West to trade, and much of the territory to agriculture, grazing, and mining. In fact, more American land was transformed into farmland between 1870–1900 than in the previous 250 years of American history. Moreover, many homesteaders, especially those lucky enough to settle on fertile plots, prospered.

At the same time, the Homestead Act and railroad subsidies fell short of the democratic ideals associated with "free land." First, while the land was almost free, farm equipment and the long trek west were costly. Few wage laborers could afford to take advantage of the Homestead Act. Second, mining and lumber companies frequently paid individuals to stake claims and then acquired the land well below market price. Third, the railroad monopolies gouged farmers who had to pay whatever the railroads charged if they were to get their crops to market. Moreover, the volume of new land put into production drove down commodity prices, strangling many farmers. Finally, Native Americans, many already removed from their traditional lands, saw the coming of white settlers as a threat to their way of life. Sporadic attacks on settlers led to confrontations with the U.S. military and eventually a war between the Sioux and the United States. When the United States defeated the Sioux in 1877, the last of the serious Native American resistance to white settlement was over. Native American tribes also suffered terrible social and economic losses as settlers killed the great buffalo herds that had formed the core of their cultures.

With the repeal of the Reconstruction amendments in 1876 and the withdrawal of the last of federal troops in 1877, southern planters returned to political power. In effect, this meant that African Americans were left without federal protections from their former slave owners. **End of Reconstruction in the South** They were intimidated by armed whites from voting, forced to sign exploitative labor contracts under threat of arrest, and subject to severe segregation in housing, education, and public facilities.

Northern business interests generally saw this as the end of political conflict in the South. With the return of the planter class to power, southern politics had stabilized, conflicts diminished, and the region was considered safe for investment. Northerners invested in the railroads to the South as well as in some southern industries. However, industrial development was very uneven, as northern capitalists tended to extract natural resources such as timber, coal, and cotton and transport it North for processing into finished products. Consequently, only the tobacco and textile industries grew much during the period. The South remained a largely agrarian, debtor region, lacking a diverse economy.

Use of Federal Troops to Put Down Strikes   As a result of a persistent depression begun in 1873 and exploitative practices on the part of the railroad cartel, railroad workers struck in 1877. As chapter 2 details, the workers protested an across-the-board wage cut agreed to by the four largest railroad companies working in collusion. It was the latest of many wage cuts the companies forced on workers, who faced dangerous conditions and long hours. The strike exploded into a national crisis, known as the Great Uprising of 1877, when federal troops were called in to keep the railroad lines open. Angry at the government's role, workers in other industries launched sympathy strikes and attacked railroad capital. The federal government, fearing a militant working class, took the part of the railroads and used troops across the nation to violently put down strikers. This action set a precedent for future interventions on the part of the federal government. Federal troops would be used throughout the era to protect property, clear the way for replacement workers, and undermine working-class strikes.

Taxation— The Protective Tariff and the Income Tax   The federal government relied primarily on steep import duties to finance its operations, though controversial taxes on alcohol and tobacco produced in the United States added substantially to the federal coffers. In fact, one of the most controversial issues of the Gilded Age was the tariff. Proponents argued that the federal government was precluded from other forms of taxation, which fell within the purview of the states. Tariffs were an easily administered way of collecting necessary revenue and, because a wide variety of products were assessed, it spread social costs out among citizens. Opponents pointed out that some citizens were more dependent on imported goods than others. The South, for example, had developed an agrarian economy and relied largely on industrial imports both from the North and abroad. Moreover, their main export, cotton, benefited little from import duties because they competed well with cotton producers abroad. British industrial wares were produced more cheaply than American goods at the time, but with high tariff rates they ultimately cost the southern consumer more. Westerners were similarly dependent on industrial imports. Westerners, however, were more likely to vote for Republican tariff supporters because so much federal tax income had been plowed into the railroads, the lifelines of western farms.

The tariff debate raged throughout the period but came to a head when the federal government began to run huge surpluses. During the Civil War and Reconstruction, the federal government incurred heavy expenses, expenses that outpaced the federal income during the depression years of 1873–77 and beyond. But with the economy prospering and Reconstruction expenses curtailed, the country began running a surplus in 1882, which continued until the federal government could no longer buy back treasury bills. The federal government literally did not know what to do with the surplus.

Long opposed to the tariff, the Democratic Party launched an offensive against it, calling for dramatic reductions. Special interests lobbied Congressmen intensively. Some thought luxuries should continue to be taxed, but necessities like lumber, fish, salt, flax, hemp, and wool should be excluded (Dewey 62). Others thought goods such as coffee and tea, which were not produced domestically and so didn't require trade protections, should be duty-free. Republicans argued in favor of trade protectionism for its own sake. They claimed that the tariff had successfully shielded American industries from those in Britain and Europe, allowing for unprecedented growth in the American economy. Individual industries lobbied to have their products protected and their raw materials declared duty free. Ultimately, the Democratic Party passed a bill that reduced the average tariff from 47 to 40 percent and favored Democratic over Republican states in its choice of goods to continue to protect (67).

Even as the tariff debate raged, many working-class Americans agitated for a federal income tax. Individual states had experimented with the income tax, as had the federal government, but they had had great difficulty collecting it. Designed to assess only the wealthiest Americans, the tax was easy to evade by simply lying about one's income. Nonetheless, during the severe depression of 1893–97, many Americans saw it as a positive alternative to the tariff and the "sin" taxes that fell heaviest upon the working class. Moreover, income from the tariff failed to keep up with federal expenditures during the depression. A new source of federal income was needed. The Wilson-Gorman Tariff of 1894 included a provision for a flat 2 percent tax on income over $4,000. While not a substantial tax, it provided a precedent for future income taxes and a fund for a more interventionist government during the twentieth century. Ultimately, income taxes provided a more predictable and lucrative source of federal revenue than the states' property taxes or the current structure of tariffs (Buenker 1–25).

THE TEXTURE OF DAILY LIFE

The ideas, events, and government policies above should provide a sense of the shared context for the widely varying experiences of people in the industrial United States. While all Americans would have been aware of the ubiquitous tariff debates and ongoing concerns about racial strife in the South, they would have responded differently depending on their own daily experiences. Racial perceptions, for example, had much to do with hiring practices in specific industries and with daily resistance to modern work discipline among the working class. For some industrial workers, the lot of African American sharecroppers seemed a positive, even idyllic alternative to industrial work. Without electric lighting and heat, work patterns followed daily and seasonal cycles. Moreover, sharecroppers were free from the tyranny of the machine. Such perceptions could lead to admiration or resentment of African Americans. In the following chapters we will contrast how people across gender, age, ethnicity, race, and class lived from day to day—what pleasures they experienced, what fears they held, what trials they faced, and how they adapted their daily lives to a rapidly changing environment.

1

The City

INTRODUCTION

The rise of the modern city is perhaps the most significant social and economic transformation of the industrial era. In fact, industrialism as we know it would have been impossible without cities that provided both a workforce for industries and a market for the goods they produced. As urban areas grew in population, in physical size, and in relative economic importance, Americans rethought their conception of the city and its place in American culture.

The modern city was an unprecedented development, and it came about with surprisingly little forethought. In the United States, where city governments tended to be relatively small, commercial interests led the development of the city. Public interests weren't entirely ignored, but development tended to occur where there was money to be made. As cities grew, Americans also developed new ways to think about private space, public responsibility, and the role of government. At the same time, some traditional practices persevered in new urban environments. For some, cities were places of mystery, menace, and squalor, and they represented a threat to traditional ways. Much writing about cities at the time took on an apocalyptic tone (as in the famous study that wrongly predicted New York City would be waist high in horse manure by the twentieth century). However, for others, cities were places of excitement and opportunity, and there is also ample evidence of the pleasures to be found in city life.

This chapter covers many aspects of the industrial city including population growth, the structure of the city, transportation, housing, and social services; there is also a section focusing on the rise of the city of Chicago. However, because the city touched so many aspects of the industrial experience, some city-related issues can be found in other chapters. For example, details on the department store are in the chapter on Consumer Culture, and the chapter on the Railroad covers important aspects of urban politics.

POPULATION GROWTH AND SHIFTS

U.S. cities had been growing throughout the nineteenth century, but their development was exceptional during the industrial era. From 1870–1900, the total U.S. population nearly doubled, increasing from 38,558,000 to 75,995,000. In 1870, only 25.7 percent of the U.S. population was urban (in fact, in the late 1860s, three-quarters of Americans lived on farms or in villages with less than 2,500 people). By 1900, almost 40 percent of Americans were city dwellers. Urban population during this time increased at triple the rate of rural areas (United States 11–12; Walker 14, 207).

At the turn of the century, there were 38 U.S. cities with more than 100,000 residents, 24 more than there had been in 1870. To highlight the scope of this change, consider that in 1790 only 3.14 percent of the U.S. population lived in cities. Between 1870 and 1900 Detroit grew from 80,000 to 286,000 residents; Minneapolis increased from 13,000 to over 200,000; Los Angeles expanded from 6,000 to over 100,000. The 1880s were the most intense period of urban growth. In this decade alone, the U.S. population increased by 56.4 percent and the cities of Chicago, Detroit, and Milwaukee doubled in size. As much as 40 percent of the rural population migrated to cities during the 1880s (Walker 126; Weber 1).

There were two main sources for this population growth: internal migration, where U.S. citizens living in rural areas decided to move to cities, and external migration, where immigrants from other countries came to the United States (other developments, such as a decline in mortality rates, played a smaller role). In the case of both internal and external migrants, people came to cities because that's where the work was. By 1900, nine-tenths of the nation's manufacturing occurred in urban areas (Trachtenberg 114).

Cities absorbed unprecedented waves of foreign-born immigrants coming into the United States during this time. Between 1870 and 1900 approximately 11.3 million immigrants came to the United States, a rate of immigration more than 10 times that which the country experienced at the beginning of the 1800s. By 1900, 14 percent of the U.S. population was foreign born. As a point of comparison, consider that a century later, in 1999, only 8 percent of Americans were born abroad. The immigrants at the beginning of the industrial era tended to be part of the wave of Northern European immigrants from counties including Ireland, Germany, and the Scandinavian countries. Starting around 1880, a new and larger group of immigrants came across the Atlantic from Southern and Eastern European countries including Poland, Russia, Italy, Greece, and Turkey. New immigrants also came across the Pacific from China and Japan (Kristof 5, Mohl 23).

Though many of the earlier immigrants had sought out available farmland in the Midwest and West, the majority of these new immigrants settled in cities to look for work. As a result, cities such as San Francisco, Pittsburgh, and Philadelphia had a population during the industrial era that was 50–70 percent foreign born. In fact, in 1880 over 80 percent of the population consisted either of immigrants or the children of immigrants in the cities of Cleveland, New York, Detroit, and Milwaukee. Add to those numbers the many internal migrants to urban areas, and it becomes clear why cities often seemed like places where everyone lived but no one was born (Gutman 40; Mohl 23).

The tale of internal immigrants is less well known but equally crucial to this period. The American frontier famously has been thought of as a "safety valve," in the words of Frederick Jackson Turner, an outlet for discontented Americans who went West to seek a fortune or start anew. But this was not the case, according to Stephan Thernstrom. He claims that the cost of land was too high to attract poor immigrants, and increased mechanization of farming also meant fewer farm workers—either native or immigrant—were needed during the industrial era. For every urban worker who became a farmer, there were twenty farmers who moved to cities. It was the cities, not the frontier, that attracted native-born Americans looking for new opportunities. In fact, despite emigration to the west, about the same percentage of the population (about half) lived in the Northeast in 1870 as in 1920 (Gordon 272; Thernstrom 399–400).

THE STRUCTURE OF THE CITY

The preindustrial city was a walking city. Businesses, shops, and residences were all clustered together in an area that usually covered less than two square miles and was often located on a waterfront. There were no zoning regulations in the contemporary sense of the term. Businesses, residences, and factories often existed side by side. Water, rather than land, was the main transportation route. Within the city, most people traveled on foot to their destinations. Only the well off could afford to own a horse and carriage in a city.

As a result the preindustrial city was both diversified and centralized. All the activity of an urban area, from manufacturing to shopping to living, occurred within walking distance. Classes also intermingled regularly. Factory owners, for example, lived in the same general area as their workers (though, of course, in vastly different housing). Where there was a geographical distinction, expensive housing tended to be located closest to the businesses. Workers' housing was further from businesses though still within walking distance. Those walks often took place along poorly paved streets or dirt roads. As late as 1870, the city of Newark, with over 100,000 residents, had paved only 27 of its 621 miles of streets (Griffith 7).

In contrast, the industrial city was decentralized and specialized. Specific areas of a city took on unique functions. The traditional heart of the city came to be dominated by manufacturing and business, creating what has come to be known as a central business district or downtown. Though elite housing from an earlier era was maintained, business expansion took over much of what was previously downtown residential space. The area immediately surrounding the downtown remained residential and was increasingly dominated by housing for the poorest segments of the population. Middle-class people often chose to live in new residential neighborhoods on the outskirts of cities and in suburbs served by public transportation.

As the city grew, social distinctions between its various neighborhoods became more prominent. Neighborhoods became identified with distinct classes or ethnicities. Though this trend was not entirely new, areas with large immigrant populations increasingly turned into ethnic enclaves that were often given nicknames such as Chinatown or Little Italy. These neighborhoods served an important social function, providing recent arrivals and native-born members of ethnic minorities with a space where common cultural practices could be shared. In fact, these neighborhoods were not just modeled after ethnic villages; in some cases, specific European villages were literally re-created in the United States. Remarkably, almost half of all Italian immigrants to San Francisco between 1850 and 1930 came from just four Italian provinces. Similarly, what appeared to many outsiders to be Chicago's various "Little Italies" were in fact neighborhoods of Italian immigrants from specific villages. Immigrants from each village settled in the same areas and reestablished many old world practices (Mohl 185–86).

Transportation   Transportation was in many ways the lynchpin of the modern city. Cities could not grow if the majority of the population needed to be within walking distance of work and shopping. This problem was exacerbated when manufacturing interests bought up waterfront properties to have access to water transport, and growing populations placed a strain on existing housing. As cities grew, there needed to be a way to move large groups of people in and out of central business districts.

In the mid-1800s, omnibuses and steam-powered commuter railroads were introduced to help bring an expanding population to and from workplaces. Omnibuses, horse-drawn carriages seating a dozen or so passengers, became popular at mid-century in large cities. They traveled fixed routes, but their cost of operation meant that fares put them out of

reach for most of the working class. They were, however, the first transportation vehicles that permitted a notable number of city dwellers to live
on the outskirts of urban areas. Commuter railroads also served wealthy
passengers and further extended the decentralization of the city. But the
dangers and expense of running railroads through existing streets limited
their spread (Mohl 30–32; Tarr 204–05).

In 1873, the first cable car line was introduced in San Francisco. Cable
cars drew power from an underground wire cable, allowing the cars to
move along tracks. Cable cars were faster than horses, moving at speeds
up to ten miles an hour. As horses often struggled with steep hills, the
cable car also proved better than the omnibus in a hilly city like San Francisco. However, cable car lines were expensive to build and repair (Mohl
31–33).

In the 1890s, the electric trolley emerged as the most popular form of
public transportation. Trolleys drew electricity from an overhead wire that
was easier to service and repair than an underground cable car wire. Trolleys could also run on the same streets used by horses and pedestrians,
though elevated train lines (and later, subways) were also constructed in
many cities. Trolleys traveled at approximately 10 miles per hour, double
the speed of horse-drawn omnibuses. They were also cleaner and quieter
than steam railroads. With fares that working people could afford, trolleys
soon came to dominate urban transportation. Between 1890 and 1902, the
miles of trolley rail in the United States jumped from 5,783 to 22,577. By
1902, 97 percent of urban transportation was electric. The trolley had all
but replaced the omnibus and steam commuter rail. However, street trolleys were not practical in all locations. On congested streets, they added
to traffic. Elevated lines were constructed in cities including Boston,
Chicago, and Philadelphia. In cities with skyscrapers, like Manhattan,
overhead trolley wires created the additional hazard of blocking fire fighters from reaching upper floors of tall buildings. This was one of the reasons for the later development of the subway (Mohl 33–34; Tarr 207).

The trolley transformed city life, with results that now appear both positive and negative. The trolley made it possible for large numbers of people to live farther away from downtown businesses. The physical space of
the city began to expand, as many who could afford to began to reside in
outlying areas. Some of these areas have been called "streetcar suburbs,"
as their very creation was predicated on public transportation. This development allowed some people to escape the congestion of the industrial
city, but it also gave them less of a stake in the conditions of the city they
left behind.

Traveling in the city became more enjoyable for many. In 1892, Julian
Ralph, writing in *Harper's*, declared street car service in Minneapolis
"nearly perfect." By the 1890s there were even "trolley parties" in cities
like Philadelphia, where people would simply ride the streetcar lines for
fun. Trolleys also brought hazards, however. The Brooklyn baseball team

A streetcar in Washington, D.C., circa 1890. (Courtesy Library of Congress)

was originally called the "Trolley Dodgers," in acknowledgment of the regular dangers pedestrians faced on Brooklyn streets (Mohl 33–34; Vreeland 48; Ralph 61).

"CHOKED WITH A CROWDED MASS OF HUMANITY"

In 1894, William Stead published *If Christ Came to Chicago,* a popular expose of the excesses of urban development in Chicago. His calls for reform of city life struck a chord with religious as well as secular reformers. In an apocalyptic tone, he draws attention to the dangers of streetcars and train crossings on the streets of Chicago in this selection.

This great city with a million and a half of population is stretched over a gridiron of rails which cross and recross the city and form a complex network of tracks, every mesh of which is stained with human blood...I do not think that it is too much to say that in the last five years we have had fewer soldiers killed in our wars all round the world than have been slaughtered in the streets of Chicago at the grade crossing. The figures are: in 1889, 257; 1890, 294; 1891, 323; 1892, 394; 1893, 431. As might be expected, the number of these railroad murders steadily increases with the growth of the population.

A Chicago car at the rush time, in the middle of the day or early in the morning or late at night, is a sight which once seen is not easily forgotten. Every seat is filled and all the space between the seats is choked with a crowded mass of humanity. The unlucky individuals are holding on by a strap from the roof. At the platform at each end of the car a crowd is hanging on by its eyelids as thick as bees when they are swarming. (Stead qtd. in Cook et al. 62–63)

Then, as now, cities were known for their distinctive street life. Especially in working-class communities, the street **Street Life** became the place where people talked, did business, played, and relaxed. Many middle-class reformers were horrified by street life in working-class neighborhoods, fearing it interfered with familial influences, exposed children to filth and vice, and broke down the distinctions between home and society. These middle-class reformers had little trouble finding illustrations for their concerns. In crowded neighborhoods, children often played on street corners and around garbage dumpsters. Others tried to make money begging or working as street vendors selling everything from newspapers to matches.

With large groups of people sharing the little public space available in many cities, it became difficult to maintain urban infrastructures using traditional methods. Cobblestone streets frequently became riddled with potholes. Garbage often piled up in alleys and in street gutters. It was not uncommon for working-class residents to keep animals to supplement their incomes, and the waste of these animals was added to the stream of garbage. The combination of all these factors often overwhelmed the senses of observers as in the excerpt below from Abraham Cahan's novel *Yekl*. These conditions provoked the ire of many reformers, who called for better zoning enforcement and urban planning. By the turn of the century, special Sanitation Commissioners were appointed to clean up filthy city streets in places like New York City. Jane Addams of Chicago's Hull-House settlement found inadequate garbage disposal to be among the greatest health threats in her neighborhood. She upset the Chicago political machine by arranging to be appointed ward garbage inspector, ensuring that regular and complete garbage collection would remove refuse from the overcrowded and underserved Halsted Street neighborhood.

YEKL IN THE GHETTO

Abraham Cahan was born in Lithuania and immigrated to the United States in 1882. He became the foremost Yiddish journalist of his day, founding and editing the *Jewish Daily Forward* from 1897 until his death in 1951. In this excerpt from his 1896 novel, *Yekl: A Tale of the New York Ghetto*, Cahan follows his protagonist through an overcrowded ghetto street:

He had to pick and nudge his way through dense swarms of bedraggled half-naked humanity; past garbage barrels rearing their overflowing contents in sickening piles, and lining the streets in malicious suggestion of rows of trees; underneath tiers and tiers of fire escapes, barricaded and festooned with mattresses, pillows, and featherbeds not yet gathered in for the night. The pent-in sultry atmosphere was laden with nausea and pierced with a discordant

and, as it were, plaintive buzz. Supper had been dispatched in a hurry, and the teeming populations of the cyclopic tenement houses were out in full force "for fresh air," as even these
people will say in mental quotation marks. (13)

As awful as the physical condition of city streets tended to be, what
some reformers misunderstood was how urban street life replicated traditional ways of life in European villages. Neighbors used the streets to con-
gregate or share information, and they kept an eye on each other's
children. The street also offered a respite from the crowded conditions of
working-class tenements or cottages. A street that appeared dangerously
crowded to some may have simply felt vibrant and alive to those who
lived there.

For example, in *Twenty Years at Hull-House*, the reformer Jane Addams
writes of a dilapidated block of houses she arranged to have torn down
and turned into a playground (in fact, the first public playground in
Chicago). Despite her good intentions, her words testify to a gap between
her understanding of her actions and that of a previous occupant.

[T]he dispossessed tenants, a group of whom had to be evicted by legal process
before their houses could be torn down, have never ceased to mourn their former
estates. Only the other day I met upon the street an old Italian harness maker, who
said that he had never succeeded so well anywhere else nor found a place that
"seemed so much like Italy." (207)

Playgrounds, as it turned out, were one of the most lasting responses of
middle-class reformers to the questions of children and the streets. Initially these efforts were led by private organizations, but soon municipalities began taking on the responsibility. Dedicated play spaces were
established for children in many areas, and a variety of groups organized
team sports for children. Part, but not all, of the motivation behind playground reform was to provide children with physically safer and cleaner
places to play. As Dominick Cavallo writes, reformers believed that physical conditioning "instilled values and aptitudes that allowed the city
child to meet the challenges of his stimulating and often dangerous environment" (4). Playgrounds were built to improve both morals and muscles, and city governments supported them. Between 1880 and 1920, over
$100 million was spent on urban playgrounds (Mohl 164).

Parks
This same desire to mitigate the influences of the city also
drove reformers to support the creation of public parks. The
most famous landscape architect of the era (in fact, the man
who virtually invented the field), Frederick Law Olmsted, orchestrated
such still-famous landmarks as New York's Central Park, the park system
of greater Boston, and the grounds of the United States Capitol in Washington, D.C. For Olmsted, parks served as a hedge against the dangerous
influences of city life, and they offered some of the inspirational qualities

of the natural world. Olmsted's parks were not like carefully cultivated European gardens. He envisioned parks as natural landscapes with open spaces and forested areas. They were to provide moral uplift and a sense of freedom to urban dwellers otherwise influenced by saloons and congested streets (Mohl 74–77).

In his writings as well as in his designs, Olmsted emphasized that the experience of park space needed to differ from the experience of city streets.

We want a ground to which people may easily go after their day's work is done, and where they may stroll for an hour, seeing, hearing and feeling nothing of the bustle and jar of the streets, where they shall, in effect, find the city put far away from them. We want the greatest possible contrast with the streets and the shops and the rooms of the town which will be consistent with convenience and the preservation of good order and neatness. We want, especially, the greatest possible contrast with the restraining and confining conditions of the town, those conditions which compel us to walk circumspectly, watchfully, jealously, which compel us to look closely upon others without sympathy. (80)

Olmsted did not exactly view his parks as part of the city, but rather as a necessary oasis from urban life. They were to allow individuals a chance to step outside of the streets, to be outside of the city, with the expectation that during those periods of time people's gentler, more civil natures would be free to develop.

Olmsted was not alone in his concern. Helen S. Conant expressed a commonly held viewpoint in an 1879 article on Central Park in *Harper's* when she wrote,

The barrenness of life in great cities is not conducive to perfect healthy development, either mental or physical. To those whose childhood has been spent in the freedom afforded by broad-spreading fields and forests, the confinement of brick walls, the incessant clatter and confusion of the city street, become positively sickening. (689)

Conant believed that the constructed nature of urban environments, their "unnaturalness," made them intrinsically harmful to both moral and physical sensibilities. Parks were not constructed simply to provide leisure or entertainment. They were thought of as a kind of environmental inoculation; they provided enough of nature to ward of the supposed diseases of city living.

Today we may question just how much parks can influence personal behavior, and we are less likely to see city living as intrinsically detrimental. That said, there is no doubt that the movement for parks made a lasting contribution to the livability of cities, ensuring public and open space in areas where space can be an expensive commodity. In fact, today we tend to think of urban parks as a feature which distinguishes cities from contemporary suburbs. Because Olmsted's model was embraced enthusi-astically during the industrial era, by the end of the nineteenth century American cities rivaled European capitals in the amount of open land dedicated as public parks, breaking up what might otherwise have been unending rows of businesses and residences (Teaford 253).

URBAN HOUSING

The most influential form of housing from the industrial era is what has come to be known as "Victorian houses," often-ornate wooden homes with a range of features including balconies, turrets, cupolas, and porches. These houses were constructed on what has been called the "balloon frame." The first balloon frame house appeared in 1833, and the model quickly became popular. Unlike earlier colonial or Greek Revival houses, Victorian houses did not use post-and-beam construction. Post-and-beam houses required skilled craftsman who would build the hardwood frame of a wall on the ground and then need as many as twenty men to raise it into position. Balloon frame houses used lighter wood (often virgin white pine newly logged in Michigan) and built frames with factory produced

A home with elaborate woodwork and detail typical of Victorian houses. From Manchester, New Hampshire. (Courtesy Library of Congress)

nails and studs. These new houses could be constructed quickly by as few as two workers. In many cases, urban workers built their own homes using this method and blueprints that could be ordered out of mail-order catalogs. The development of the balloon frame changed house building from a craft to an industry. Outlying sections of cities and new suburbs catering to the emerging professional-managerial class were besieged by subdivisions. Houses in these projects tended to be built by construction companies as speculative ventures rather than with a specific occupant in mind (Kunstler 161–63; Foner and Garraty 76).

When most people think back on working-class housing of the industrial era, the image of the tenement comes to mind, particularly as pictured in Jacob Riis's landmark book on the tenements of New York City, *How the Other Half Lives*. However, though tenements could be found throughout the country, they were not where most working-class people lived. Working-class housing took the form of cottages, row houses, boarding houses, back alley houses, and shantytowns, in addition to tenements.

Working-class housing varied by region. In northeastern cities like Philadelphia, the brick row house was typical, whereas in Midwestern cities like Chicago, Detroit, and Buffalo, one- and two-family wooden cottages were the norm. Home ownership was a high priority, particularly for urban immigrants who purchased homes at a higher rate than native born urban dwellers. In Joseph Bigott's study of working-class housing in Chicago during the industrial era, he found that immigrants often invested in two- and three-family housing units, occupying one unit and renting the others. The effect was to keep money within ethnic communities; rents paid by poorer immigrants went to the upwardly mobile immigrant investors of the area (Bigott 119, 145).

Boarding Houses

A boarding house was typically a single-family home that had been converted to take in boarders, each of whom rented one room of the house and ate or "boarded" at a common table. Boarding houses were a commonplace feature in nineteenth century America. During that century as many as 70 percent of American citizens may have been boarders at one time or another, and as many as 20 percent of city households may have taken in boarders. Boarding houses catered to both rich and poor. Some of these houses were converted mansions that offered extravagant menus. Others housed people in shacks and provided poor food. Though moralists of the period often voiced concern that boarding houses were disruptive of "proper" family life, their omnipresence made them a way of life for a large number of families (Sutherland 48–49).

Row Houses

The ideal of home ownership loomed large for many Americans. But in cities where property taxes could be high and housing shortages common, it was not feasible for many people to own separate, unattached houses. The row house emerged as a compromise in cities including Baltimore, Cincinnati, Pittsburgh and Philadelphia (in the latter city, row houses were in such demand that they were even built in outlying suburbs). A standard row house measured sixteen to thirty feet across and three to five stories high. A block of identical, narrow row houses would typically line city streets. Each would contain as many as a dozen rooms throughout its multiple levels. Though less expensive than traditional housing, most urban row houses still cost more than average city dwellers could afford to spend on housing (Sutherland 48; Walker 210).

Apartments and Tenements
Although we now tend to think of apartments as synonymous with city life, they were still relatively rare in industrial America. The first American building developed specifically to house multiple apartments (as opposed to converting an existing building) was not constructed until the late 1860s. The early apartment buildings were modeled on luxury hotels and designed for the wealthy. Apartment buildings of six to eight stories for middle-class tenants appeared only gradually. Moralists at the time feared that apartments would undermine family life and referred to them contemptuously as "French flats." But for city dwellers who had lived in boarding houses or row houses and saw little possibility of owning their own homes, apartments provided privacy and independence within an urban atmosphere (Sutherland 49–50; Walker 209).

The term "tenement" also describes an apartment, but whereas apartment is a generally neutral term, tenement has taken on a negative connotation, largely as a result of the awful condition of tenement housing during the industrial era. *How the Other Half Lives,* Jacob Riis's 1890 photo documentary exposing the desperate conditions of New York's poorest citizens during the industrial era, concentrated attention on the crowded, multiple family tenements and back alley houses of New York City. Tenements were not typical working-class housing structures nationwide (only New York City and Providence, Rhode Island, had a preponderance of tenements), but they were seen by many as symptomatic of the changes wrought by industrialization. Some multiple family dwellings were quite luxurious, but the vast majority were built to house the maximum number of people in a minimal amount of space and led to extremely unhealthy conditions.

In the 1880s, Riis reported on life in the tenements for the *New York Tribune* and later the *New York Evening Sun.* His daily columns on the exploitation of hard-working immigrants by greedy slumlords fostered support for the Tenement House Commission in 1884. With advances in photography that allowed photographers greater mobility, reporters could capture stunning images for their papers. Riis initially published 38 of his photographs in the first edition of *How the Other Half Lives* in 1890. The pictures, along with his text explaining the degradation inherent in tenement life, encouraged Progressive Era reforms such as housing and

Before municipal street cleaning, it was not uncommon for garbage to collect in
the streets of crowded urban areas, as in this picture from around 1890 taken by
Jacob Riis in a tenement neighborhood on East Fifth Street in New York City.
(Courtesy Library of Congress)

park developments. The picture above from his volume gives a sense of
the crowded, unsanitary conditions that prevailed in New York's poorest
tenement neighborhoods. Dozens of families sharing a common tenement
yard used it for multiple purposes—laundry, playground for children,
well water, and, most alarmingly, disposal of human waste. Under such
conditions, it is no wonder that tenement dwellers suffered tragically high
rates of communicable diseases, transmitted through unsafe drinking
water and extremely close quarters.

The typical "dumbbell" tenement, which, ironically, initially won a
competition for its supposed combination of profitability for the landlord
and healthfulness for the worker, consisted of six floors and four apartments per floor squeezed onto a 25-by-100-foot lot. An airshaft 28 inches
wide going through the center of the building was to provide light and air
for the interior rooms of each apartment. Instead, the airshaft became a
repository for each apartment's garbage and a fire hazard. A fire on the
first floor quickly spread to each apartment through the airshaft. The front
apartments contained four rooms, all in a row, and the back apartments

contained three rooms, also in a row. To make rent, many families rented out one of the rooms to a boarder.

Back Alley Houses

If possible, back alley houses were even more crowded and unsanitary than the dumbbell apartments that fronted the street. Located behind tenements and single-family dwellings, alley houses arose in response to limited transportation networks and rising urban populations. Developers would build "fill-in" housing between existing homes. In Washington, D.C., for example, absentee owners squeezed two-story 12-by-30 brick row houses onto the back properties of other houses. Alley population peaked in Washington, D.C., in 1897 at nearly 20,000. Alley dwellers were the poorest of a city's residents and were often viewed by outsiders as "the dangerous classes." In Washington, D.C., back alleys were more racially segregated than the street population. James Borchert notes that 70 percent of alleys in 1897 were totally segregated and "nearly half of all alley residents in 1880 lived in all-black alleys" (610, 619).

Shantytowns

As housing shortages beset many industrializing cities, a number of the poorest residents were unable to find or afford even poor quality tenement or back alley housing. As a result, shantytowns began to appear on the outskirts of metropolitan areas. Shantytowns were unofficial villages not serviced by cities and lacking even basic sanitation. Typically, shanties were single rooms built out of available wood, scrap metal, or any other material that could be obtained. H. C. Bunner, writing in 1880 of New York City's Shantytown (then located near Central Park between 65th and 85th Streets), was struck by the diversity of building materials in these makeshift dwellings.

There are bits of wood from the docks, from burnt-out city houses, from wrecks of other shanties; there are rusty strips of roofing-tin; sheets of painted canvas; the foundations are of broken bricks, neatly cemented, the top of it all is tin, slate, shingle, canvas and tarred paper. No bird's-nest ever testified to more industrious pickings and stealings. (861)

Though some shantytowns later became part of cities, more frequently, as cities expanded, these squatters were often driven into even further outlying areas or inward toward congested working-class housing (Sutherland 51–52).

THE GROWTH OF URBAN GOVERNMENT

The lasting image of urban government during the industrial era is that of "machine politics" led by a "boss." "Machine politics" described an approach to governing in which a group of organized politicians were able to control the reigns of governmental power through delivering (and sometimes manipulating) votes. They often accomplished this by delivering patronage jobs and services back to those same voters. The "boss" of such a system was not necessarily the mayor of a city but instead someone who could leverage his power to both give and get favors.

Historians generally agree that in a situation in which urban governments were structurally weak and fragmented, there was a great incentive for strong leaders to find ways to seize power and coordinate unwieldy municipal forces. Beyond that, however, there is a vast division of opinion on the state of urban government in the industrial era as is illustrated by the titles of two well-known histories of the era: Ernest S. Griffith's *A History of American City Government: The Conspicuous Failure, 1870–1900* and Jon C. Teaford's *The Unheralded Triumph: City Government in America, 1870–1900*. Both authors found illustrations to support their titles. City governments at this time were the site of corruption and incompetence as well as flexibility and innovation.

Ernest Griffith argues that during this period city charters (the regulations setting up the organization of city governments) were "a hodge-podge and a patchwork" (10). Few were written in anticipation of massive growth, and entrenched interests often made charter revision difficult. Furthermore, as urban areas grew, the amount of revenue passing through city coffers without adequate controls, and the control of patronage jobs, led to widespread corruption. According to Griffith,

Of the ten largest cities, five (New York, Philadelphia, Cincinnati, Chicago, and San Francisco) were unquestionably corrupt; Boston, Brooklyn, and New Orleans varied by departments (for example, an honest and public-spirited mayor and a corrupt council). Two, Baltimore and St. Louis, may have been essentially honest. ("Honest," in the context of the times, meant an unwillingness to accept bribes, to tolerate rigged elections, and to use public office for direct personal gain in conflict-of-interest situations.)...The centers of corruption were police graft election frauds, public works and other contracts and favors to businesses. (10)

For Griffith, what the cities needed was a professionalization of government as was championed by many middle- and upper-class Progressive reformers in the 1890s and up through World War I.

Jon Teaford measures the role of industrial city governments differently. Though he does not deny that cities faced a litany of difficulties or that they were often beset by corruption, he says that urban governments had many successes to show during the latter part of the nineteenth century. They developed modern schools, sanitation, and infrastructures in the midst of immigration that brought unprecedented ethnic and religious diversity to cities. But within the context of nineteenth-century thinking, it was difficult to appreciate the role city governments played in mediating and compromising between different constituencies.

Late-nineteenth-century urban government was a failure not of structure but of image. The system proved reasonably successful in providing services, but there was no prevailing ideology to validate its operation...[There was] no system of beliefs to bolster the existing government structure. Thus late-nineteenth-century city government survived without moral support, and to many urban dwellers it seemed a bargain with the devil. (10)

City government was the place that brought together "the municipal professional, the downtown business leader, and the neighborhood shopkeeper and small-time politico," as well as the immigrant leader or union supporter (7). No one group always got its way, but through compromise and negotiation, the modern city nevertheless came to be.

For every Boss Tweed—the notoriously corrupt New York City politician of the Tammany Hall machine—there was also a Brooklyn Bridge—a major architectural and infrastructural accomplishment made possible by municipal government. Dramatic improvements as well as scandalous waste were hallmarks of the city governments of this period.

Electricity   Cleveland, Ohio, was the site of the first demonstration of an electric lighting system in the United States. In 1879, Charles Brush, a local inventor who had installed early lighting systems in some factories, convinced the Cleveland City Council to allow him to outfit a section of the city with a dozen of what were called "arc lights." On the evening of the display, crowds gathered in downtown Cleveland (some had brought smoked glasses fearing, erroneously, that the light might be too bright). At 8:05 P.M., the signal was given and the dozen lights (each as strong as a modern-day floodlight) were illuminated. The crowd cheered, a municipal band struck up a song, and an artillery salute was fired on the lakeshore in honor of the occasion. Following the success of this demonstration, other cities clamored for outdoor electric lighting. Soon Boston, New York, and Philadelphia had their own arc light projects powered by Brush's equipment (Rudolph and Ridley 24–26).

Arc lights gave off a bright light and worked well for lighting large areas, but they were not practical for domestic use. Thomas Edison's incandescent lightbulbs, which eventually emerged as the standard for lighting, gave off a softer light than the arc lights. Edison ran a successful demonstration project from his Pearl Street plant in 1882, lighting up the offices of 50 Wall Street businesses. Soon, a fierce competition erupted between these two lighting systems for municipal contracts. In the early days of electric power generation, all the systems, whether arc or incandescent, were small in scope, rarely stretching more than a mile from the central generating station. Nevertheless, by 1884, most major cities had some type of limited electric lighting system, as electric light was viewed as superior in quality and cost to older gas lighting systems. However, lighting for homes remained limited during the industrial era, costing as much as $100 a year, which was almost a quarter of an average wage earner's income (Bowers 66; Rudolph and Ridley 26–30).

By the late 1880s, many major cities had competing electric companies running their own wires alongside one another, leading to wire congestion and overbuilding in lucrative markets. At one point, New York City had 32 separate electricity companies. Meanwhile, many rural areas were left without electricity altogether. Competition between electricity firms increased, and a consolidating industry began to increase prices. As companies competed for the favor of city governments, many municipal authorities feared a repeat of the bribery scandals over the railroads. A number of reform mayors in cities including Chicago, Detroit, San Francisco, and Toledo created city-owned, municipal power utilities. In Detroit, private electricity cost an average of $132 a lamp per year in 1894; in 1898 the new Detroit municipal power authority provided electricity at $87 a lamp per year. Although not without controversy, municipal power often proved able to offer cheaper electricity and wider service. It remains to this day an alternative to private electric companies (O'Dea 102; Rudolph and Ridley 31–33).

Today it is easy to take for granted the sanitary infrastructure of a city. But in the industrial era, the availability and quality of water, sewers, garbage collection, and street cleaning varied widely. The growth of the city created life-threatening conditions for both rich and poor and led to substantial governmental actions on behalf of what Martin V. Melosi calls "The Sanitary City." Still, creating such a city was an expensive undertaking, as municipalities had to assume substantial debt for the expense of constructing public water works and sewer systems. A whole field of public health reform emerged to cope with the sanitation crisis.

Modern Sanitation

To understand the uneven development of sanitary reforms, it helps to appreciate the different understanding of the nature of disease at this time. Up until around 1880, most experts believed that epidemic diseases such as typhoid, cholera, and yellow fever were caused by miasmas, a term for foul smells or dirt. Decomposing organic material was thought to be the cause of epidemics. It was only after 1880 with the general acceptance of germ theory, and growing understanding of the role of microorganisms in the spread of disease, that miasmas were seen as a symptom rather than a cause of disease.

Water emerged as the first substantial public utility in most American cities. Clean water was a primary concern for urban residents, and a modern water system was seen as a sign of a city that was prepared to grow. In the mid-nineteenth century, waterborne illnesses were a leading cause of infectious diseases. Though some cities had long had primitive waterworks run by private companies, others still relied on individual wells. As the population of cities grew and they became centers of industrial production, traditional waterways and urban wells quickly became polluted with both manufacturing and human waste. Industrial cities increasingly invested in large scale water projects, despite the enormous expense. The cost of not centralizing water supplies could be even higher. Twice in the 1870s, the city of Memphis suffered yellow fever epidemics, the second of which killed one-sixth of the city's population (Melosi 119, 153).

Today, we tend to think of water and sewage systems as interrelated, but this was not how they emerged in most cities. Even after public water supplies were established, sewage was largely handled through individual septic systems. However, old-style privy-cesspool septic tanks often could not handle the amount of water used by people with access to a public water system, leading to appalling conditions. For example, the Baltimore harbor in summertime during this era was "often a stinking mass of decaying garbage and other pollution." But a growing appreciation of germ theory allowed many to see the need for the safe disposal of human waste; sewers appeared in (or, more accurately, below) American cities throughout the industrial era (Melosi 91–92, 149).

Garbage was a constant problem in urban areas. Cities not only had large numbers of people living in small geographic areas, but the growth of consumer culture also increased the amount of throw-away material used on a daily basis. It was not uncommon at the beginning of this era for garbage removal to be solely taken care of by scavenger pigs that would roam wild through city streets. Less than 25 percent of U.S. cities had public garbage collection as late as 1880. Piles of festering garbage on curb sides and in alleys were a constant nuisance and a common danger in many cities (Melosi 186; Walker 112).

Not surprisingly then, street cleaning proved a huge challenge for municipal authorities. Not only did unprecedented numbers of people produce huge amounts of trash, but horses also created an astonishing quantity of waste. Experts estimated that each horse produced 20 to 30 pounds of manure a day and that in the mid-1880s over 100,000 horses were used in public transportation alone. By the turn of the twentieth century, there were probably 3.5 million horses in American cities. Chicago had to cope with 600,000 tons of horse manure a year, and 15,000 dead horses were removed from the streets of New York City in 1880 alone (Melosi 179; Mohl 174).

Many cities began to professionalize their street cleaning agencies (which were notorious for patronage hiring and make-work jobs). In 1895, Col. George E. Waring, Jr. was appointed street cleaning commissioner for New York City by the reform mayor William L. Strong. He put an end to patronage hires, instituted curbside trash sorting, opened the nation's first rubbish reclamation plant, and dispatched 2,000 street sweepers who were nicknamed "White Wings" after their impractical but nevertheless eye-catching white uniforms. His successes prompted many other cities to adopt similar sanitary engineering techniques (Melosi 190–91).

Social Services   Considering the details of city life noted above, it should come as no surprise that institutions dedicated to public welfare were woefully inadequate during this time. Part of the reason for this was that industrial cities grew first and only later obtained what we think of as an urban infrastructure. Government was not organized to provide necessary services for a burgeoning city population, and a disconnected array of existing organizations—from settlement houses to churches to hospitals to schools—were strained to meet the demands placed upon them. However, the creation of what we would now consider modern social services faced difficulties beyond those confronting bridge building or road construction. The prevailing ideology of individualism hindered the development of social institutions, as historian Raymond Mohl notes:

Public attitudes toward the poor were often uncharitable, to say the least. Most 19th-century Americans accepted the distinctions generally drawn between the so-called worthy or deserving poor and those considered unworthy and thus undeserving. The American gospel of individualism fostered the belief that any hard-working, virtuous man could support his family in independence and dignity. Those in need, it was generally believed, had come to their dependent state through such personal failings as immorality, ignorance, idleness, and alcoholism. (155–56)

Between 1870 and 1900, as immigrants made up an increasing percentage of those in need, public programs to assist the non-institutionalized poor actually declined. Over a dozen major cities—including New York, Kansas City, New Orleans, and San Francisco—were without any formal public welfare program by 1900. Immigrants and other poor people were often left to fend for themselves in the midst of dire conditions. One reason ethnic enclaves and machine politics took root in American cities is that ethnic and local political leaders were among the few institutions to which people in need could turn (156).

CHICAGO

No city changed as much in the nineteenth century as Chicago. In 1830, it was a village of less than a thousand permanent residents built on a marshy piece of land. Overall, though, geography worked in Chicago's favor. The city's location along Lake Michigan gave it water access to eastern and even European markets. This allowed Chicago to become a main stopping and processing point for Western goods, such as cattle or grain, headed east. The city was also a primary route whereby industrial farming equipment and processed foods were shipped west via rail. In the industrial era, Chicago became the world's largest rail center. As industry grew in Chicago, the city's population rapidly increased, as shown in the table below (Griffith 23).

CHICAGO POPULATION GROWTH

1830:	less than 1,000 persons
1850:	30,000
1870:	300,000
1890:	1,100,000
1900:	1,500,000

(Farr 87; Teaford 5, 217; Thernstrom 399)

Chicago's largest industry during the industrial era was slaughtering and meatpacking. However, by the turn of the century the city's economy had grown more diversified and its leading industries included machine tools, men's clothing, steel and iron, agricultural tools, and railroad cars. Chicago was the most quickly industrializing city in the United States, and it also had some of the most horrifying social conditions. It was a city known for both the luxury of its millionaires and the misery of its large population of poor people. In Chicago, all the majesty and all the tragedy of the Industrial City could be witnessed firsthand.

Before the Fire In 1870, Chicago was still a preindustrial or walking city in its layout. Though its population stood at 300,000 at this time, and it had more ship traffic than New York City, most of the commerce of Chicago was clustered around a downtown area that took up less than one square mile. Similarly, a lack of building codes meant that neighborhoods were not segregated by income. Rich and poor often lived side by side with mansions abutting pine shanties; residences and businesses were intermixed; and only 88 of Chicago's 530 miles of road were paved. That said, Chicago in 1870 was also a city of stark contrasts. More than half of the city's population was foreign born and two-thirds were poor, but a small elite controlled much of the city's wealth. Chicago in 1870 was a city that seemed poised for growth, but first it would have to confront tragedy (Miller 134–35).

The Great Chicago Fire On the night of October 8, 1871, in the midst of one of the worst droughts Chicago had faced, a fire broke out on the west side of the city. Though Chicago had both a network of fire-alarms and a group of fire spotters who watched over the city from observation towers, a screen of coal smoke made it difficult to determine where the origin of the fire was, and volunteer fire fighting units were sent to an area about a mile away from where the fire actually began. This delay turned out to have disastrous consequences. By the time firefighters reached the blaze an hour later, it had already engulfed the wooden shanties and stables of a west side immigrant neighborhood. Gusts of wind quickly spread sparks and soon the fire jumped the Chicago River, igniting the South Side Gas Works. The river itself, coated with oil and grease, caught fire. A recently built million-dollar courthouse fell in the fire's path (destroying the title records for all properties in Cook County), in addition to banks, churches, hotels and theaters (Miller 143–58).

It took two days before the fire burned itself out on the prairie grasses on the city's outskirts. In the end, an estimated 300 people were dead, 100,000 persons were left homeless, and $190 million dollars in property was destroyed (including 17,450 buildings). Parts of Chicago looked like a charred prairie. Relief aid quickly poured into the city as makeshift shelters and distribution sites were established. Although the fire made no distinction between rich and poor, the disaster relief agencies worked differently. Agencies brought aid directly to wealthy victims, while the poor had to line up at distribution centers and prove that they were in need (Miller 159–68).

In the aftermath of the fire, it must have seemed hard to believe that Chicago would ever again reach the same level of prominence. But while the fire forever altered many individual lives, and certain businesses such as insurance would not recover for many years, Chicago began to rebuild at a rapid pace.

The greatest physical change brought about by the 1871 fire was the transformation of downtown Chicago. New building codes, designed at the behest of city business leaders, created a larger downtown area devoted to retail and business. Former downtown slum areas such as Conley's Patch and the Wells Street vice district disappeared. When streetcar lines were established to bring middle-class shoppers and workers from the new suburbs into downtown it took on the designation of "the Loop," a nickname it still has today. Chicago's distinctive skyscrapers also appeared in the decades after the fire. Advances in steel and elevator technology made it possible for buildings over ten stories tall to be built and productively used, and Chicago businesses and real estate developers clamored for them (Miller 275–76, 306–11).

Chicago Rebuilt

As Chicago developed as an industrial city, it became simultaneously decentralized and specialized. Its population spread out into new, economically stratified, suburban areas connected to the downtown by an expanding set of streetcar lines (and eventually an elevated system of trains that is still a mainstay of public transportation in Chicago today). "Instant suburbs," as they were called, were quickly constructed on speculation by builders and developers. Middle-class families and some well-paid working-class families soon filled them up. As developers realized the attraction of nearby park land to suburban residents, parks and boulevards were laid out all along the city's outskirts in the 1880s and 1890s (Miller 277–90).

Chicago's poor remained in crowded neighborhoods outside the Loop and outside the new fire-code districts. Though Chicago had relatively few buildings constructed with the aim of being tenements, many formerly one-family frame and brick houses were subdivided into apartments with the aim of fitting as many people as possible into a structure. Yards became filled with shoddily constructed wooden additions designed to house the ever-growing population of workers arriving in Chicago. These crowded sections of the city were some of the worst slums in the world. Parts of Chicago had three times the population density as the most crowded parts of Tokyo or Calcutta. Many sections remained unserved by streetcars and were far from the new parks. And, of course, this was where the vast majority of Chicagoans lived (Hunter 127; Miller 191, 275–76; Putnam 373).

Sanitary Chicago   As late as 1855, Chicago had no sewers at all. Up until that time, human waste and other garbage was simply dumped into ditches along the sides of roads. Providing Chicago with sewers posed engineering difficulties, as the city had been built on low-lying land. The solution, provided by Ellis Chesbrough, one of the new breed of sanitary engineers, was to lay the sewers at street level and raise the streets ten feet. This project required immense amounts of dirt fill as well the deployment of a screw-operated lift system to raise most of the city's buildings. As ingenious as this solution was, however, it had a fatal flaw. Adopted before germ theory was widely understood, Chesbrough's sewer plan had its water intake close to where sewage entered Lake Michigan. As a result, this new sewage system worsened Chicago's water supply and led to an increase in waterborne diseases. To solve this problem, more incredible engineering feats were undertaken. In 1863, Chesbrough supervised the digging of a tunnel two miles under Lake Michigan to a new water-intake point. In the 1880s, engineers actually reversed the flow of the Chicago River, connecting it to the Illinois-Michigan canal so that sewage from the city stayed out of Lake Michigan and flowed southward toward the Mississippi River (Mohl 175–76).

Within the city, however, sanitation standards followed along class lines. The wealthy and middle classes had access to water and sewage services, while running water remained a scarce commodity in poor neighborhoods. By the end of the 1880s, barely 25 percent of poor households had indoor plumbing. In the 1890s, over 250,000 poor residents had no bathing facilities (D. Ward 82; Miller 457).

A Tale of Two Chicagos   In the last decade of the century, Chicago made two substantial but very different contributions to daily life in the United States. The city hosted the 1893 World Columbian Exposition, a hugely successful World's Fair that set new standards for urban and suburban development. Chicago also was the site of Hull-House, the influential American settlement house founded by Jane Addams in 1889. While there is much that can be said about these institutions (they have both been written about extensively), they are interesting in the context of this study for how they influenced the way that Americans thought about the city and the possibilities of transforming urban life.

Officially, the 1893 World's Columbian Exposition was held to commemorate Columbus's 1492 voyage to America. But for Chicago, the city that beat out New York to serve as host for the celebration, the Exposition served as an unofficial coming out party to announce Chicago as a world-class city. Certainly, the Exposition attracted a worldwide following. An estimated 27 million people attended the fair, and half of them were international visitors. At the time, it was the most popular tourist destination there had ever been in the United States (Miller 488).

As with other World's Fairs, the Exposition featured rides, exhibits, and food. But its greatest influence on American culture was its architecture. The centerpiece of the fair was the elaborate "White City" constructed at the heart of the fairgrounds. Built primarily on a neo-classical model (i.e., modeled after the ancient buildings of Greece and Rome) and laid out along a landscape designed by Frederick Law Olmsted, the White City was everything American cities at the time were not: carefully planned, meticulously clean, and at the forefront of technology. Complete with its own electricity, sewage, and water plants (as well as the world's first Ferris wheel), the White City also was designed with pedestrians in mind. The streets were made to handle large crowds, there were no peddlers selling their wares, and a transportation canal system wound through the grounds.

For many fairgoers, the White City was an image of what an urban center could be, and it helped to spawn a movement in the first decade of the 1900s known as City Beautiful. The reformers who were part of this movement, men such as Arnold Brunner, Daniel Burnham, and Charles Mulford Robinson, envisioned their work as both aesthetic and moral. They wanted to coordinate city planning efforts and emphasize the inspirational impact of carefully constructed buildings and landscapes. The end result, they hoped, would be not only to do away with the visual clutter of most American cities, but to clean them up morally. The White City provided the model for what such a city would look like and it inspired the development and redevelopment of cities from Washington, D.C., to Denver to Chicago itself.

Of course, the problem of the model of the White City was that it was only an edifice. Behind its display lay the lives of the men and women who worked to construct and run the Exposition. Many of these men and women lived in the slums of Chicago, often in appalling conditions. It was this unbeautiful city that was the focus of Hull-House and the American Settlement movement.

Hull-House was founded by Jane Addams, who was herself among the first generation of college educated women in the United States. Inspired by a post-graduation visit to the Toynbee Hall settlement house in London, Addams aimed to establish a similar model in Chicago in a rundown

The Exposition grounds at the 1893 World's Columbian Exposition in Chicago. (Courtesy Library of Congress)

mansion she rented on Halsted Street. Settlement houses brought middle-class reformers into some of the poorest urban neighborhoods. Addams and the women who worked with her lived among the people they aimed to serve. Their goal was to provide both material as well as cultural uplift, or as the Hull-House charter stated, "To provide a center for a higher civic and social life; to institute and maintain educational and philanthropic enterprises, and to investigate and improve the conditions in the industrial districts of Chicago" (Addams 89). As a result, Hull-House soon came to be the site of everything from soup kitchens and public baths to art galleries to book discussion groups.

However, as Addams's early idealism was tempered by her experience with the material deprivations of the people she served, she quickly turned against a model of providing charity and became more broadly, and more politically, involved in the conditions of Chicago's poor. As

Addams wrote, "One of the first lessons we learned at Hull-House was that private beneficence is totally inadequate to deal with the vast numbers of the city's disinherited" (219). This belief led Addams and her compatriots to become immersed in the politics of the time. Florence Kelly, an early Hull-House resident, headed an investigation of sweat shop and child labor conditions in Chicago that eventually led to passage of the state's first law regulating factory employment. This law regulated sanitary conditions and barred children under fourteen from working in factories. As a result of Addams's lobbying for better trash collection, she herself was once appointed to the unlikely position of ward garbage inspector (149–51, 203).

Hull-House captured the imagination of many middle-class reformers, and its many successes with the immigrant population that made use of its services led to larger undertakings. Eventually Hull-House came to encompass thirteen buildings as part of what Donald L. Miller calls "a veritable department store of social welfare" (420). Hull-House's successes led to similar settlement houses in other cities (6 by 1891, 74 in 1897, and almost 400 by 1910). This movement of settlement houses also provided on-the-job training for some of the leading reformers of the progressive era (Putnam 393–94).

However, Hull-House did have some conspicuous failures. For example, an effort to establish a public kitchen failed largely because the volunteers of Hull-House looked down on and refused to provide the traditional food of immigrant cultures. As Jane Addams noted, the failure of the kitchen "was best summed up by the woman who frankly confessed that the food was certainly nutritious, but that she didn't like to eat what was nutritious, that she liked to eat 'what she'd ruther (sic)' " (102). Where the efforts of Hull-House floundered, it was often because of the efforts of middle-class reformers to impose their beliefs on immigrant and working-class populations (Spain 227).

It is important to recognize that at the time of Hull-House's founding, there were almost no government supported relief or welfare programs. Poor and immigrant populations could only rely on each other or perhaps the patronage of ward bosses. Addams's reform efforts represented an unprecedented attempt to rethink how services should be delivered in the industrial city. In doing so, she launched new ways of thinking about the city itself. One of Addams's early projects was a study called *Hull-House Maps and Papers*. The first study of its kind, it attempted to map out scientifically the ethnic and socio-economic makeup of the neighborhood Hull-House served, as a means of calling for reform. Working in a period before the establishment of the fields of social work or sociology, Jane Addams and the individuals of Hull-House were important precursors of both.

Visitors to Chicago were often taken aback by the city's congestion and busyness. As William Stead wrote in his reform-minded 1894 book, *If Christ Came to Chicago,*

Accounting for Chicago

The first impression which a stranger receives on arriving in Chicago is that of the dirt, the danger and the inconvenience of the streets. Those accustomed to the care that is taken in civilized cities to keep the roadway level and safe for teams and carriages stand simply aghast at the way in which the thoroughfares are corduroyed by ill-laid, old-fashioned street car lines...If a stranger's first impression of Chicago is that of the barbarous gridironed streets, his second is that of the multitude of mutilated people whom he meets on crutches. (Stead qtd. in Cook et al. 62)

Though written in a hyperbolic style, Stead's concerns were not without merit. There were no limits on train crossings within the city and by the late 1880s, an average of two persons per day were killed or injured in street-level railroad accidents (Miller 184).

However, for other observers the growth of Chicago was nothing less than a cause for celebration. As Charles Dudley Warner wrote in 1888 in *Harper's*,

The growth of Chicago is one of the marvels of the world. I do not wonder that it is incomprehensible even to those who have seen it year by year. As I remember it in 1860, it was one of the shabbiest and most unattractive cities of about a hundred thousand inhabitants anywhere to be found; but even then it had more than trebled its size in ten years...Yet I am not sure that even then the exceedingly busy and excited traders and speculators did not feel that the town was more important than New York. For it had a great business. Aside from its real estate operations, its trade that year was set down at $97,000,000, embracing its dealing in produce, its wholesale supply business, and its manufacturing. No one then, however, would have dared to predict that the value of trade in 1887 would be, as it was, $1,103,000,000. Nor could anyone have believed that the population of 100,000 would reach in 1887 nearly 800,000 (estimated 782,644), likely to reach in 1888, with the annexation of contiguous villages that have become physically a part of the city, the amount of 900,000. Growing at its usual rate for several years past, the city is certain in a couple of years to count its million of people. And there is not probably anywhere congregated a more active and aggressive million, with so great a proportion of young, ambitious blood. (870–71)

The same frenzy of activity that had taken Stead aback was a source of excitement to Warner. He marveled at the increase of both business and population in Chicago, and he saw it as a city of the future, slated (correctly, as it turns out) for even greater growth.

In 1899, the city of Chicago increased its physical size from 36 to 170 square miles by annexing adjoining suburbs. With that act, it became a city of 1,400 miles of paved streets, 38,000 street lamps (many electric), and almost 1,000 miles of streetcar lines. 500 million gallons of water passed through the Water Works per day, it had 1,500 miles of sewers, 2,000 acres of parkland, and more than 20 skyscrapers. However, the successes of Chicago were not shared equally. Donald L. Miller writes that by the 1890s Chicago had become "an intensely centralized, economically segregated city with a belt of despair rimming the Loop. There, newly arrived immigrants living in horrific poverty, surrounded by ring after ring of rising affluence, a settlement pattern shaped by the city's transit system" (275–76). Chicago was a city with much to offer and much to take. In this, Chicago had become the Midwest's most prominent city and, to many, the quintessential American city (Melosi 105; Miller 177).

2

The Railroad

INTRODUCTION

It is difficult to overestimate the importance of the railroad in the industrial era. Americans responded to the rise of the railroads with both great excitement and great anger. Railroads made many new experiences possible, but they also made many people dependent on the trains for their livelihoods and survival. Though the railroad became a crucial part of public life, railroads in the United States were almost exclusively private enterprises.

Railroad construction and operation became the largest U.S. industry at this time and was the main market for the nation's second largest industry, steel production. Railroad operation was a highly competitive business with huge fixed costs that made it vulnerable during periods of economic turmoil such as the depressions of 1873 and 1893. The contradictory economy of the railroad business also played a role in engendering both hopefulness and cynicism. As Ernest S. Griffith notes, "many of these early railroads brought their promoters great wealth through land speculation, timber, coal, watered stock, profitable contracts in their construction—in almost everything except in the operation of the railroads themselves" (28). Not surprisingly, the interests of owners, passengers, and shippers were often at odds. When railway owner William Vanderbilt was asked by a reporter about the railroad's responsibility to the public, his response, "The public be damned," confirmed for many Americans the attitude of the railroad "robber barons" (qtd. in Daniels 78). When railroad workers and their allies revolted during the Great Uprising of 1877, the worst fears of the owner class were confirmed.

Furthermore, railroads did not simply supplement American society with a new means of transportation. Railroads, because of their scope of operation, the vast amount of money involved in their construction and operation, and the technological leap they represented, transformed fundamental aspects of American culture. They changed the nature of urban and rural life, made possible the settlement of the west by European-Americans, led to corruption and labor strife on a scale never before seen, and even altered the way Americans experienced time.

THE TRANSCONTINENTAL RAILROAD AND ITS AFTERMATH

Though the first railroad appeared in the United States in 1828, the event that truly set the railroad era in motion was the 1869 completion of a transcontinental railroad connecting New York City to Sacramento. The transcontinental was an engineering achievement but a political and financial scandal. It was the cause of national excitement as well as widespread cynicism, setting the stage for Americans' contradictory feelings toward the railroad in the industrial era (Daniels 19).

On May 10, 1869, dignitaries, onlookers, and workers of both the Central Pacific and Union Pacific converged on Promontory, Utah, where the two railroad companies building the transcontinental line had agreed to meet. A drunken crowd gathered for a ceremony in which California Governor Leland Stanford, with assistance from a Union Pacific work boss, drove a golden spike into a railroad tie connecting the two lines of rail (Stanford quickly had the golden spike removed in fear that it would be stolen). At the time, the completion of the railroad was seen to herald the beginning of a new era of trade with Asia. However, the railroad turned out to be historic for very different reasons. Trade with Asia never fully prospered; for example, Asian trade made up only five percent of the Union Pacific's business in 1891. In the five years after the completion of the transcontinental, California's population actually decreased by 35,000 (Ambrose 370–71; Daniels 54; Wormser 83).

The importance of the railroad developed, not in the area of international trade, but along the railroad's own lines, as Rudolph Daniels writes:

Towns sprang up along the track around water and coaling stations for the locomotives. There were restaurants for passengers. Just as important, station spacings were at a convenient distance for farmers to bring their produce to the depot within one day's wagon ride from nearby farms. Moreover, the railroads sold the land at prices affordable to the average homesteader. Many times, the men who laid the tracks purchased property and settled down on farms. (54)

The transcontinental railroad made expanding American settlement on the continent feasible, drawing unprecedented numbers of internal and external migrants to the Plains and West. In fact, between 1870 and 1900, more U.S. land was brought under cultivation than during the previous 250 years. But the railroad was not constructed without financial and social costs. To get the transcontinental built, the U.S. government had given the railroads unprecedented grants of land along the right of way for the rails. Soon after the railroad was completed, scandals surrounding its construction engulfed the nation. Governmental hearings revealed that railroad companies and their financers had bribed congressmen and pocketed huge government subsidies while paying the lowest possible wages to the largely immigrant Chinese and Irish workers who built the line. Furthermore, some of the lines were laid inadequately and almost immediately had to be replaced. Though government loans to the railroads were eventually paid back, the impression of railroad corporations as influential, corrupt, and greedy became a common refrain in the industrial era (Ambrose 374–75; Daniels 55; Gutman 518).

A TYPICAL DAY BUILDING A RAILROAD

In the morning the men were up at first light. After their toilet they went to wash faces and hands in a tin basin, had a hearty breakfast, and went to the job, whether plowing, shoveling, placing ties or rails, spiking them in, or putting on the fish-plates at the junction of two rails. At noon, "Time" was called and they had an hour for a heavy dinner that included pitchers of steaming coffee, pans of soup, platters heaped with fried meat, roast meat, potatoes, condensed milk diluted with water, sometimes canned fruit and pies or cakes. There was little conversation: the men were there to eat, and they made a business of it.

Afterward, they sat around their bunks smoking, sewing on buttons, or taking a little nap. Then back to work, with the bosses cursing and excoriating to overcome the noontime lassitude. "Time" was called again an hour before supper, to allow some rest. The evening meal was more leisurely. Then to the bunkhouses, for card games, a smoke, lots of talk ("railroad talk" was said to consist entirely of "whisky and women and higher wages and shorter hours"), perhaps a song, such as "Poor Paddy he works on the railroad" or "The great Pacific railway for California hail." Then to bed, the whole to be repeated the next day and the next and the next.

—From Stephen E. Ambrose, *Nothing Like It in the World*, 179

TRAVELING BY RAIL

The technology that made transcontinental travel possible and freight shipments profitable did not always make passenger travel comfortable. Over time, a variety of means were undertaken to make the experience of rail travel more enjoyable. However, the quality of commercial travel by rail varied greatly during the industrial era, primarily on the basis of how much passengers were willing to pay and what region of the country they were in. The rich were more likely to take long excursion trips while the middle and working class often used trains for day trips or regional vacations. During a time when the only other mode of land-based transportation was a horse, the railroad opened up unprecedented opportunities for travelers to see sections of the country that most only read about prior to the arrival of the rails.

Standard Accommodations With the exception of the long rail journeys made by immigrants and other homesteaders, the distance one traveled by train usually conformed to one's social class. Working-class urban dwellers may have been able to afford the occasional day trip out of the city, from Manhattan to Coney Island or from Boston to Revere Beach. Middle-class vacationers have been more likely to take the train farther, perhaps from Boston to a summer cottage in Cape Cod. Middle-class organizations and professional groups were often able to get group rates for national meetings or for trips to World's Fairs. Most transcontinental vacationers were wealthy, however. A typical Boston to California luxury tour in 1889 cost $400 to $630 at a time when the average working-class yearly salary was less than $500 (Gordon 180, 284, 306).

Railroads, with their enormous fixed operation costs, were eager to encourage transcontinental travel, especially among the rich. They built luxury hotels on the sites of famous Indian battles. They were among the most vocal lobbyists for the creation of the first national park, Yellowstone. But making rail travel comfortable created a series of logistical problems for the railroad industry. For example, among the dangers of commercial rail travel were sparks cast off by the massive railroad engines. Cinders from passing trains frequently set fire to wooden bridges and private land, and, despite the development of spark arresters, passengers often found their clothing burned by bits of debris that would drift in through open windows. Similarly, providing light in train coaches was a constant problem. Kerosene lamps were an improvement over the candles used before the Civil War, but they were dirty as well as a fire hazard. By the turn of the century, compressed gas lamps had become widespread, but it would be another decade before electric lighting was common on trains (Bianculli 211–12; Daniels 94; Gordon 304).

Pullman Cars Though sleeping cars had been in existence before the Civil War, the innovation of George Pullman's cars was to provide elite accommodations at a time when transcontinental railroads made it possible for the wealthy to take extended train trips. Pullman's sleeper cars brought the feel of a luxury hotel to the railroad, both in furnishings and service. Pullman cars looked like well-appointed passenger cars by day, but at night the seats were folded up and private sleeping quarters were folded down from hinges in the wall. Pullman cars also came with a standardized and well trained staff. Of course, a berth on a Pullman car was much more expensive than a standard fare (costing $2 extra, typically), but the Pullman name quickly became associ-

An 1894 advertisement for Pullman dining cars. Note the idyllic factory scene through the train window and the African American porter bringing alcohol and cigars to the traveling businessmen. (Courtesy Library of Congress)

ated with elegant travel, and Pullman expanded into exclusive dining cars and private cars (Daniels 30, 66; Gordon 182; Wormser 105).

Trains could travel for a much longer time than the human stomach could. As a result, keeping passengers well fed became an immediate concern for railroads, and the industry developed a variety of ways to keep their passengers from getting hungry. Pullman built the first dining car in 1867, but many railroads operated their own restaurants-on-wheels as well. Some featured elegant dining with specialty food and fine silver. Others provided more rudimentary offerings. Dining cars were a convenient service for passengers, but they proved difficult for railroads to run profitably, as they had large fixed costs and were limited in the number of passengers they could serve at any one time (Daniels 95; Reinhardt 269).

Food on the Railroad

Trackside restaurants sprang up to provide travelers with food quickly (though passengers who paid for second class fare usually were not

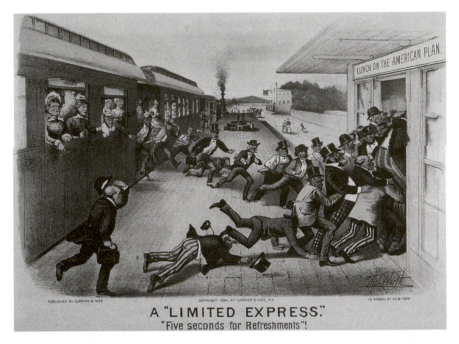

A "LIMITED EXPRESS."
"Five seconds for Refreshments"!

"A 'Limited Express.' " A Currier & Ives print parodying the short time rail passengers were given for meals at railroad stations. (Courtesy Library of Congress)

allowed to leave the train). Travelers would only be given ten or twenty minutes at a stop, leading to hurried attempts to order and eat. Some rail lines would take orders in transit and telegraph them ahead to the restaurant to further hasten the stop. Among the most famous of the rail side refreshment stops were the Fred Harvey restaurants (a precursor of today's roadside chain restaurants) along the western Santa Fe line. "Harvey Houses" were spread out every hundred miles or so along the rails, providing an elaborate menu with fresh food for set prices (Daniels 95–96; Reinhardt 265–66).

If a train had no diner car, the only other source of food was the "news butchers." These young men would walk from car to car offering travelers an assortment of food, newspapers, tobacco, trinkets, and, in some cases, pornography. They would work from one end of a train to the other, shouting to announce their arrival, frequently to the irritation of those who were trying to sleep (Reinhardt 266–67).

Recruiting Immigrants   Once the western railroads were built, they needed employees as well as a population to serve. The generous land grants provided to railroads gave them ample acreage to entice potential farmers. The Northern Pacific sent more than 800 agents to Europe and Russia to recruit potential farm families. The Union Pacific advertised in over 2,000 papers, sometimes offering deceptive promises of highly fertile land and free housing (Gordon 158; Wormser 123).

Immigrants that took the railroad companies up on their offer had a difficult trip to the West. Immigrant trains provided few services for what was often a long journey. Usually they were old passenger cars with wooden seats or converted freight cars. Immigrant trains were slow, since express or mixed passenger/freight trains had priority for track use. There were no dining services or sleeping cars. Passengers cooked on heating stoves, slept on baggage shelves, and used coats as blankets (Gordon 224–25).

Railroads struggled to establish themselves in the South. Prior to the Civil War, the South had far fewer miles of line than the North, and most of those lines had been destroyed during the war. Though there was a great deal of post-war **Railroads in the South** northern investment in southern railroads (and rail connections were seen by many as a way of reuniting the South with the North), southern rail lines were rebuilt primarily as local lines linking interior regions to the sea. The first direct rail connections between the South and the North were not built until after Reconstruction ended in 1877. Southern lines relied more on mail order business than passenger service, and the limited passenger service they provided was expensive. Southern train coaches were more likely to be mixed (with a combination of passenger and freight) and slow (even the fastest Southern line—from Mobile, Alabama to New York City—took four or five days). Southern passengers also paid more for worse service, on average, six cents per mile, which was twice the average cost in the North (Gordon 167–72).

BUILDING RAILROADS AND BUILDING RESENTMENT

The transcontinental railroad was just one of many prominent railroad construction projects following the end of the Civil War. By 1871, 160 million acres in land grants had been given to railroads (space equal to the size of California and Nevada combined). Between 1862 and 1872, the railroad industry received more than $64 million in tax breaks and loans. Of the 35,000 miles of track laid down in the decade after the Civil War, almost two-thirds was west of the Mississippi. But growth in the railroad industry was anything but stable, following the booms and busts of the economy (Gutman 517; Wormser 97, 100).

Though most rail lines began with great fanfare and promised to open up a world of travel to passengers, the everyday realities of railroad operation were more mundane. Even on profitable railroads, more money was to be made from freight transportation than from passengers. For example, as Sarah Gordon writes, "The Chicago and Northwestern, a link on the transcontinental route, in its fiscal year 1874–1875 earned $3,205,059 from its passengers and $8,837,828 from freight" (185). Such numbers were not atypical. Freight sometimes accounted for three to four times as much income as passenger travel on some railroads.

The possibilities of rail shipment transformed many aspects of the American economy. The mail order business was created when Joseph Sears realized he could market goods directly to far-flung locations through the Sears & Roebuck catalog and deliver the merchandise by rail. Most major American retailers soon followed suit. Similarly, the creation of the refrigerated rail car in 1867 changed the nature of the American beef industry. Previously, cattle had to be driven or shipped to the place of consumption before being slaughtered. But refrigeration allowed steers to be slaughtered at Midwestern locations, like Chicago and Kansas City, and then shipped east. California fruit growers were quick to make use of the technology, also (Daniels 92–93).

Because rail lines were financed primarily through government bonds, getting money to build a railroad was a highly politicized and lucrative affair, and it often led to bribery and corruption. For example, from 1868–69, the North Carolina legislature issued $17,640,000 in bonds to thirteen different railroads, but by 1871 only 93 miles of rail had been constructed. Much of the bond proceeds went into the pockets of the railroad operators or were used for bribes. One railroad promoter went as far as to set up a bar in the west wing of the Statehouse to dispense free alcohol and tobacco to legislators. Another promoter paid out more than $133,000 in bribes to government officials. By 1897, North Carolina railroads curried favor by handing out 100,000 passes for free travel by rail in a single year at an estimated cost of $325,000 (Stover 98–99, 115).

"As much as the traffic will bear" While there was a great deal of support for constructing new rail lines, making money running a railroad proved to be more problematic. Railroads had extremely high fixed costs, both from the equipment they had to maintain and the interest they had to pay on the bonds that were issued to finance construction. The 1873 collapse of Jay Cooke and Company, a leading investment bank and the primary backer of the Northern Pacific Railroad, led to a panic. The Panic of 1873, as it came to be known, closed the New York Stock Exchange for 10 days and directly led to the longest economic depression of the nineteenth century. Many smaller railroads were unable to stay in business, and a long process of consolidation in the railroad industry began, led by one of the most notorious figures of the industrial era railroad, Samuel Huntington. Huntington was the owner of the California-based Central Pacific railroad. When revenues dropped in the early 1870s, Huntington attempted unsuccessfully to sell his railroad. When that didn't work, he developed a more ambitious plan to monopolize the railroad industry in California. First, he bought up smaller lines and changed the name of his company to Southern Pacific. Then he pressured competing steamship companies not to undercut the freight rates of his trains. Although the Southern Pacific had large fixed costs and had taken on huge debts, it was a virtual monopoly. With a virtual monopoly, Huntington began to raise rates on all his customers, charging, as the famous phrase went, "as much as the traffic will bear" (Gutman 521; Wormser 113–14).

Huntington's tactics were ruthless. He played towns off of each other, demanding subsidies and payments to run a line through a particular location. In one instance he threatened to bypass Los Angeles for San Diego in order to gain a $610,000 subsidy from Los Angeles. He bribed legislators and judges to ensure that efforts to rein in his business practices were fruitless. By the 1880s, he had bought off the leadership of both California political parties (Griffith 26–27).

In one famous confrontation, farmers in San Joaquin Valley had made an arrangement to settle and irrigate an arid region of land owned by the Southern Pacific. Their agreement with Huntington allowed them to purchase the land after they had made it fit for cultivation at a fixed price of $2.50 to $5 per acre. When the farmers had turned the land into a lucrative agricultural region, Huntington reneged on his offer and put the land up for sale at $40 to $50 an acre. The farmers banded together to fight the railroad both in court (where they lost, since Huntington controlled the judges) and through vigilante actions. The railroad hired its own guns and, in a confrontation in Mussel Slough, half a dozen farmers were killed and more were forced to leave the valley (Wormser 114–16).

Not long after, two masked bandits began targeting trains on Southern Pacific lines. Police and detectives were unable to capture the robbers for a time, but suspicions centered on two men with grievances against the railroad, George Sontag, a former Southern Pacific brakeman who had been crippled in a work related accident, and Chris Evans, whose family had been evicted from land owned by the Southern Pacific. Sontag and Evans were able to elude police for over a year and a half, primarily because they were able to find many people who had a grudge against the railroad and were willing to hide them. Though Sontag was eventually killed and Evans wounded and captured, the guilt of the two men was never clear, and Evans eventually received a pardon.

The tactics of the Southern Pacific eventually provoked widespread outrage, leading to the rise of anti-railroad politicians and railroad regulations (as well as serving as the basis of Frank Norris's novel, *The Octopus*), but the Southern Pacific was not alone in inspiring anger and banditry (Wormser 116–19).

In the face of actions by railroad industry executives like Huntington, there was an enormous amount of popular support for anyone who could beat the railroad corporations. The rise of train robbers and hobos into figures of folklore needs to be appreciated within that context. As John H. Stover writes, "Farmers who felt cheated by high freight rates, investors who had lost in wildcat rail investments, railroad workers who remem-

Train Robbers and Hobos

bered the strike violence of 1877—all were little worried if other men successfully robbed cars" (157). In the last third of the 1800s, train robbers such
as Jesse James and Thomas Younger inspired sympathy, not so much for
their crimes as for their targets, railroads (as well as banks). Jesse James, in
particular, became a popular figure in the dime novels of the day, inspiring
dozens of titles, many of which presented him as a Robin Hood-like figure,
or, to use Eric Hobsbawn's term, a social bandit. As Hobsbawn argues
(using banks as his example, though the point would apply equally well to
railroads), "the period which turns institutions like banks into quintessential public villains and bank robbery into the most readily understood form
of robbing the rich marks the adaptation of social banditry to capitalism"
(qtd. in Denning 163). The dominance of railroad corporations turned
some bank robbers, deservedly or not, into popular heroes.

A similar social context accounts for attitudes toward hobos, homeless
and unemployed men who rode the rails from town to town. As Rudolph
Daniels notes, "The figure of an unshaven man wearing tattered clothes
and carrying all his possessions in a bag, called a 'bindle,' became a common figure along the tracks" (97). While some hobos paid conductors a
portion of a fare, many more hopped trains without paying and hid
between cars or would "flip" into unlocked freight cars. Riding this way
was dangerous, not in the least because, in an effort to limit hobos, railroads hired detectives nicknamed "bulls" who were known to throw hobos
off of moving trains. Other dangers can be found in this first-hand account
from a hobo who was riding on the roof of a railcar to escape detection.

There were three of us on top of that car, two lying down and one sitting up reading a paper. We came to a tunnel, and when we had passed through the man who
was reading the paper was gone. When the train made its next stop I and my companion (*sic*) went back and found the missing man lying dead on the track. That
ended my riding on top of freight cars. ("Life Story of a Greek Peddler" 75)

Some hobos inspired sympathy because they were Civil War veterans, but
others, known as "tramps," were viewed favorably for a very different reason. As Michael Denning writes, the idea of the tramp was a new concept,
"…constructed in the wake of the 1873 depression and the 1877 railroad
strikes to designate migratory and unemployed workers" (151). Tramps
were seen by many as victims of the new industrial order. Though train
robbers, hobos, and tramps could also become the subject of fear, in the
context of the railroad in the industrial era, they manifested the insecurity
and anger of many average Americans (Daniels 97; Denning 149–51).

THE RAILROAD AND THE CITY

The perception that a city's future rested with the railroad led to fierce
competition (and frequent bribes) to attract a railroad. As Raymond A.

Mohl writes, "the coming of a rail line could make a town spectacularly successful. By the same token, towns bypassed by railroads were often doomed to certain failure, or at least slow growth" (71). Railroad operators demanded, and often received, substantial subsidies to run a major line through existing urban areas, often by playing one city against another. However, attracting a rail line could be a mixed blessing. While losing out on a railroad could diminish a city's future, getting one was no guarantee of success.

For example, railroads held great risks for cities, particularly during the turbulent economic conditions of the industrial era. The city of Duluth, Minnesota, had invested heavily in the Northern Pacific railroad. But when the Panic of 1873 caused the Northern Pacific to declare bankruptcy and suspend construction, the ripple effect led to the closure of more than half of Duluth's businesses. The city itself was forced to temporarily forfeit its charter and write down its debt. It was years before Duluth regained its previous stature, though with the eventual completion of the railroad, it became the nation's largest recipient of wheat shipments by 1886 (Griffith 28–29).

Engraving of the exterior (with interior inset) of Washington, D.C.'s Pennsylvania Station in the 1880s. (Courtesy Library of Congress)

As the railroad became identified with progress in many urban areas, cities attempted to outdo each other with elaborate railroad stations located in downtown central business districts, such as the Pennsylvania Stations in both New York City and Washington, D.C. In many cases, these new terminals extended the traditional reach of downtowns, taking land that had formerly housed low-income residents. However, there was a functional reason for locating rail stations in a downtown area, as that placed them close to the industrial center of most cities (Mohl 41–42).

Rail stations in traditional downtowns created logistical problems as well. Many urban railways used what were termed "grade level crossings," tracks laid out along existing streets. Such crossings were extremely dangerous, as they required people to cross active tracks as part of their day to day lives. For example, in Albany, New York, one crossing that required pedestrians to pass over four different sets of rail lines was located a block from a hospital, a school, residences, saloons, and grocers. That crossing acquired the nickname "the Terror." Trains posed huge dangers to people who had to live in close proximity to them. In the 1870s, the most common type of steam engine weighed 70,000 pounds and had wheels standing six feet high. In New York state alone, 150 people (not including railroad employees or passengers) were killed by railroads in 1868; the number of deaths climbed to 238 in 1880, and 370 in 1889 (Stowell 13, 47, 90–91).

THE RAILROAD COMES TO TOWN

The arrival of a railroad was often a time of great hope and optimism for residents of small towns. Many civic and business leaders saw train travel as integral to an area's growth and success. Inhabitants of many towns, particularly those without water transportation, viewed trains as essential to their future. The railroad would connect previously isolated regions to the rest of the country, providing new markets for farmers and new sources of goods for consumers. However, as Sarah H. Gordon notes, "The arrival of a railroad and the construction of a station marked the transformation of towns once identified by local or regional self-sufficiency. In their place developed towns dependent on the national economy" (201).

Railroad companies aimed to establish depots at the heart of an existing town's commercial center. Soon, services catering to travelers (hotels, cafes, liveries) clustered around the station, as did industries dependent upon freight deliveries (grain elevators, factories, coal, and lumber mills). Depots became landmarks in small towns and, though privately owned by railroads, they quickly became social centers and community institutions. As H. Roger Grant and Charles W. Bohi write, "Since the railroad brought virtually all visitors to town, communities commonly sought to beautify the track area so as to make a good impression on the traveler, just as civic types today seek to avoid 'visual pollution' along urban inter-

An 1888 parade in Deadwood, South Dakota, celebrating the completion of a section of railroad. (Courtesy Library of Congress)

state highways and near airports" (3). It was common for towns to place public parks near stations. Railroad companies tended to be less interested in investing money into the upkeep of small depots, however. In one case, residents of Stanton, Iowa took matters into their own hands. When the Chicago, Burlington & Quincy Railroad refused to repaint a worn depot in Stanton, citizens took up brushes and painted it themselves (Grant and Bohi 3, 8).

In some cases, railroad companies literally made the town, laying out town sites and even naming towns that had no inhabitants in anticipation of future arrivals. In the early 1870s the town of Primghar, Iowa got its name when a town site promoter created a name out of the first letters of the names of the first eight train passengers to arrive at a newly constructed rural station (Grant and Bohi 10).

FARMERS AND THE RAILROAD

Midwestern and western farmers had perhaps the most contentious relationship with the railroad. On one hand, railroads made home-steading possible in the first place. Trains brought many farmers west to begin with and shipped necessary provisions to them after that. Rail shipments also connected farmers to their markets in the more heavily populated East. However, whereas eastern farmers may have had the option of personally bringing their goods to market, most western farmers were entirely dependent upon the railroad to deliver their crops, and since few farms were serviced by more than one railroad, they had no alternative but to pay whatever rate their local railroad charged.

Beginning in the 1870s, agricultural production increased dramatically—corn and wheat production more than tripled—but the amount farmers were paid for their crops declined. For example, Robert C. McMath, Jr. writes that "By the end of the 1880s the price that one bushel [of wheat] would bring had dropped from $1.19 to $0.49" (46). At the same time, railroads engaged in fierce interstate competition and attempted to make up the difference by charging more along lines where they had a monopoly, particularly for transporting freight for short trips rather than over long distances. John Stover notes that during this time, "The grain rate from the Twin Cities to Chicago in the nineties was 12.5 cents a hundred pounds, while the rate from many Minnesota towns to St. Paul was 25 cents a hundred" (114). In what became known as the "Long Haul—Short Haul" controversy, farmers' organizations such as the Grange (which had over 800,000 members in 1873) lobbied state and federal authorities to pass regulations, and they achieved some measure of success when the U.S. Congress passed the Interstate Commerce Act in 1887, the first legislation that regulated railroad operations nationally (Daniels 78–79; Meyers 67; Stover 113–15).

The Long Winter, one of the books in Laura Ingalls Wilder's "Little House on the Prairie" series based on her childhood experience, details the struggles of the Ingalls family, led by her parents Charles and Caroline, to persevere through the winter of 1880–81 in present day De Smet, South Dakota. The railroad made it possible for the family to become homesteaders, but it also made families like the Ingalls dependent on the railroad for basic necessities. In this novel, Wilder tells of a year when constant blizzards and snow drifts made it impossible for trains to get through. By April, the Ingalls are burning hay for fuel, they are unable to repair their shanty due to a shortage of materials, and they are starting to run out of food. The Ingalls are down to their last week's supply of grain when news finally arrives that a freight train is heading toward them. When the whistle sounds, announcing the train's arrival, Charles Ingalls joins a group of men from the town who go to meet the train. However, instead of carrying supplies, the train turns out to be a combination freight-immigrant train. The angry townsmen force Mr. Woodworth, the local stationmaster, to break into the immigrant car and demand a share of the food the immigrants had. Charles then brings potatoes, flour, and fat salt pork back to his family. When Caroline Ingalls suggests that it was wrong to break into the immigrant car, Charles uncharacteristically explodes:

"I'm past caring what he ought to do!" Pa said savagely. "Let the railroad stand some damages! This isn't the only family in town that's got nothing to eat. We told

Woodworth to open up that car or we'd do it. He tried to argue that there'll be another train tomorrow, but we didn't feel like waiting. Now if you'll boil some potatoes and fry some meat, we'll have us a dinner." (322)

Because so much of rural life in the industrial era depended on trains and because railroads made such enormous profits, even honest Charles Ingalls could be driven to anger against them.

WORKING ON THE RAILROAD

Building a railroad and running steam engines along it required a great deal of cooperative work among workers in both skilled and non-skilled positions. Nostalgic writings on the "Era of Steam" (of which there are many) view railroad work as a romantic undertaking, but it could be difficult and poor paying. Additionally, railroad work was often extremely dangerous and, until 1887, there were no federally mandated safety regulations. Many railroad workers were termed "boomers," which meant they moved around to where the work and wages were best, following the "booms" of construction and operation rather than settling down in one location.

The job of building railroads was physically grueling and often hazardous. Railroad construction workers had to labor in extreme weather conditions, and they would break through mountain ranges by dynamite and pick ax. As **Railroad Builders** Rudolph Daniels writes of the first transcontinental railroad, "it was the last grand project completed before the use of mechanized tools. Except for the use of black powder, the workers used the same techniques as the Egyptian pyramid builders or those who put up the Great Wall in China" (51). Railroad construction tended to be work taken on by those with limited employment options, often young Irish men, or male Chinese immigrants.

RAIL MILEAGE

The number of miles of rail grew enormously in the industrial era. From 1869 (the year the transcontinental railroad was completed) to 1900, total rail mileage more than quadrupled. The peak year for operating miles of rail in the United States was 1916 when 254,057 miles were in use.

Year	Total miles of rail in operation
1869	46,844
1875	74,096
1880	93,296
1885	128,320

Year	Total miles of rail in operation
1890	163,597
1895	180,657
1900	193,346

(Daniels 228)

The Chinese railroad workers played a unique role during the period. They were hired directly from China under what was called "contract labor." This system, which was similar to indentured servitude, required Chinese immigrants to work for a certain period of time for a specific railroad to pay for their passage across the Pacific. Chinese workers tended to be given the most dangerous jobs and they were often exploited, but they also proved to be very productive workers.

The presence of Chinese workers on construction crews proved controversial, both because contract labor employment could depress wages for other workers and because the Chinese were victims of racism and violence from their co-workers and the population at large. Following the completion of the transcontinental railroad (for which 12,000 Chinese were hired), California passed a law in 1870 that it used to refuse Chinese women the right to immigrate. In 1882, the Federal Chinese Exclusion Act forbid the immigration of all Chinese. Nevertheless, Chinese workers remained vital in building railroads from Washington to Texas (Daniels 52; Okihiro 15, 84, 180).

Engineers   The figure of the engineer has become most prominent in the folklore of the railroad. Engineers like Casey Jones, an actual engineer, became legends for narrowly avoiding accidents or sacrificing their lives for the safety of their passengers. Engineers were among the only railroad employees during the 1870s to maintain a union, the Brotherhood of Locomotive Engineers, largely because good engineers could make a huge difference in the functioning of a railroad, and the rail corporations could not afford to fire them (as they were quick to do with non-skilled workers with union sympathies). In the early years of the industrial era, engineers would not only drive the locomotive but were responsible for its repair and maintenance as well. The skill of an engineer, or "hogger" as they were commonly known, made a huge difference in the cost of running trains. An engine pulling forty freight cars could use anywhere between forty and two hundred pounds of coal per mile, largely depending on the skill of the engineers. Those hoggers who burned a great deal of coal earned the nickname, "pounders" (Daniels 89; P. Foner, *Great* 16; Reinhardt 129; Stromquist 105).

Firemen   Firemen on locomotives did not put out fires; they started and maintained them. The fireman worked alongside the engineer and was responsible for maintaining the engine's steam boiler and supplying it with coal. His most dangerous task entailed climbing out onto the boiler of a moving train to oil the valves with a long nosed can of liquid tallow. Failing to oil the boiler properly could cause the entire engine to explode. On coal-fed steam engines, a fireman might also be expected to shovel as much as a ton of coal per hour. Undoubtedly, it was an anonymous fireman with a sore back who scornfully came up with the term "pounder" to describe engineers who made his job more difficult (Daniels 31; Reinhardt 107).

The industrial era conductor was far more than just a ticket taker. Conductors wore dress uniforms and were gen- **Conductors** erally accorded respect by passengers and crewmembers alike. As one commentator at the time wrote, "The American conductor is usually a well-to-do, intelligent, gentlemanly person, with a fair place in society, a great deal of popular consideration, and as good a claim to it as is enjoyed by the captains of our ocean steamers" ("American" 491). It was the conductor who determined when trains left stations and how long they stayed. Conductors were responsible for maintaining order among the passengers, and they were known to order a train stopped to discharge an unruly passenger. They would also put out fires set by cinders from the engine (Daniels 31, 76; Reinhardt 285).

It was the rare brakeman who made it through a career on the railroad without the loss of fingers or injuries from a **Brakemen** serious fall. Braking a train at this time was very dangerous. The only brakes a train had were located on each car, and they had to be manually applied by turning wheels located on the car's roof. When the engineer signaled for a stop, brakemen had to leap from roof to roof, turning the braking wheels. At night or in bad weather, it was easy for brakemen to slip and fall on a roof, sometimes to their deaths.

One of a brakeman's other jobs was to join together individual cars on a train by what was called a link-and-pin coupler (though in rail yards, putting together cars in this manner also would be the job of a switchman). In this procedure, a brakeman would have to stand between cars and use his hands to guide the pin of a slowly moving car into the socket of a stationary car and then quickly move out of the way. A slight miscalculation could result in death or a serious injury, as in this firsthand account by Herbert E. Hamblen:

I was making a coupling one afternoon. I had balanced the pin in the drawhead of the stationary car and was running along ahead of the other car, holding up the link. Just before the two cars were to come together, the one behind me left the track, having jumped a frog. Hearing the racket, I sprang to one side, but my toe caught the top of the rail. I was pinned between the corners of the cars as they came together. I heard my ribs cave in like an old box smashed with an ax. (86)

Hamblen recovered and was able to work again, but the story of his accident was not unique. The most dangerous job on industrial era railroads was that of brakeman (Stromquist 105).

Sadly, automatic couplers and air brakes operated from the locomotive had been available soon after the Civil War, making the brakeman's hazardous tasks unnecessary. Railroads were unwilling to undertake the expense of installing them, and it took the passage of the landmark 1893 Safety Appliance Act for these devices to become standard on all railroads. In the thirty years that these safety devices had been available but unused, 65,000 railroad men had been killed and 750,000 injured. In the decade after the law went into effect, the yearly death rate was cut in half and the injury rate declined by more than two-thirds (Reinhardt 280).

Pullman Porters

The work of a Pullman porter was neither glamorous nor lucrative, but among the limited employment options open to African Americans in the industrial era, becoming a Pullman porter ranked among the most reliable. The reasons George Pullman chose to employ only African American porters remain unclear (theories range from a promise Pullman made to President Lincoln to the ability to pay these employees low wages). Pullman porters, who were almost exclusively addressed by customers as "George," were expected to meet all needs of passengers, from moving luggage to offering a final "dust off" at the end of a journey. They had to put up with demanding and sometimes insulting passengers, and, as they made most of their money from tips, they quickly learned how to size up travelers, as in this account by H. N. Hall.

I have been asked quite often who are the best passengers and tippers. That question is hard to answer, but my first choice goes to the regular riders, such as traveling salesmen, who ride weekly or monthly. These men know service; they are reasonable; and your tip, though only standard, is sure. Then there is the working class, who work a year to take a vacation. They have itemized every little detail for the two weeks' trip, and they never forget the porter. Newlyweds are also good. The groom tips fast and heavy, especially in the presence of the bride, and he is always in her presence. Women traveling alone are very conservative with their tips. (300–301)

The work of a Pullman porter involved extremely long hours and a great deal of time away from family, but it was not unusual for a son to follow his father into the same profession (Daniels 129; Reinhardt 298; Wormser 105).

THE RAILROAD AND SOCIAL LIFE

Segregation

The main distinction railroads made among passengers had to do with the price of their tickets. This meant, as James Alan McPherson writes, "Traditionally, American railroad coaches have provided a greater degree of democratic interaction than any other mode of transportation in the history of the world" (79–80). Trains were places where people of different classes and races interacted, often in a manner unlike that which law and custom would have allowed outside the train.

As interstate railroads grew, the culture of the train began to come into conflict with local or regional laws and standards, particularly segregation regulations in southern states after Reconstruction. Segregation, the legal separation of peoples of different races, was the law in many southern states, but it was a regulation many railroads were reluctant to enforce. It wasn't that the railroad companies were necessarily more enlightened on racial issues. Rather it was an additional expense to provide racially seg-regated cars, particularly on small lines. This was especially the case for railroads traveling across the Mason-Dixon line from northern into south-ern regions.

One of the most infamous Supreme Court cases of the era, Plessy vs. Ferguson (1898), arose out of this very situation. Homer Plessy, a biracial Louisianan, challenged the Louisiana statute that mandated segregated coaches in railroads, arguing that as someone of seven-eighths European ancestry, he should not be forced to ride in "colored" railroad coaches. However, the Supreme Court ruled against Plessy in its famous "separate but equal" decision, paving the way for the segregation of public facilities throughout the South.

The everyday indignities of segregation on the railroad were illustrated in Charles Chesnutt's 1901 novel, *The Marrow of Tradition*. In one chapter, the novel's protagonist, Dr. William Miller, an African American doctor, takes a train from Philadelphia to North Carolina. Along the way he meets his former teacher and mentor, Dr. Alvin Burns, who is white. The two men sit together and catch up on old times, but, when the train passes through Virginia, a conductor informs Miller that he will have to move into a "colored" coach. When Burns angrily objects to this treatment of his friend, the conductor informs him, "'The law gives me the right to remove him by force. I can call on the train crew to assist me, or on other passen-gers. If I should choose to put him off the train entirely, in the middle of a swamp, he would have no redress—the law so provides" (55). Eventually Miller chooses to defuse the situation by removing himself to the dirty and worn car set aside for black passengers, though he remains embit-tered by the experience.

Traditional timekeeping methods, what was called "sun time" or even "God's time," involved measuring noon by when the sun had peaked in the sky and adjusting clocks and watches accordingly. This meant that noon occurred at a different time depending on how far east or west a partic- **Railroad Time vs. Sun Time** ular city was. These small differences were of little importance in an era when nothing moved any faster than a horse, but by the early 1870s there were over 150 railroad companies in operation, and many towns and cities were serviced by more than one line. Wisconsin had thirty-eight different local times and Illinois had twenty-seven. Travelers making transcontinental trips had to reset their watches twenty times (Daniels 81; Stover 146; Wormser 106).

"SUN TIME"

Prior to the adoption of Standard Time in 1883, the exact time of noon varied greatly, even within the same region of the country. According to what was called "sun time," the following local times would all occur at the same moment.

11:27	Omaha
11:50	St. Louis
Noon	Chicago
12:07	Indianapolis
12:09	Louisville
12:17	Toledo
12:24	Cleveland
12:31	Cincinnati

(Stover 145; Wormser 106)

Because of the confusion brought about by so many different times, railroad companies formed an organization called the General Time Convention that aimed to establish standard and uniform time zones for railroads. In 1883 the General Time Convention adopted a system of four time zones (Eastern, Central, Mountain, and Pacific) throughout the country to be followed by all railroads. Soon, industries that relied on the railroad adopted the new time zones as well. By the 1890s most people in urban areas lived by "railroad time." Railroad time did have its opponents, however. Some areas passed resolutions professing their refusal to adopt standard time. Newspaper editorials railed against the idea of having to follow railroad time for everyday activities, and some saw it as a casting off of the natural rhythms of a life lived upon the land. One editorialist wrote that he'd rather run his clock on God's time than Vanderbilt's. But gradually, railroad time grew in acceptance and it became the official U.S. time in 1918 during World War I (Daniels 81; Gordon 251; Stover 146; Wormser 106–08).

CONCLUSION: THE GREAT UPRISING OF 1877

In July 1877, a strike among railroad workers became a national uprising, engulfing the United States in a wave of protest and reaction that left over 100 people dead and millions of dollars in property damage. Historians note that while the Great Uprising proved unsuccessful in the short run, it inaugurated a period of intensive labor and political organizing in the United States. Appreciating how a decentralized labor action by railroad workers became a general strike with surprisingly wide popular support requires accounting for the animosity much of the public felt toward the railroad industry.

In 1877 the United States was in the fourth year of what would be a six year economic depression following the Panic of 1873. Unemployment, underemployment, and wage cuts were widespread. As Philip Foner notes, "By 1875, there were as many as three million unemployed, and two-fifths of those employed were working no more than six or seven months a year, while less than one-fifth worked regularly. The wages of those still working had been cut by as much as 45 percent, often to little more than a dollar a day" (20). In the railroad industry, construction had temporarily stalled, and a series of wage cuts had already been levied against railroad employees. Furthermore, railroad workers tended to be erratically employed. Though brakemen or firemen on the major lines would have earned $59.70 if they took thirty trips per month, because of the lack of work, most railroad employees actually made only $30 a month. Add to that the facts that railroad work was dangerous, workers were paid on an irregular schedule, and those same workers were expected to perform unpaid labor such as general maintenance and cleaning, and you have a recipe for dissatisfaction (18).

But the event that set the Great Uprising into motion was the decision by four already profitable rail companies—the Pennsylvania, New York Central & Hudson, Erie, and Baltimore & Ohio lines—to pool together and simultaneously reduce employee wages by 10 percent across the board. On July 16, the day the cuts went into effect, Baltimore & Ohio workers walked off the job in Martinsburg, West Virginia. Strikers in all major cities along the Baltimore & Ohio line joined them the next day. The day after that, President Rutherford B. Hayes sent federal troops into West Virginia to put down the strike, which he termed an "insurrection," producing a backlash of anger that federal troops would be used against U.S. citizens. Strikes soon broke out in Baltimore, Pittsburgh, Buffalo, St. Louis, San Francisco, and other locations within fourteen U.S. states and Canada. The effect of the strike was to halt grain and freight shipments in much of the country.

In many communities, strikers found themselves warmly supported, and the rail strikes quickly grew into general strikes in which workers in many industries walked out in support of railroad workers. In some cases, the crowd supporting the strikers was more militant than the strikers themselves. As David O. Stowell notes, the 1877 strike happened in the context of rising urban anger and protests against further railroad encroachment into residential neighborhoods.

The railroads' injurious intersection with streets and neighborhoods killed and injured people with appalling regularity. Passing locomotives had even set homes on fire. The noise of locomotives frightened horses, causing innumerable "run-aways," some of which ended in injury to people and property, all of which were part of the hazardous disorder railroads sowed in urban areas. (83–84)

In Buffalo, strikers and their supporters gathered at key crossings and refused to let trains pass. In one instance a train from the Buffalo and Jamestown railroad approached the strikers. Since the Buffalo and Jamestown line was not among the companies that imposed the 10 percent wage cut, the strikers asked the crowd to let the train go on. However, the crowd wanted to stop all trains from passing and they uncoupled the pins before strikers could hold them back and allow the train through (Stowell 103–4).

While strikers' grievances against the railroads tended to be specific, the crowds that joined the uprising had more wide ranging goals. The strike was unplanned and decentralized, and its development varied by city. Pittsburgh, for example, had suffered disproportionately from the depression, and anger against the Pennsylvania Railroad was widespread. The strike had broad popular support there, even among the local militia. Troops called in from Philadelphia to put down the strike found themselves facing a crowd of 10,000 people. Nervous troops fired into a crowd, killing 20, including three children. In response, a larger crowd, drawing workers from throughout the city, gathered at the rail yards and set fire to the main roadhouse and scores of engines and freight cars. Federal troops were then called in to put down the strike (P. Foner, *Great* 55; Gutman 557; Wormser 120).

In St. Louis, the strike had broad support, even among government officials, and it was generally peaceful. At the forefront were Socialists from the Workingman's Party. Not only did most of the city's industries temporarily close, in what was perhaps the most successful general strike of the Great Uprising, but the strike had a high level of racial unity, as whites supported black workers who shut down the city's canneries and river shipping (P. Foner, *Great* 157; Gutman 557).

San Francisco's strike took a different turn, however. In that city, the Workingman's Party called for a mass meeting in sympathy with the railroad strikes. However, talk of labor solidarity soon devolved into hostility toward Chinese immigrants (a common refrain at this time in the West during periods of high unemployment). Some people in the crowd led attacks on Chinese sections of the city that lasted for several nights and led the Workingman's Party to call off future meetings (P. Foner, *Great* 117).

While the contours of the Great Uprising varied from city to city, a number of general themes emerged from this astonishing event. Railroads had become an omnipresent force in the United States, and their way of doing business had caused widespread disenchantment. The federal government put itself squarely on the side of the railroads and used troops to put down the strikes. Thousands of men found themselves blacklisted from working on the railroads, but the strike had the effect of increasing union support and activity. The strikes of 1877 were by no means the last labor actions taken against railroad corporations, but they did mark a turning point in U.S. history, making clear the polarization of American society and the uncertain social order left in the wake of industrialization.

3

The Factory and Organized Labor Responses

INTRODUCTION: MAJOR INDUSTRY TRANSFORMATIONS

"They don't waste anything here. They use everything about the pig except the squeal," commented tour guides as they led curious spectators through the vast slaughterhouses of Chicago's "Packingtown." At any one time, Chicago's stockyards held up to 75,000 hogs, 21,000 cattle, and 22,000 sheep; all waiting to be "processed" through the slaughterhouses (Halpern 11). In a vast procession the hogs would be driven up long staircases to the top of the five- or six-story slaughterhouses. In an exposé of the packing industry, Upton Sinclair described what visitors saw. Middle-class consumers and working-class factory operatives alike were in awe of the tremendous mechanization, efficiency and, at times, inhumanity of the new factory system. They came in droves to see how the slaughterhouses of one city managed to produce inexpensive meat for the entire northeast.

PORK MAKING BY MACHINERY

Upton Sinclair's novel *The Jungle* is based on his detailed investigation of the meat-packing industry. Here he describes what visitors saw during their tour of a factory.

It was a long narrow room, with a gallery along it for visitors. At the head there was a great iron wheel, about twenty feet in circumference, with rings here and there along its edge. [. . . Men] had chains which they fastened about the leg of the nearest hog, and the other end of the chain they hooked into one of the rings upon the wheel. So, as the wheel turned, a hog was suddenly jerked off his feet and borne aloft.

At the same instant the ear was assailed by a most terrifying shriek; the visitors started in alarm, the women turned pale and shrank back. The shriek was followed by another, louder and yet more agonizing—for once started upon that journey, the hog never came back; at the top of the wheel he was shunted off upon a trolley, and went sailing down the room. And meantime another was swung up, and then another, and another, until there was a double line of them, each dangling by a foot and kicking in frenzy. [...]

Meantime, heedless of all these things, the men upon the floor were going about their work. Neither squeals of hogs nor tears of visitors made any difference to them; one by one they hooked up the hogs, and one by one with a swift stroke they slit their throats. There was a long line of hogs, with squeals and life-blood ebbing away together, until at last each started again, and vanished with a splash into a huge vat of boiling water.

It was all so very businesslike that one watched it fascinated. It was pork-making by machinery, pork-making by applied mathematics.

—From Upton Sinclair, *The Jungle*, 38–39

While factories existed in the United States prior to the Civil War—textile mills were the largest and most automated—they were anomalies in an otherwise agricultural nation. Most northerners produced for a local market and worked on capital owned by themselves or their families. To these people, wage work was considered a temporary stage en route to independence, associated with the acquisition of a farm or a craft shop. Most historians of the United States refer to the period between 1870 and 1900 as the industrial revolution, and the most marked development of that period is the rapid expansion of factories and the "factory system."

Manufacturers "rationalized" production; they broke a production process down into discrete, uniform tasks. Workers were responsible for just one task, decreasing the need for skilled artisans. Factories used new technological inventions to reduce their reliance upon skilled workers still more; machines performed tasks people once had. Workers were increasingly referred to as "operatives," appendices to the machines that were the real producers. Factories reduced the prices of many goods, benefiting many, but they also led to more severe forms of worker exploitation.

While many industries changed with technological advances and new management practices, some so fundamentally altered the lived experience of American workers and consumers that they deserve special attention. After a brief explanation of the forces moving production into factories, this chapter will focus on the textile, steel, and meatpacking industries.

The textile industry was one of the first to incorporate large-scale, labor-saving technology. Important changes in working-class culture resulted from the transformation of the New England textile mills from "model," paternalistic factories employing a native-born, female labor force into centers for labor unrest, employing a predominantly immigrant population. These changes illustrate important changes in working-class culture. The new steel industry, with its massive machinery requiring extensive capital investment, fueled the growth of crucial industrial developments such as the railroads and steel-framed skyscrapers. It also offers a place to study the newly forming professional-managerial class. Lastly, the meatpacking industry, with its effective monopoly power and its infamous working conditions, represented a new phase of industrial development. All three industries employed large numbers of industrial era workers in highly mechanized, rationalized settings. They offer insights into the strategies workers used to secure living wages, safe working conditions, and some sort of safety net in the event of tragedies.

FROM OUT-WORK AND CRAFT SHOP TO FACTORY

Several factors account for the transition from piecework accomplished in the home or small craft shops to much larger factories. Many point to technological advances that made work in the home or craft shop less viable, but that tells only part of the story. True enough, in some industries the sheer size and expense of the new technology made it impossible for individual workers or even small business owners to acquire the new equipment. For example, the large steel manufacturers put small blacksmith shops out of business because these blacksmiths could not afford the Bessemer converters that made inexpensive steel. And the Bessemer converter, because it was such a massive, expensive piece of equipment, necessitated a large plant that would manufacture and then transport finished steel products.

But in other industries, workers could and did acquire the necessary technology for production in the home or small craft shop. Nevertheless, these small operations were gradually absorbed into larger factories for a number of reasons. In many instances, employers preferred factory production because they could control waste materials—which could be quite valuable. In the out-work system, a capitalist delivered raw materials to workers who were then paid a specific sum for each item they produced. In the boot and shoe industry of Lynn, Massachusetts, for example, employers paid "freighters" to deliver leather hides to cutters who cut shoe parts and then sewed them together. Generally, skilled men did the cutting and then other members of a family or shop sewed the shoes or boots. Because of the odd sizes and shapes of leather hides, there were scraps of leather left over that the cutters could then sell to leather merchants for extra money. By bringing the cutters into the factories, shoe manufacturers could keep these valuable extra pieces and could pay cutters hourly to eliminate the incentive to work quickly and perhaps waste material. The effect on cutters, however, was to eliminate a source of substantial income (Christiansen and Philips 24–31).

Another advantage employers gained by moving work into the factories was the ability to "sweat" workers. In the out-work system, an employer could increase production in two ways, by offering an incentive to existing workers to produce more in a shorter period or by hiring more workers. In both cases there were downsides for the employer. Either the employer paid more per item or the employer took a risk with new, perhaps less skilled or less honest, workers. In the factory, the employer had the opportunity to speed up the work process, eliminate breaks, and lengthen hours. For example, during the spring and fall, when farmers were most likely to purchase shoes and boots, manufacturers increased workers' hours and work intensity. They avoided the risk of large inventories of shoes—which might fall out of fashion or tie up necessary capital—by speeding up production during the peak season and laying off workers during the slow season. Such fluctuations were more difficult to accommodate in the out-work system (Christiansen and Philips 40–41).

Finally, employers could make production more efficient through the division of labor, breaking up the production process into smaller tasks. In 1880, David N. Johnson, a superintendent in one Lynn, Massachusetts, shoe factory, listed 33 different processes required to assemble a single shoe. Each task was accomplished by a different employee, which meant that each employee spent his or her entire day repeatedly performing the same small task. For example, one person was responsible for cutting buttonholes for shoes, while another sewed on the buttons (Hazard 120–21). While this made production more tedious for the individual worker and led to repetitive stress injuries, it sped up the overall process because each worker became more proficient at his or her task. Moreover, in some industries the division of labor transformed skilled positions into unskilled positions. For example, a great deal of expertise was required to carve an entire pig, but when the process was broken down into many pieces, a very limited amount of skill was necessary to simply bleed it or skin it. Hiring less skilled workers in factories, employers no longer had to pay the higher wages of the skilled workers or endure the threat of strikes from the limited pool of skilled workers. The division of labor made individual workers more easily replaced.

Even as factories sprung up throughout urban America, many industries continued to rely on piecework done in homes or tenement shops. But even these work environments changed substantially as the factory system dominated production. For example, the sewing machine gave an advantage to those men and women who could afford the initial investment. They could produce more in less time compared with the hand-sewers. But as sewing machines became cheaper and more people had them, piece rates for outwork declined and soon even those with sewing machines saw their incomes decline. By then, working in the home had become even less comfortable. Conrad Carl, a New York tailor for thirty years complained in 1883:

During the time I have been here the tailoring business is altered in three different ways. Before we had sewing machines we worked piecework with our wives, and very often our children. We had no trouble then with our neighbors, nor with the landlord, because it was a very still business, very quiet; but in 1854 or 1855, and later, the sewing machine was invented and introduced, and it stitched very nicely, nicer than the tailor could do; and the bosses said: "We want you to use the sewing machine; you have to buy one." Many of the tailors had a few dollars in the bank, and they took the money and bought machines. Many others had no money, but must help themselves; so they brought their stitching, the coat or vest, to the other tailors who had sewing machines, and paid them a few cents for the stitching. Later, when the money was given out for the work, we found out that we could earn no more than we could without the machine; but the money for the machine was gone now, and we found that the machine was only for the profit of the bosses; that they got their work quicker, and it was done nicer. [. . .] The machine makes too much noise in the place, and the neighbors want to sleep, and we have to stop sewing earlier; so we have to work faster. We work now in excitement—in a hurry. It is hunting; it is not work at all; it is a hunt. (Garraty 20)

Contrary to expectations, technological improvements had not shortened the workers' hours and in many cases they had not improved wages. Technological improvements, however, had decreased the prices for many goods. Displaced, skilled workers may have lost ground, but the new professional-managerial class of supervisors and engineers, as well as some workers, gained ground.

TEXTILES

The textile industry, which produced a wide variety of cloths and silks for clothing and domestic use, was among the first sectors of the American economy to be industrialized. As textile factories in the United States multiplied, social commentators expressed concern over the importation of a British-style laboring class—desperately poor, uneducated, physically deformed, and rebellious. Francis Cabot Lowell traveled to England in 1810 to observe British mills. He returned to the United States determined to reproduce the labor-saving machinery he had seen, but equally determined not to reproduce the labor conditions he had seen. He expressed horror at the large number of children he saw in English mills working long hours and being flogged by overseers for slowing their pace. Lowell developed a vision of a new, paternalistic system of employment.

The Birth of the Integrated Factory

Lowell successfully reproduced machines he had seen in England—machines to clean cotton, machines to make thread from cotton puffs, and, most importantly, the power looms that wove the threads into cloth. None of the other mills in the United States had power looms, so they sent their thread to independent weavers as out-work or to Lowell's new mill. All of Lowell's machines were powered by the Charles River, which turned an enormous water wheel linked through a series of gears and leather belts to all of the machines in the factory. But the most innovative part of Lowell's business plan was his decision to recruit young, female farm-workers to make up the bulk of his work force.

For Lowell, the advantage of using female factory operatives was that they were stronger than children, could be paid less than men, and were unlikely to strike. If they became dissatisfied or disabled for work, they generally returned to their homes on neighboring farms, rather than forming the base of a disgruntled work force. Moreover, the women he employed seldom had direct dependents, which reduced their financial needs. In a society in which there were few occupations for women, he had little competition for their labor. Hundreds came to work in the mills and live in Lowell's new, clean, tightly managed boarding houses, each presided over by substitute mothers whose job it was to protect the virtue of their "girls." Lowell was so proud of his "mill girls" that he advertised his products with sketches of fresh-faced, female operatives.

The Transformation of the American Working Class By the end of the Civil War, Francis Cabot Lowell had long since died and many more mills had been established in Lowell, Lawrence, and Fall River, Massachusetts as well as in Rhode Island, Connecticut and New York. Lowell's ideal faltered in the face of far more competition and a wider dissemination of his labor-saving technology. The integrated factory, which took raw cotton and turned it into finished cloth, was now the model, and wages had been greatly reduced over time.

No longer did native-born farm girls from New England's countryside staff the mills. Immigrant families came, knowing the mills were looking for women and children in addition to men. Children as young as six worked 11-hour days and factory operatives endured speed-ups in which the machines ran faster to force operatives to work more quickly. Conditions became far worse even as pay failed to keep up with rising living expenses. The native-born women left the factories, preferring the higher status position of schoolteacher to the once better paying positions in the mills. This transformation in the working class was hardly unique to the textile industry; the vast majority of workers in the manufacturing sector were either foreign born or the children of foreign-born parents.

THE IMMIGRANT WORKFORCE

Place	Industry	Number of Workers in Industry in 1880	Percentage Foreign-Born and Children of Immigrants
Paterson, NJ	Iron/steel	2,352	78%
Scranton, PA	Iron/steel	1,022	85%
Cleveland, OH	Iron/steel	4,776	86%

Place	Industry	Number of Workers in Industry in 1880	Percentage Foreign-Born and Children of Immigrants
Youngstown, OH	Iron/steel	1,784	90%
Covington/Newport, KY	Iron/steel	1,884	87%
Joliet, IL	Iron/steel	800	87%
Lackawanna Co., PA	Anthracite Coal	6,440	97%
Clearfield, Mercer, Cambria, and Westmoreland Counties, PA	Bituminous Coal	8,130	74%
Mahoning, Trumbull, Stark, Lawrence, and Perry Counties, OH	Bituminous Coal	6,062	86%
St. Clair and Will Counties, IL	Bituminous Coal	1,910	98%
Waterbury, CT	Brass	4,500	79%
Haverstraw, NY	Brick	1,143	87%
Saginaw and E. Saginaw, MI	Lumber	1,242	85%
Cleveland, OH	Oil refining/barrels	1,050	96%

(Gutman and Berlin 388)

In the place of native-born female workers came Irish, French-Canadian, and German immigrant families, but the largest group to staff the mills was made up of Irish-born women. In the 1870s, Irish-born women constituted 57.7 percent of all cotton textile employees (Diner, *Erin's Daughters* 75). They fled social oppression and poverty in Ireland and came searching for better lives for themselves and their families in America.

Upon arriving in a mill town, a young Irish woman was likely to be met by kin who had already "found a place" at the mill. Sisters, brothers, cousins, aunts, and uncles saved their meager earnings, sometimes sending some home to their families in Ireland but often saving to purchase the ship's passage of another family member. Whereas females in other immigrant groups generally had their passage paid by husbands or fathers, Irish women were usually brought over with the help of their female kin (Diner, *Erin's Daughters* 38). Often the day after arrival, the new immigrant accompanied a relative into the mill and got a job with the relative's recommendation.

Rural, Irish-born women would likely work in the lowest skilled occupations; they replaced bobbins full of thread with empty bobbins on the spinning machines or delivered the full bobbins to the power looms. Filling bobbins, while simple work, required constant, rapid motions. It was exhausting work, but frequently reserved for children and "greenhorns" because of its simplicity. As a woman acquired more skill, she might tend spinning machines that combined thin strands of cotton into cotton yarn or thread. Under pressure, these strands sometimes broke, requiring the skillful spinner to quickly tie a knot in the strand while the spinning machine ran. Over time, some women could acquire the skill to become weavers, the best paying positions for women in the mills.

Types of Work in the Mills and Grievances
The integrated factories generally moved the new cotton from the first floor up to the top of the factory and as the product moved up it became progressively more finished. In sheds next to the mill, men unloaded 500-pound bales of cotton and operated machines that shook them free of dirt and leaves. They delivered the clean cotton to the first floor of the mill where mule spinners, traditionally men, operated machines that drew the cotton into dense strands of fiber. These machines had to be frequently oiled while running and the cotton lint swept regularly to prevent sparks from the machine from causing fires. Operatives kept pails of water nearby to douse new fires quickly. The spinning operation took place on the second floor where skilled women ran the spinning machines that turned the cotton strands into thread. Weavers operated the huge

These young boys work as doffers, transporting spindles between floors in a textile mill in Gastonia, North Carolina, in 1908. (Courtesy Library of Congress)

power looms at the top of the factory and then men used enormous print machines to create colorful, patterned fabrics. Skilled women in the finishing room inspected the fabric for defects and then the newer recruits folded the fabric for delivery to stores.

Children were often introduced to the mills at very young ages. Schools gave them time off during the mills' lunch breaks so that they could deliver lunch pails to their kin. Once inside the mill, they learned to clean machines, replace bobbins, or run errands. In this way they became familiar with the mills' operation even while in school (Moran 20–21; Cumbler 153).

For rural folk who had worked in the quiet countryside, the deafening roar and vibration of machines, the dirty air filled with cotton lint that could cause fatal illnesses, and the humidity could be overwhelming. In the spinning rooms, for example, it was necessary to spray the thin strands of cotton with water to minimize the incidence of threads breaking. Operatives became drenched, especially in the summer months. Children unable to afford shoes ran barefoot on the rough wood floors sweeping, delivering bobbins and running errands. One operative described the condition of women working in these spinning rooms:

It is dreadful to see those girls, stripped almost to the skin, wearing only a kind of loose wrapper, and running like a racehorse from the beginning to the end of the day; [. . . T]hey come out so tired, and so thirsty, and so exhausted, especially in the summer months from working along steadily from hour to hour and breathing the noxious effluvia from the grease and other ingredients that are used in the mills, and they are so exhausted when the time comes to quit, that you will find that all their thoughts are concentrated on something to drink to allay their thirst. (Howard qtd. in Garraty 24)

Whereas farming people could organize their day and build in periodic breaks, textile workers were at the mercy of their machines in the mills. The manufacturers tried to keep the machines running for as long as possible with as few breaks as possible, requiring operatives to work intensely hour after hour in all weather. Moreover, operatives frequently worked in poorly lighted areas, straining the eyes. Still, new recruits could begin replacing bobbins in the spinning room or sweeping in the weaving room, learn the trade, and eventually become spinners or weavers. Mills encouraged workers to find gratification in their speed and productivity, paying some workers piece rates and posting their productivity rates in the work place. Some workers found this challenge rewarding, but many expressed frustration at the pace of their work.

Manufacturers studied ways to make both their machines and their workers more productive—without having to pay higher salaries. They fined workers for defective products, sometimes docking a worker half of his or her pay (Moran 158). They also sometimes withheld pay during a new worker's first week or weeks, calling this a learning period. Some workers complained of their employers "stealing time." They would close and lock the gates 10 minutes before the official start of the workday and 10 minutes before the bell signaling the end of lunch. If workers weren't there, they were shut out for part of the day. At the end of the day they would expect operatives to work another 10 minutes past quitting time. In this way, even after legislation prohibited days longer than 10 hours for women and children, the manufacturers still got more than a 10-hour day out of operatives.

A particularly egregious practice of manufacturers involved defining particular jobs as more than any individual man could do. Workers referred to this as "the grind," and protested this aspect of millwork vehemently. The mule spinners in Fall River, Massachusetts, in particular, suffered from this practice. Fall River specialized in low-grade textiles sold at very low prices. The owners tried to dominate the market by paying low wages, speeding up their production processes, and hiring fewer assistants in some departments. Mule spinners, for example, generally employed "back boys" to repair broken strands. They also employed "doffers" and "tubers" to carry the yarn up to the spinners and to replace tubes on the machines. In Fall River, the mule spinners had only one assistant and walked over twenty-five miles each day, six days a week. The mill supervisors knew this was an impossible pace for the workers and kept a list of "sick spinners" who came in to substitute for the mule spinners when they fell ill. Every mule spinner was expected to miss several days a month due to exhaustion. The practice undermined their self-respect in addition to their health (Blewett 186–87).

In 1874, "the grind" contributed to the disastrous Granite Mill fire in Fall River. A young mule spinner in Granite Mill #1, anxious to keep up with the production rates of the older, more experienced men in his room, neglected the task of oiling his machine. Traditionally, men had been allowed a certain amount of down time to oil machines, but in Fall River the mule spinners were expected to oil the machine while it ran. They were also expected to sweep up the cotton lint dusting the entire room and to fill the pails of water for putting out fires. The combination of sparks from the machinery and lint dust caused the fire in Granite Mill #1 and when spinners tried to put it out, they discovered empty pails. The fire quickly spread to the higher floors. Without fire escapes, the women and children working in the weaving rooms tried to jump to the ground. Others died of suffocation or were consumed in the fire. Forty workers died and another 80 were injured, some permanently disabled. These numbers represented nearly one-third of the workers in Granite Mill #1. Because the conditions of the mill were so widespread in other mills—most had no fire escapes and supervisors seldom monitored the safety of equipment or supply of water—the mill owners were not held responsible for the disaster (Blewett 135–37).

Sketch of 1874 Fall River, Massachusetts, fire from *The Daily Graphic*.

Speed-ups, wage cuts amid owner prosperity, fines for defective products, and "stealing time" led to widespread dissatisfaction among workers. Coming from impoverished and often oppressive circumstances, they were willing to work hard and tolerate much. Nonetheless, they believed themselves to be the "producing classes" and the basis of the nation's wealth, and they eventually rebelled against their exploitation. Some engaged in spontaneous walk outs. Others joined unions and pressured management with well-organized strikes. Others worked through the political system to push through government level reforms. Many turned to benevolent organizations, often ethnically based, to ameliorate their circumstances and provide some social security.

Worker Responses to Conditions in Mills

Commentators often remarked upon the frequency of worker protests in Fall River compared with the other major Massachusetts mill towns, Lowell and Lawrence. One reason for the unrest stemmed from the number of operatives immigrating to Fall River from the mills of Lancashire, England where workers had a long tradition of organizing and striking for better conditions. Even the large number of Irish immigrants in Fall River had frequently spent some years in Lancashire, accumulating the fare to come to the United States. In the United States, working-class men replicated patterns originating in Lancashire, meeting in taverns after the last bell to discuss working conditions and political issues. New immigrants frequently came to the local taverns to secure their first position in the mills. The taverns were the nexus of a system of patronage. In fact, three of the Fall River city councilmen who routinely voted for the workers' causes were tavern owners. Moreover, workers who were blacklisted by the mills for union activity regularly became tavern owners. Mill owners came to view the taverns as centers of dissension (Cumbler 109, 150).

Mills responded to the threat of unionization and strikes with both carrots and sticks. They proffered favors to skilled workers considered loyal; in Fall River the mills established savings programs and acted as intermediaries with local banks who approved home mortgages for some operatives. More often, however, they intimidated operatives considering organizing. Often workers were forced to live in company-owned tenements as a condition of employment. In this way the mills could not only collect rents and profit on workers, but they could also suddenly evict those deemed agitators. The mills also employed detectives to uncover union organizing (Cameron 59–60; Cumbler 108).

One Fall River union leader who had emigrated from Lancashire described his experience of trying to organize skilled mule spinners in Lawrence, Massachusetts. Frustrated by the inability of Fall River mule spinners to better their wages in the face of substantially lower wages at competitors in Lawrence, Robert Howard traveled to Lawrence in 1883:

When the time came that was appointed for the meeting, there across the road stood Filbrook, the corporation detective, and Russell, the overseer, watching every man that came in. There was one man at that meeting who was looking out of the window at them, and he said, "I never belonged to a union in my life, Howard, but nothing does so much as the presence of those in there to convince me that there must be some good for the workingmen in unions, for unless there was, those men would not stand there spying us as we come in." (23)

Many workers were too intimidated by their employers to join in union actions. Large employers could almost always survive a work stoppage for longer than their workers, especially if those workers were paid a bare subsistence and had little or no savings. When the Knights of Labor created a federation of labor unions, one of their primary goals was to provide a general fund that could be used to support striking workers so that they could hold out long enough to force concessions from employers. In this way, workers could have some assurance of achieving their demands. Robert Howard describes another form of employer intimidation:

In Lowell some two years ago I went to start the men to ask for more wages, because we in Fall River could not do anything until Lowell made some advance. I went down there and we had a petition drawn up. No name was signed to it, because all of the men were afraid, but the petition was sent in asking for an advance in wages. In about two weeks after that petition was presented to the Lowell manufacturers the three men that had had the drawing up of the petition were discharged from the mills. (25)

One important lesson union organizers derived from such events was that unity among workers had to precede demands or actions.

Such unity often faltered in the face of ethnic, gender, and occupational differences. In Fall River, for example, Irish- and English-born operatives, often having experienced organized protest in Lancashire, easily understood their interests to be opposed to those of their employers. They perceived themselves as a class. The more recent French-Canadian immigrants, recruited by the corporations because of their reputation as docile and hard-working, had no experience with unionization but a great deal of experience with the anti-Catholic policies of the English-speaking, Canadian government. Their cool reception by the English-speaking operatives, who felt threatened by these cheap workers, did little to make them feel a sense of solidarity. The French-Canadians also had less to gain from unions. As rural people, they seldom held skilled positions, the positions for which the unions were most successful in winning advances. Finally, the local French Catholic Church—rather than the working-class tavern or union hall—became the center of their communities, opening French-speaking schools and offering assistance to the most needy. One French-Canadian worker remembered:

Immigrants from the province of Quebec settled not only in Manchester but in other New Hampshire mill centers, Salmon Falls and Newmarket, to name only a few. In each community, they [a] built church first of all, then a presbytere or residence for the pastor, as soon as possible a school for their children (which the children had to attend), and they finally bought a tract of land on the outskirts of the city for a cemetery. To protect their homes and families, they later organized mutual benefit or fraternal societies. (Lemay)

Hostilities between the more militant operatives and the new immigrants, who threatened to undermine the union, stoked ethnic tensions.

Traditional understandings of gender also undermined union solidarity. When the Pacific Main Mill of Lawrence imposed wage reductions that fell disproportionately on female frame spinners, they protested in 1882.

Wages were to be reduced from ninety cents a day to sixty-eight cents a day and the work was to be sped up by 25 percent. The pay was not enough for the many women who supported themselves as well as children or disabled adults. Male workers also suffered reductions, but their pay remained far higher than the women's pay. Mule spinners, who were among the most highly paid workers in the mill, had a wage reduction from $11.50 per week to $10.25 with no additional work. Working six days per week, the female frame spinners only earned $4.24 per week. Both the mill owners and the skilled, male workers believed that women should be supported by men. When they were not—because they were unmarried, widowed or abandoned by their husbands—they became social pariahs.

Many working-class men turned a deaf ear to women's complaints. Labor organizers repeatedly claimed that women in the mills represented a threat to male operatives precisely because they were so poorly paid that they were cheaper for the mills to hire. Technological innovations made it possible for smaller and comparatively weaker people to take over traditionally male occupations. Instead of working with women to raise their pay, so that they would not offer such an attractive alternative to male workers, the men frequently sought to emphasize distinctions between themselves and female workers. They agitated for a "family wage" that would enable them to keep their wives and daughters at home. Not only did the men not join in the strike, but many male, pro-labor representatives spoke out against the striking women. John Breen, the pro-labor Mayor of Lawrence, gave voice to the men's belief that the city's large population of working women was a social drag. Addressing strikers, he encouraged the women to migrate west and marry the men settling rural homesteads. Referring to newspaper editor Horace Greely, he said "It is a source of regret that many of the young ladies, of whom there are a surplus in this city, do not take Horace Greely's advice and make many young men in the West happy" (qtd. in Cameron 61). Ultimately, many of the strikers did leave town and the strike leaders were blacklisted. The Pacific Mill reorganized production with new looms and produced a different kind of cloth requiring fewer skilled workers, male or female.

Some strikes did win higher wages and better working conditions. Nonetheless, technological changes and the continuous stream of immigrant workers willing to accept low wages and unfamiliar with union actions undermined the bargaining strength of organized labor.

One strategy that did prove effective for improving work conditions was the textile workers' campaign to pass state legislation limiting the length of the work day to 10 hours for women and children. Massachusetts legislators had repeatedly voted down proposals to limit the workday to 8 or 10 hours on the grounds that an important liberty of adult males was the right to form individual contracts. Labor activists countered that individual liberties were worthless without the power to exercise them. Individual workers had no bargaining power against the large manufacturers. They were easily replaced. Moreover, only the exceptional worker had the drive and energy to become an enlightened voter after 12- or 14-hour days. Angry at the defeat of 8-hour legislation, workers mobilized to defeat Massachusetts state senators who were beholden to the textile manufacturers. Supporting a vigorous pro-labor press and holding large demonstrations in the mill towns to keep the issue continually in the news, workers turned 10 anti-labor senators out of office in 1873. In 1874, Massachusetts passed a 10-hour bill. While only women and children were covered by the legislation, hours were reduced for men as well (Blewett 126–35).

Textile workers also developed cooperative arrangements that helped them to achieve a measure of social security despite seasonal bouts of unemployment, workplace injuries, and low wages. The various ethnic-based clubs and some labor unions offered small life insurance policies as well as insurance against disability. Women pooled their resources to share housekeeping and child care responsibilities. Single mothers fre-

TIME TABLE
OF THE
PACIFIC MILLS.
SUMMER ARRANGEMENT.
WORKING TIME:
Ten Hours per Day, or Sixty Hours per Week

COMMENCE WORK,	6.30 A. M.
LEAVE OFF WORK, except Saturdays,	6.24 P. M.
LEAVE OFF WORK SATURDAYS,	12.00 M.
HOURS FOR DINNER THROUGH THE WEEK,	12.00 M. to 1.00 P. M.

☞ Bells will be rung and Gates opened and closed to meet the change made in Starting and Stopping the Mills.

Commencing March 29th and continuing to September 25th, 1880.

Workers won an important victory when the workweek was limited to 6 days per week and 10 hours per day. Nevertheless, as this 1880 time table shows, this still translated into long days. (Courtesy American Textile History Museum, Lowell, MA)

quently ran boarding houses where they cooked and did laundry for other women who worked in the mills and paid rent. Women too old or weak to work in the mills cared for young children whose mothers worked in the mills. Some workers supported cooperative stores that bought food and basic supplies at wholesale prices for distribution among members. During strikes, many sympathetic store owners extended credit or offered lower prices to striking workers.

The textile workers' difficulties in winning strikes during the late nineteenth century resulted in part from the differences of skill level, ethnicity, and gender dividing the working class. Even while a more militant working class, experienced with union activism, immigrated from Lancashire, England, textile owners offered free railroad passage for French Canadians. They played different groups of workers against one another, replacing comparatively well paid male workers with poorly paid female workers when technology allowed. But even a comparatively well-organized and homogenous labor union faced formidable obstacles. Textile manufacturers used their wealth to control state and federal officeholders. They also could threaten to shut down unionized mills and open mills in the South, a section of the country notably hostile to labor organizing. Eventually in the twentieth century, textile manufacturers did just that. They ceased to invest in their New England mills, allowing them to grow technologically outmoded, and they opened new mills in the South.

STEEL

Development of the Bessemer Converter
Just as the development of the power loom dramatically changed the nature of work in the textile industry, the invention and improvement of the Bessemer converter revolutionized the iron and steel industry. Prior to the Bessemer converter, steel was made from pig iron by a process called puddling. Workers melted down limestone, coal and iron ore to make the pig iron. The pig iron could be used for cooking implements but was too brittle for rolling. A skilled workman called a puddler refined the pig iron into wrought iron that could be rolled and made into rails for the railroads. The puddler stirred the pig iron over a furnace until it made a large ball of pasty, fibrous iron that was hammered into bars and sent to rolling mills. To roll the bars of wrought iron, the substance had to be reheated.

Rails for the new railroads were initially made from this wrought iron, but the iron rails were still too brittle for the heavier and faster trains of the 1870s. Steel had greater tensile strength; it could bend slightly without crumbling or breaking, making it better able to withstand the frequent application of pressure from trains. Steel was manufactured in much the same way as wrought iron except that the product had to be completely melted so that all of the particles of slag, cinders, and carbon flecks had been melted and fused into a single, homogenous whole. Moreover, unlike wrought iron, steel contained some carbon, which gave it greater strength and allowed it to be quickly hardened by quenching, a process by which a newly molded piece of steel is put into a vat of water (Temin 131; Misa 4, 31–32).

The Bessemer converter allowed for the extremely hot temperatures necessary for steel production. The pig iron was heated in a giant, cone-shaped crucible that could be tipped. When air was pumped into the heated wrought iron, making the temperature of the wrought iron spike, an explosion took place in the enormous heat, suddenly fusing the disparate parts of the pig iron into a homogenous whole. After the blast, the crucible was tipped to pour the molten steel into malleable ingots that proceeded to the rolling mills (Misa 7–9).

Work in the new mills was hot and strenuous. The enormous mills, housing 90-foot tall Bessemer converters, dwarfed the workers. Men were surrounded by the sulphurous fumes of the open hearths, the screeches of

In 1889 *Harper's Weekly* included this sketch of a Bessemer steel converter, showing how the massive vessels periodically contain an explosion that rapidly converts iron to steel. (Courtesy Library of Congress)

overhead trolleys, the banging of heavy machinery, and the hot blasts from the converters themselves. The mills could also be dangerous places. Poorly timed blasts injured and killed some workers. Trolleys delivering materials sometimes ran over men. Chains carrying steel rails overhead sometimes broke. The heat and strain overwhelmed others. Injuries were common when workers were tired. One worker commented:

They wipe a man out here every little while. Sometimes a chain breaks, and a ladle tips over, and the iron explodes. [...] Sometimes the slag falls on the workmen. [...] Of course, if everything is working all smooth and a man watches out, why, all right! But you take it after they've been on duty twelve hours without sleep, and running like hell, everybody tired and loggy, and it's a different story. ("Andrew Carnegie")

Despite a brief, 2-year experiment with 8-hour shifts, Andrew Carnegie's steel works ran on 12-hour schedules, meaning all workers in continuous operations worked 6 days a week, for 12 hours. The steel mills ran a night shift to keep the mills in operation round the clock. On Sunday, the day shift reported at 6 A.M. and worked 24 hours until 6 A.M. Monday, resting for twelve hours before reporting for the night shift at 6 P.M. on Monday. In this way, the workers rotated shifts. Every other Sunday, workers would have a 24-hour break from the mills (Livesay 149; Eggert 8). Few men over forty could stand the pace. A worker in Carnegie's Homestead mill described his experience, "Hard! I guess it's hard. It sweats the life out of a man. I often drink two buckets of water during twelve hours; the sweat drips through my sleeves, and runs down my legs and fills my shoes" ("Andrew Carnegie").

Steel workers had some advantages compared with other workers. They were part of a great transformation in America. Once the period of railroad building tapered off, steel was used to construct modern sky-scrapers and bridges, transforming the appearance of American cities and laying the groundwork for more densely populated cities. Steel mills also offered steady employment. As a general rule, steel workers did not have seasonal periods of unemployment, unlike workers at the textile mills and packinghouses. Plus, they made comparatively high salaries. The mule spinners in the textile industry making $11.50 per week in 1882 repre-sented the top of the textile industry wage scale. These men, with careful purchases, could perhaps keep their wives and children out of the mills, but without wives' and children's work, families would be unlikely to be able to buy homes. In comparison, founders at the Lucy Furnace in Pitts-burgh (owned by Carnegie Steel), brought home $3.25 per day or $22.75 for a seven-day week in 1880. That same year, keepers, who tended the giant furnaces, brought home $2.45 per day or $17.15 for a seven-day week. Common laborers, who comprised nearly half of all steel workers, brought home only $1.25 per day or $8.75 per week. Nonetheless, they could hope to achieve the higher paid positions (Eggert 13; Hogan 80).

Competition in the iron and steel industry was intense because the field was crowded by many small companies during the first railroad-building boom of the 1860s. During the severe depression of 1873–78, many mills went bankrupt and others contracted their operations. A period of rapid consolidation ensued with just a handful of steel titans emerging. The sur-

Andrew Carnegie and the Development of the Professional-Managerial Class

vivors drove others out of business by massive expansion to increase the scale of production and to reduce per-unit costs. Moreover, these heavily capitalized companies invested in each wave of the rapidly changing technology, continually lowering their costs. No one was more shrewd at navigating the system than Andrew Carnegie, the Scottish immigrant who embodied the American "rags to riches" story.

Though Andrew Carnegie participated in several steel pools, combinations of separately owned companies seeking to fix steel prices and capture more profit, he generally believed these doomed to failure. Manufacturers couldn't trust one another to limit their production in order to restrain supply and keep prices higher. Instead, Carnegie sought to control the price of his raw materials and labor costs. He did this by owning a controlling interest in Frick Coke Company, assuring a steady supply of cheap fuel for his machinery. Moreover, he hired a battery of accountants, chemists, and engineers to strictly monitor his production processes. Carnegie's white-collar crew established a voucher system by which all raw materials were weighed and all tools and building materials entered into a ledger. Every department then had cost sheets correlated with their production. Carnegie reviewed these cost sheets weekly, insisting that if costs were kept down, profits would follow (Livesay 122–24).

Carnegie had a similar faith in engineering expertise and invested in the latest technology even if it meant making relatively new and useful machinery obsolete. He hired chemists and engineers to analyze the production process and make needed adjustments. He adhered to the new philosophy of scientific management, reducing his reliance on skilled labor by reorganizing and further dividing up the production process. He made sure every employee had a limited and well-defined job and a single superior evaluating his or her work. If the workers no longer had a comprehensive understanding of the process by which steel was produced, the managers and engineers had to have this knowledge to avoid waste or slow downs in the process. Carnegie's strategy of sweating his working-class employees and rationalizing production by relying increasingly on a professional-managerial class was typical of many industries. Even as these industries reduced the numbers of skilled laborers, they swelled the numbers of what is now called the professional-managerial class, workers with some degree of specialized training in business or technical schools. These were the men whose families populated the new fringe neighborhoods around large urban areas, the neighborhoods that would become suburbs. Unable to afford homes on the elite boulevards of the old cities and unwilling to settle among the increasingly crowded working-class neighborhoods, they became the first Americans to regularly travel to work on trains or ferries (Ohmann 123–24; Biggs 37–42).

As Carnegie's empire expanded and was further combined with steel fabricating companies into what became the U.S. Steel trust, lawyers and financiers came to dominate the business. Meanwhile, in 1892, the Amalgamated Association of Iron & Steel Workers, the labor union representing steel workers, lost power in the face of a dramatic confrontation between locked out union workers at Carnegie's Homestead mills and 8,000 troops sent by the Governor of Pennsylvania. The union was effectively crushed in the confrontation and the company henceforth refused to recognize the union. Shortly afterward, Carnegie eliminated the sliding scale that had tied wages to the company's profits. Despite enormous profits, wages declined and the union was unable to negotiate improved working conditions. Superior technology and organization—supplied by managers, engineers, accountants, and financiers—had defeated artisan skills and worker organization. Not until later in the twentieth century would unions effectively bargain with the steel giants or would government agencies force the industry to establish safer working conditions.

MEATPACKING

The Growth of Chicago's Meatpacking Houses
As in the textile and steel industries, technological innovations and the division of labor dramatically altered the work experiences of those in the meat industry. Traditionally a highly skilled craft, carving animals into meat required a great deal of training, strength, and frequently an extended period of apprenticeship. Butchers had to understand the anatomy of several different kinds of animals, in all their variations. They also had to possess a variety of tools, from scrapers and hooks to many sizes and shapes of knives. Every town had its local butcher because fresh meat had to be purchased for immediate consumption. There was no way to keep meat frozen as it traveled for days or even weeks across country, except in the winter. Only cured pork products like salt pork, ham, and bacon could be transported without refrigeration. Even after the meatpacking factories introduced canned meats during the Civil War, better cuts of meat had to be purchased locally. Western ranchers transported their animals live to butchers in cities and towns until Gustavus Swift hired Andrew Chase to perfect the design of the refrigerated railroad car. By the end of the 1880s Swift developed the first vertically integrated meatpacking enterprise. He owned stockyards, slaughterhouses, refrigerated railroad cars, icehouses located along the railroads, and even smaller, "peddle cars" for delivering meat to towns located some distance from the nearest railroad (Halpern 8, 13).

With the introduction of the refrigerated cars, the meatpacking houses had two advantages over local, urban butchers. First, it was cheaper to transport meat rather than live animals who required feeding and watering. Secondly, they could take advantage of efficiencies of scale by automating some of the "disassembly" process and breaking down the remainder of the process into many distinct tasks performed by different, specialized workers. The various sizes and shapes of animal carcasses resisted mechanized carving of any sort. Machines required standardized materials—uniform grades of cotton or predictable chemical composition in iron ore. Packinghouses used overhead conveyors to move carcasses about the "disassembly line" and they used a mechanical scraper to take the quills off of a hog, but they still relied upon skilled workers to carve the meat. While the packinghouses couldn't displace the skilled workers with machines, they did find a way to displace them by dividing their work into many discrete tasks (Halpern 8).

If New England was the center of the textile industry and Pittsburgh the center of the steel industry, Chicago was the unquestioned center of the meatpacking industry. It was the largest Midwestern city, located relatively near the enormous ranches of the great plains, and it was the hub of the nation's rail system. Cincinnati had initially been the great meatpacking center of the country, but its dependence on river travel, which was more limited and more expensive compared with rail travel, put it at a disadvantage compared with Chicago.

Four Chicago companies sold fully half of the country's meat supply by the mid-1880s; however, competition among the big four (Swift, Armour, Morris, and Hammond) was intense, because they had dramatically increased the supply of meat for year-round consumption. Moreover, their integrated operations required extensive capital, capital that the manufacturers couldn't afford to let lie idle in the event of a work stoppage or inadequate meat supplies.

The manufacturers improved their profit margins in three ways: by manufacturing products related to meat processing, by lowering their labor costs, and by combining to fix price floors. They produced lard, tanned hides, bone meal for animal feed, oleomargarine, fertilizer, and pharmaceuticals. By 1900, these additional product lines contributed a quarter of the income of a steer. They lowered labor costs by introducing new technology, eliminating skilled positions, and speeding the line. Such work speed-ups, however, led to a high incidence of injuries, especially in the carving rooms where men wielded sharp knives. Finally, in 1886, the big four meatpackers, along with pork packer Samuel Allerton, agreed to common prices they would pay ranchers for livestock and divided up the northeast market so they would not compete with one another. Over the next 17 years, until the Department of Justice disbanded the trust, the packers absorbed smaller, rival companies, squeezed ranchers, and gouged consumers.

The big packers faced their own pressures. Even while
Working in the   the division of labor made it possible to eliminate many
Packinghouses   skilled positions, the dependence of each operation on
the operation before it left the packers vulnerable to sudden work actions. Workers regularly protested speed-ups in the line by walking out. If just one department walked out, the entire moving conveyor belt had to stop. Unlike some other manufacturing processes, the packers couldn't keep stockpiles of partially processed meat on hand in the event that one department stopped working. If spinners in a mill stopped working, enough full bobbins could be found to keep weavers busy for some period of time. But if men in the hog scraping department walked out, all of the carvers had to stop work as well. Workers had found a powerful tool for exercising some control over their work process (Halpern 14).

While small, localized work actions did prove an effective way to control the pace of the line, they did not prove an effective way of regulating wages. If workers stayed out any length of time, they were quickly replaced. Only the skilled workers in the meatpacking industry had effective craft unions that could negotiate wage increases.

At the turn of the nineteenth century, a typical cattle-killing gang was comprised of 200 men, only 14 of whom made the top salary of 50 cents an hour. One group of skilled men were the floorsmen who removed the steers' hides, carving quickly and accurately to avoid harming the hide or wasting the meat. The other group was the cattle splitters who separated the carcasses into halves using heavy cleavers that required great strength and dexterity. A slightly larger group of semi-skilled workers, including backers and rumpers, who made precise cuts along the cattle's hind end, received slightly less. Another notch down on the scale were the gut-snatchers who removed the animals stomach and intestines. These men earned 40 cents an hour.

The remaining two-thirds of the cattle-killing gang was comprised of common laborers. These workers did things such as make fertilizer, stuff sausages or sweep intestines, fat, and other by-products along the kill floor and down chutes to various specialized departments. In his novelistic exposé of conditions in the packinghouses, Upton Sinclair described work in the fertilizer department this way:

To this part of the yards came all the "tankage," and the waste products of all sorts; here they dried out the bones—and in suffocating cellars where the daylight never came you might see men and women and children bending over whirling machines and sawing bits of bone into all sorts of shapes, breathing their lungs full of the fine dust, and doomed to die, every one of them, within a certain definite time.... The person entering would have to summon his courage as for a cold-water plunge. He would go on like a man swimming under water; he would put his handkerchief over his face, and begin to cough and choke; and then, if he were still more obstinate, he would find his head beginning to ring, and the veins in his forehead to throb, until finally he would be assailed by an overpower blast of ammonia fumes, and would turn and run for his life, and come out half-dazed. (129–30)

A man from a sausage-making department described conditions there, saying, "The work is not difficult in and of itself, but it couldn't possibly be more unhealthy. All day long the floor is flooded with water. The electric lights burn all day to ensure sufficient light in case the room—as often happens—fills with smoke and steam. The smells are unbearable for a newcomer" ("From the Stockyards" 74). Common laborers earned

Men and children worked in putrid, standing water while stuffing sausages at Armour's packing house in Chicago in 1893. (Courtesy Library of Congress)

approximately 16 to 18 cents per hour. Not every one earned even this much; women and children, working largely in the specialized departments such as the sausage department and the canning operations, frequently earned far less. Unlike the skilled workers, common laborers also experienced seasonal bouts of unemployment in the summer or whenever demand for meat tapered off (Halpern 25–28; Barrett 28, 44, 51).

Older groups of immigrants—the Germans and Irish—as well as old-stock Americans dominated the skilled positions. In the semi-skilled and unskilled positions, more recent waves of immigrants, largely from Eastern Europe, dominated. (See following text for one Eastern European worker's initial experience of life in Packingtown.) Some African Americans immigrating from the South on the railroads found relatively permanent positions, but many were only offered work in the event of a strike. Because Union Station, the nation's largest railroad hub, was located only a few miles northeast of the stockyards, a large transient population regularly came through the stockyards looking for short-term work. Moreover, heavy immigration meant that many newcomers turned to the packinghouses for work. The large unemployed population kept wages in the unskilled positions very low. Many of the common laborers were hired by the day or even the hour. Hundreds reported to the packinghouses during the morning "shape up," when a lucky fraction of the workers was hired to round out a gang. The segmentation of the labor force along occupational and ethnic lines also undermined workers' ability to organize (Halpern 29).

A LITHUANIAN IMMIGRANT TO PACKINGTOWN

My job was in the cattle killing room. I pushed the blood along the gutter. Some people think these jobs make men bad. I do not think so. The men who do the killing are not as bad as the ladies with fine clothes who come every day to look at it, because they have to do it. The cattle do not suffer. They are knocked senseless with a big hammer and are dead before they wake up. This is done not to spare them pain, but because if they got hot and sweating with fear and pain the meat would not be so good. I soon saw that every job in the room was done like this—so as to save everything and make money. One Lithuanian who worked with me, said, "They get all the blood out of those cattle and all the work out of us men." This was true, for we worked that first day from six in the morning till seven at night. The next day we worked from six in the morning till eight at night. The next day we had no work. So we had no good, regular hours. It was hot in the room that summer, and the hot blood made it worse.

I held this job six weeks and then I was turned off. I think some other man had paid for my job, or perhaps I was too slow. [...]

Those were bad days and nights. At last I had a chance to help myself. Summer was over and Election Day was coming. The Republican boss in our district, Jonidas, was a saloon keeper. A friend took me there. Jonidas shook hands and treated me fine. He taught me to sign my name, and the next week I went with him to an office and signed some paper, and then I could vote. I voted as I was told, and then they got me back into the yards to work, because one big politician owns stock in one of those houses. Then I felt that I was getting in beside the game. I was in a combine like other sharp men. Even when work was slack I was all right, because they got me a job in the street cleaning department. I felt proud, and I went to the back room in Jonidas's saloon and got him to write a letter to Alexandria to tell her she must come soon and be my wife. [...]

[...] I had been working hard in the cattle killing room and I had a better job. I was called a cattle butcher now and I joined the Cattle Butchers' Union. This union is honest and it has done me a great deal of good.

It has raised my wages. The man who worked at my job before the union came was getting through the year an average of $9 a week. I am getting $11. In my first job I got $5 a week. The man who works there now gets $5.75.

It has given me more time to learn to read and speak and enjoy life like an American. I never work now from 6 A.M. to 9 P.M. and then be idle the next day. I work now from 7 A.M. to 5:30 P.M., and there are not so many idle days. The work is evened up.

With more time and more money I live much better and I am very happy. So is Alexandria. She came a year ago and has learned to speak English already.... We have four nice rooms, which she keeps very clean, and she has flowers growing in boxes in the two front windows. We do not go much to church, because the church seems to be too slow. But we belong to a Lithuanian society that gives two picnics in summer and two big balls in winter, where we have a fine time. I go one night a week to the Lithuanian Concertina Club. On Sundays we go on the trolley out into the country.

—From "The Life Story of a Lithuanian," 25–31

Packingtown itself was isolated from other Chicago neighborhoods. It was bordered by Bubbly Creek on the **Living in** north, a branch of the Chicago River used as a dump for **Packingtown** decaying animal matter from the slaughterhouses. The city dumps formed Packingtown's western border, railroad tracks formed its southern border, and the Union Stockyards, where animals congregated before entering the slaughterhouses, made up its eastern border. Cut off from the rest of the city, Packingtown was noted for its overpowering odor and its utterly inadequate sewage system that left wide troughs of raw sewage by the side of its unpaved streets. One recent immigrant, pausing before Bubbly Creek, described it this way, "It was so full of grease and dirt and sticks and boxes that it looked like a big, wide, dirty street, except in some places, where it boiled up. It made me sick to look at it" ("The Life Story of a Lithuanian" 23). Overcrowding, dangerous work conditions, and inadequate sanitation led to high rates of infectious diseases and high rates of infant mortality.

To cope with this harsh environment, people socialized in ethnically homogenous groups that supported a wide array of benefit organizations, church parishes, and parochial schools. Early sociologists surveying the Bohemian community of Packingtown recorded 30 savings and loans, 259 benefit societies, 35 gymnastics clubs, 18 singing societies, 5 bicycling clubs, and 4 drama groups in 1902 (Barrett 68, 75). Within these ethnic enclaves, individuals could communicate in their first language and continue cultural traditions that gave them a sense of strength and continuity.

Given the frequent periods of unemployment, the unhealthy conditions of Packingtown, and the inadequacy of government relief programs, families in desperate straits often turned to ethnic benefit societies. One poignant appeal to the German Society in Chicago read:

Because I find myself in a terrible situation I am turning to you through this letter with a large request if there would be some kind of aid left over for me as my husband hasn't had much work and now it's unsteady and I am in childbed where I've needed 2 doctors and now after 8 days I had to have a relapse with bleeding and the 5 little children and in my illness I'm turning to you distinguished German Society. ("Three Cases" 124)

According to German Society records, this family lived in a basement apartment where the mother sewed trousers for about $2.25 per week. The father had had little employment and the children were still too young to work. The baby mentioned in the letter died shortly after the mother's appeal. With slim resources for its large number of applicants, the German Society allocated $5, less than a week's rent, to this family. Cases such as this one give contemporary readers a sense of the tremendous risk associated with working-class life. Illness or economic downturns could kick off a downward spiral of gradually more unhealthy living quarters, sparser food, more exhausting work, and mounting doctors' bills. Such downward spirals frequently were reversed only when sick family members died or children grew old enough to work.

Each ethnic group established its own churches. Even though the majority of Packingtown residents were Roman Catholic, they did not generally attend church with members of other ethnic groups. Moreover, most children attended parochial schools taught in their parents' languages. As a result, residents of Packingtown were slow to assimilate to American culture; many spoke little English and received their news from local newspapers printed in their native languages. As another measure of ethnic segregation, fewer than 2 percent of 284 Packingtown couples surveyed in 1905 had married outside of their ethnic group (Barrett 75).

Not only did ethnic organizations offer a safety net, skimpy though it may have been, but family organizational patterns also made it possible for people to survive. Though the packinghouses offered employment to women, very few married women chose employment outside of the home. Because wages in the meatpacking sector were so low for common laborers, wives could contribute more to family incomes by taking in boarders or doing the kind of piecework, such as sewing, that could be accomplished in the home. Moreover, with small budgets, wives could conserve expenses by carefully shopping for food and household supplies. Some women took on episodic employment as midwives. As historian James R. Barrett notes, women in the yards earned only six or seven dollars a week, whereas a woman who took in three male lodgers could earn about thirty dollars a week minus food costs. Of course, the practice of taking in boarders contributed to the overcrowded conditions of Packingtown. Large families did not generally take in boarders, but relied more upon the earnings of their older children.

CONCLUSION

The growth of the factory system during the industrial era provided opportunities for some. Engineering and business schools flourished as increasingly complex industrial operations required greater accounting and engineering expertise. As even skilled laborers increasingly accomplished only a small part of a much more complex production process, knowledge of the entirety of the process rested with this new professional-managerial class.

Aggressive capitalists and financiers, particularly in the steel and meatpacking industries, discovered ways to dominate their industries, restrict competition, and maximize their profits at the expense of their suppliers, workers, and consumers. Company towns springing up around the textile and steel giants often provided the means for manufacturers to doubly exploit their workers. Paying their employees in company scrip or in checks that could only be cashed at company stores, the manufacturers could charge higher than market rates for household necessities.

Some rose out of the ranks of the working class by opening their own small businesses, frequently saloons. Others achieved middle-class status through education and white-collar employment. Andrew Carnegie, a poor, Scottish immigrant and one-time bobbin-boy, took bookkeeping classes after his 12-hour shifts in the textile mill. The lesson he drew from his experience was that the truly hardworking could rise to the top. By contrast, one of his protégés, William Dickson, left school at the age of 11 to work and by 15 found a position in the steel mills. Dickson transferred to clerical duties at 20, as a result of a program of self-education and a few night courses at a local business college. His experience taught him a very different lesson. He worked to eliminate the seven-day workweek in steel, and to track, then reduce, workplace fatalities.

Consumers benefited by the industrial economy, finding a greater range of products at lower prices as a result of the factory system. Canning and refrigeration technology made it possible to have a far more varied diet, especially in the winter, than most had enjoyed before. Moreover, ready-made clothes and soap (a by-product of the meatpacking industry) came within the range of even a working-class family's income.

Those who lost by this process did so because their livelihood became less certain; they lost control over their work processes, and frequently their real incomes fell. These were the working class, largely immigrants or the children of immigrants, who had left traditional, agricultural economies in which they organized their own tasks and provided most of their necessities from the land they farmed.

They responded with both confrontational and cooperative strategies. They unionized to match the strength of the large manufacturers. They elected pro-labor representatives on federal, state, and local levels to push pro-labor legislation such as 8- and 10-hour legislation, as well as laws restricting child labor. They supported a vigorous pro-labor press that drew workers together to support labor unions, socialism, and legislative reforms. Often they were defeated in these measures. Manufacturers hired spies to ferret out and blacklist organizers. State and federal governments took the manufacturers' side in labor disputes and deployed soldiers and police to intimidate or attack strikers and organizers. The mainstream press generally viewed working-class organizations negatively.

Suffering major defeats in confrontations between large manufacturers and strikers or demonstrators (e.g., the Great Strike [1877], Haymarket Riot [1886], Homestead Strike [1892], and Pullman Strike [1894]), workers were, perhaps, more successful in the short run with their cooperative strategies. A range of formal and informal working-class organizations helped individuals at crucial moments. The new immigrant reported to a relative, the local tavern, or an ethnic club to find his or her first job. Through boarding arrangements, single employees found cheap lodging and food, and women found a means to support their families. Benevolent societies and church parishes, usually ethnically based, provided emergency help to the most destitute. Cooperative buying clubs reduced the cost of essential purchases. All members of a family contributed what they could to the family budget; even small children scavenged in the dumps of Packingtown or ran errands in the textile mills. Later in the twentieth century, the tide of public opinion would shift, and labor unions would more successfully bargain for higher wages and safer working conditions.

4

Housework, Houses, and Women at Home

The way in which American women experienced home and housework changed considerably in the industrial era. This chapter describes how women's roles were gradually redefined. Even while women continued to do physically demanding work within the home, and increasingly outside of it, society put greater value on their spiritual role in the family. The self-disciplined, cheerful worker celebrated by early nineteenth-century writers like Susan Warner and Harriet Beecher Stowe was supplanted by more ethereal heroines like Mark Twain's, or the degraded working women of Stephen Crane, Upton Sinclair, and Edith Wharton.

Similarly, homes were increasingly seen as spiritual centers where men could recover from their harrowing work in the public sphere and where children could be safely shepherded. While the houses of the wealthy reflected this ideological transformation, working-class houses more readily revealed the constant round of work to which most women devoted themselves. This chapter describes the characteristic housing of the era, the most significant technological innovations affecting the home, and the typical work of a woman in the home.

WOMEN'S WORK: THE IDEOLOGY OF SEPARATE SPHERES

By 1870 in the industrializing North, most production for the marketplace had moved out of the home, dramatically changing cultural understandings of women's roles and home life. In 1800, 8 out of 10 Americans worked on family farms where women were integral parts of the family's agricultural business. Many of the remaining Americans worked in small craft shops attached to the home of a master craftsmen. Consequently, the majority of homes in 1800 were sites of production where men and women labored in close proximity. While men did most of the work for the marketplace, women pitched in during periods of peak activity such as planting and harvesting seasons. They cooked for all of a farm's or shop's workers. In addition, women made the family's clothing, their soap, their candles, and most of their other consumables. Men and women recognized that housework was essential to the family's economic prosperity.

By 1870, however, families produced few of their own consumables and much production had shifted from artisan craft shops and farms to factories. The home was no longer understood to be an extension of the commercial and political world. Americans began to think of the home as a sanctuary from these competitive arenas. They idealized the home as a "haven in a heartless world," a place where women were to nurture their harried husbands, educate their children, and compensate for a spiritually impoverished world outside of the home. With the rapid growth of a wage-dependent population and a shift toward a more market-oriented economy, Americans' understandings of men's and women's roles underwent a dramatic shift.

Most American women and men of the late nineteenth century were expected to live in "separate spheres." Men were expected to enter the competitive, impersonal marketplace and political arena. In this public sphere, Americans believed that a Darwinian logic ensured that only the strong and shrewd prospered. According to Herbert Spencer's theory of Social Darwinism, the widespread poverty and frequent workplace injuries characteristic of industrializing economies were akin to the natural forces which weeded out the weak among animal species. The resulting competition for survival was a positive force leading to human progress. It was the role of women, according to this line of thinking, to compensate and spiritually heal men brutalized by the public sphere. Women were expected to remain in the home, caring for children, cleaning, cooking, washing, and overseeing the physical and spiritual health of the family. In this private sphere, an alternative ethic of cooperation and self-sacrifice was supposed to prevail. According to Spencer, social disaster would quickly ensue if the home became a competitive arena or if the public realm protected the weak by taxing or regulating the strong. Through both high praise for the "angel in the home" and often heavy-handed condemnation of the so-called unnatural women who entered the public sphere, women were pressured to confine themselves to the home.

Ann Douglas refers to this shift in women's roles as "feminine disestablishment." Women lost power, according to Douglas, because "feminine labor and its function in society were *visible* in the earlier period, and this visibility assured a minimal recognition, and a minimal degree of directness in the assessment of the feminine contribution" (55). With the movement of production out of the home, women's labor ceased to be considered an important contribution to the family's economic well-being. As Douglas notes, even women who quite visibly produced goods—western women and working-class women in the industrializing northeast—were subject to the ideology of separate spheres. They "often had the worst of two worlds" because they worked when such work was thought to degrade women's nature (55). Women were increasingly valued for their spirituality, their beauty, and their remoteness from the everyday strife of the marketplace and political realm. Americans of this era expected women to be concerned with their children and husbands but not with larger political and economic issues.

A typical statement of this ideology of separate spheres appeared in an 1869 article from the women's magazine *The Household*. Entitled "Woman's Relations to the State," the article claims "Woman is the divinely commissioned teacher of her race" (79). According to the article, she is charged with the sacred and nationally crucial task of rearing and educating men who "become citizens" and determine "the condition of the State" (79). Women are equipped, moreover, to educate the future citizens of the nation precisely because women are excluded from the "strife" of the "noisy world." Should women "make speeches, edit papers, and hold office" their "scepter falls to the earth" (79). The logic of "separate spheres," in other words, claims that two incompatible ethics govern public and private life, and that participation in public life would unfit women for their role as the spiritual leaders of their families.

Women's restricted status was somewhat elevated, however, by new beliefs about childhood and the development of domestic science. Because children were increasingly understood to respond better to loving influence rather than stern punishment, women raising young children were given greater esteem than childless or older women. The advent of "domestic science" also served to elevate women's sphere. While domestic advice articles, books, and magazines were first published in the United States in the mid-nineteenth century, it was only toward the end of the century that this advice was linked to Americans' growing respect for science. Starting with the widely read 1869 volume *American Woman's Home*, advisors encouraged women to apply scientific methods and the latest technology to improve the health and happiness of their homes. Harriet Beecher Stowe, the renowned author of *Uncle Tom's Cabin*, and her sister Catherine Beecher, famous in her own right as an educator, penned *American Woman's Home* to "elevate [...] woman's true profession" and to "embody the latest results of science" (13, 15). For example, the sisters began their chapter on "a healthful home" with a short anatomy lesson demonstrating the importance of pure air and a properly ventilated home to the heart and lungs. They advanced women's status, not by arguing for an enlarged

Women's Status

sphere, but by attempting to professionalize the private sphere. They—and a host of their contemporaries—argued that women's domestic responsibilities were just as important as men's political and economic responsibilities, and that they consequently should have just as much formal preparation for their daunting labors.

The labor of women, whether working-class or middle-class, was daunting indeed. In an era when public schools were still relatively rare in some sections of the country, women were responsible for educating their children. They also nursed family members through many common, contagious diseases, diseases that often resulted in months of bed rest. They cleaned the home without the aid of vacuum cleaners, washed clothes without the aid of motorized washers or dryers, cooked on wood or coal burning stoves that had to be refueled frequently, ironed using irons placed in the fire, sewed much of their family's clothing, and often carried water or fuel into the home. Middle-class women may have had servants to help them with this multitude of chores, but such women often commented on the difficulty of managing their servants. In addition, working-class women sometimes worked in factories or took in piecework to support their families. It is no wonder then that Lydia Maria Child commented in frustration to her brother Convers, "Thank God that you are not a woman! Great labors do but strengthen the intellect of a well-balanced character; but these million Lilliputian cords tie down the stoutest Gulliver that ever wrestled in their miserable entanglement" (qtd. in Karcher 264).

Domesticity and Its Discontents While many women might have felt similarly overwhelmed by the volume and physical demands of housework, the ideology of separate spheres discouraged them from considering their duties as work. Domestic writers often portrayed housework as an expression of love rather than as labor. As Elizabeth H. Pleck points out, "It was crucial to the ideology of domesticity that women not think of themselves as workers, for if they did so, the home would become simply another artisan's shop rather than a haven against a hostile, even corrupt, world" (24). Consequently, artists and writers often represented the home as a work-free environment, what historian Jeanne Boydston calls, "a new Eden—a paradise delivered up to husband and children from a benevolent and bountiful nature, without the curse of labor" (147). The early nineteenth-century farm wife did strenuous work and was valued for that work. But as Americans increasingly entered a money economy and left the barter economy, they accepted that money was a "neutral index of economic value" (Boydston 160). The unpaid work of the household ceased to seem like real work. The angel in the home seemingly produced a clean house, a plentiful and tasty meal, and well educated children through her virtuous nature rather than through strenuous exertion.

To be sure, there were women who protested the restriction in women's roles. Elizabeth Cady Stanton and Susan B. Anthony emerged from their long work in the abolitionist movement as advocates of women's right to vote and to participate fully in public life. Anthony traveled extensively, earning women's right to vote in many school districts and local governments across the country. Reformer Rheta Childe Dorr argued that it was women's special duty to protect the welfare of children, widows, and society's weakest members. She explicitly questioned the ideology of separate spheres when she commented, "Woman's place is in the Home, but Home is not contained within the four walls of an individual home. Home is the community" (S. J. Diner 327). Still, such protests were often ridiculed in the popular press. While working-class women may have engaged in paid

This cartoon from 1909 reflected a familiar criticism of women's rights advocates, that they were selfish, manly, and unnatural, and that they emasculated their husbands. Similar satires of women's rights advocates dated back to the 1840s. (Courtesy Library of Congress)

labor outside of the home, they were still responsible for the "women's work" inside the home. They could expect little help from the men in their families and little support for their ambitions in the public realm.

Because this volume focuses on geographic areas greatly impacted by industrialism, housing and women's work in the South will not be addressed. Even with the emancipation of slaves, the southern social system was based on a more rigid class hierarchy, a less fluid labor market, and a far less industrialized economy. A southern model of family life placed less stress on the private, nuclear family. Even housing differed significantly in the warmer climate of the South. The kitchens in large homes, for example, were commonly detached from the main house to keep the house from becoming over-heated in the summer. Consequently, southern family life reflected different norms.

HOME, SWEET HOME

The Upper-Middle-Class House
Contrary to nostalgic notions of nineteenth-century families, most individuals lived in nuclear families consisting of parents and their dependent children. While grandparents and aunts and uncles seldom lived in the same house, they did commonly live nearby, making it possible to share some responsibilities, especially for young children.

Depending on a family's income, there was a wide variety of housing. A prosperous family might live in a sumptuous multi-story home. People would first enter a central hall, which operated as a transitional space between the exterior, male sphere, and the domestic, feminine sphere (Ames 8). The formal hall would serve as a place to store outerwear and a connector between the other rooms of the house. A central, ornately carved stairway would take people from the hall to the upper rooms. On the first floor, the hall would lead to a formal parlor, dining room, kitchen, and perhaps library. This transitional space made it possible to preserve the privacy of the family and their company when visitors, especially those of a lower social class, came to the house. "[T]his form of hall," historian Kenneth L. Ames comments, "emphasized control and hierarchy" (13).

The formal rooms of the house such as the parlor, dining room, and library were located in the ceremonial, elaborately decorated front of the house. The more functional rooms, such as the kitchen and pantries on the first floor or the nursery and sewing room on the second floor, were located at the back of the house. Company would generally be entertained in the parlor, though it was common for men to socialize separately in the library or in a smoking room after dinner.

Upper-middle-class homes often had one and sometimes two pantries separate from the kitchen and designed to store food and sometimes dishes. The larger pantry was generally located just off the kitchen and connected to no other room in the home. A butler's pantry would primarily store serving dishes and glasses and it was generally located between the kitchen and dining room, operating as a passageway between the two.

Upstairs were the bedrooms, a separate nursery, often with an adjoining room for the nurse, a bathroom, and sometimes a sewing room. If the house had a third floor, it was generally designated as servants' quarters. A relatively small and plain staircase carried servants and the family during more private periods of the day between the functional spaces at the back of the house.

The Skilled Worker's and Professional-Managerial Class's House

The family of a skilled worker would likely live in a one- or two-story cottage or a one-and-a-half-story bungalow. At an earlier moment in history, such a family would also have had a central hall and parlor, less to preserve a formal space in the house than to provide for a large, central fireplace in the hall. With the advent of smaller and more efficient stoves, the central hall lost one important function. Moreover, by dispensing with the central hall, the same size home contained more living space and could more easily fit in the narrow 25-by-125-foot lots common in urban areas. The cottage or bungalow without central hall became the dominant house type for the skilled working class.

For example, Edwin Thompson, a unionized carpenter, lived with his family in a two-story cottage in Chicago. The home consisted of seven rooms—a wood-trimmed study, parlor, dining room, and kitchen on the first floor, and three bedrooms on the second floor. The front door led directly into the parlor. They had many amenities, including a phonograph, a dining room chandelier, ornate rocking chairs, and china. The growing professional-managerial class whose income consisted primarily of wages—lawyers, doctors, accountants, engineers, and the like—would live in similar housing (Bigott 4–6).

The Unskilled Working Class's House

Contrary to misperceptions of the industrial era, the unskilled working class did not typically live in large, multi-unit tenement buildings. Only in New York City and Providence, Rhode Island, did the preponderance of the unskilled working class live in tenements. Elsewhere, even very poor families generally lived in one- or two-family cottages. An unskilled worker's family might, for example, share a two-story cottage with another family. One family would live in the two to four rooms on the first floor and the second family would occupy the two to four rooms above.

Unskilled workers in some areas could buy small homes on fairly easy terms; in Harvey, Illinois, for example, a family might buy a two-room cottage for $500 (Bigott 40). A more prosperous family with multiple wage earners or a boarder, might afford the common five-room cottage. Very small, seven-by-eight-foot bedrooms made it possible to squeeze two bedrooms into the narrow, five-room cottages. Such houses were generally built without amenities; there were no sidewalks, paved roads or trees planted by the developers. Open sewers proved to be health hazards, particularly to young children who played near them.

Older working-class houses seldom came with "improvements," meaning that there was no indoor plumbing. The family used an outdoor privy and hauled water from an outdoor pump. If the family did have running water and an indoor toilet, the toilet would likely be located behind the kitchen so that it could share the same set of pipes as the kitchen sink.

MAJOR TECHNOLOGICAL ADVANCES FOR THE HOME

Sewing Machine   From women's perspectives, the most important invention of the nineteenth century was likely the sewing machine. It transformed both the work women did and the work they no longer had to do. Prior to the invention of the sewing machine, most women made all of their family's clothing by hand. With the invention of the sewing machine, people could sew much more rapidly and the cost of ready-made clothing declined significantly. Most women continued to make women's and babies' clothing in the home, but by the 1880s very affordable men's and boys' clothing could be purchased at department stores or through mail-order catalogs.

The first operational sewing machine was patented in 1846 and by 1860 companies such as Singer were selling more than 30,000 per year. Improvements in manufacturing techniques and the expiration of exclusive patents resulted in much more affordable sewing machines by the late 1870s. In 1851, for example, a Wheeler and Wilson sewing machine cost $125—a third of an unskilled workingman's annual salary. After the patent pool expired in 1877, the same sewing machine cost approximately $50 (Brewer 12). Most households, even poor ones, owned sewing machines by 1880—in part because manufacturing methods had made them affordable and in part because they could be used to supplement a family's income.

Prior to the widespread use of sewing machines, the over-worked, emaciated seamstress had become an icon for exploited and impoverished workers. The seamstress took piecework home from large factories, accepting minimal pay for her work. Often she was limited to this type of work because she had children at home she had to watch while she worked. Many viewed the sewing machine as a way for the seamstress to increase her earnings. However, the affordability of the sewing machine made piecework an even more widespread and exploitative form of labor. Huge garment manufacturers employed thousands of women and children, many of them immigrants, to make clothes for the growing ready-made garment market. Because these women and children worked in separate tenements, the industry was very difficult to regulate, leading to terrible working conditions. Sometimes several immigrants and their children would crowd into a small tenement, sharing a sewing machine and working extended hours for very little pay. While the sewing machine made ready-made clothing far more affordable for many, it did not improve working conditions for those employed in the industry.

There is a certain irony to the 1885 *Good Housekeeping* ten-part series on "Domestic Sanitary Appliances." It was *Good Housekeeping*'s first year in publication and it emerged amid a host of magazines and books devoted to domestic life. While **Indoor Plumbing** the masthead proclaimed the magazine was devoted to "the interests of the higher life of the household," it was the household's indoor plumbing, literally the underpinning of the house that the lead articles addressed.

Indoor plumbing and ventilation were major themes in the domestic literature of the period. Indeed, Mrs. Henry Ward Beecher's popular *All Around the House; or, How to Make a Home Happy* (1878) began with a defense of "why women should understand the details as well as the theory of sanitation." Women were in league with doctors, plumbers, and scientific "sanitarians" to prevent illness. "Women," Beecher wrote, "are more interested in preventive medicine and household hygiene than men" (3) and therefore were charged with the responsibility of seeing to their homes' safe implementation of indoor plumbing.

The advent of indoor plumbing had a profound effect upon the daily life of late nineteenth-century Americans. Indoor plumbing potentially included many things. In most homes, by 1870, water heaters permanently attached to the back of stoves replaced kettles of boiling water on the stove (Ogle 70). These water heaters were sometimes filled by hand with pails of water from an outdoor pump located near the kitchen door. Homes that had been improved or recently built generally had a set of pipes that would carry the hot water to the kitchen sink and perhaps an upstairs sink and bathtub. Another set of pipes carried the waste water to an outdoor cesspool or municipal sewer system.

Other plumbing innovations were common in the homes of the middle and upper classes by 1900 but were rare among the working class who constituted the majority of Americans. For example, water closets, the forerunner to modern toilets, replaced outdoor privies in the homes of the wealthy. Similarly, wash stands and bath tubs with piped water supply and drains were common features in the homes of the middle and upper classes. Most of the working class, however, continued to use portable pitchers, bowls, and bath tubs filled by water buckets.

Waste water from homes generally went into underground cesspools near the home. Some cesspools were built to keep waste entirely enclosed. These had to be emptied regularly and the refuse transported elsewhere. Others were made to leach into the yard and these sometimes had the unintended consequence of leaking into the home's basement or contaminating the home's water supply.

Modern plumbing was a mixed blessing. Leaks and splashing often caused the wood frames of bathtubs and sinks to rot, and the rotting wood attracted cockroaches and water bugs (Ogle 90). Poorly insulated pipes situated on outside walls burst in cold weather, causing extensive water damage to floors and ceilings. Poor ventilation systems produced noxious odors.

According to the scientific sanitarians of the end of the century, however, the worst effect of poorly designed indoor plumbing was the ubiquitous "sewer gas" it produced. While Americans increasingly valued the convenience of indoor plumbing, the sanitarians strongly rebuked them for creating grave health risks. Waste water that leached from pipes or cesspools, as well as back drafts from sewers, produced what they believed to be poisonous gases that filled the home. In the 1870s they credited this sewer gas, or "miasma," with creating diseases such as typhus and cholera. They also believed that leaking pipes and cesspools permitted poisonous liquid to contaminate nearby water wells. The latter was nearer to the truth. By the 1880s, ample evidence of germ theory began to convince the public that bacteria caused dangerous, widespread illnesses. The gases they associated with human waste were frequently symptoms, though not causes, of the illnesses many nineteenth-century people died from.

The scientific sanitarians studying the infectious diseases of crowded tenements and Civil War camps discovered that decaying organic material could lead to dreaded diseases such as cholera and typhus, diseases to which children, the old, and the weak were particularly vulnerable (Ogle 110). Maureen Ogle notes that "while medical experts in the 1860's and after still assumed that the urban poor, especially immigrants, constituted an especially troublesome public health hazard, now they also recognized that the homes of the middle and upper classes posed many of the same kinds of health threats found in the tenement" (108).

Vocal scientific sanitarians convinced Americans to invest in clean water and more sanitary waste removal systems. The most important development in indoor plumbing of the period was that urban Americans exchanged private, self-contained plumbing systems for networks of underground municipal sewers and water mains. These networks carried potentially dangerous organic material away from homes and delivered a uniform standard of clean water to homes throughout urban areas. By 1900, close to half of the country's population and most urban dwellers had access to public water (Strasser, *Never Done* 93). New water treatment plants sprang up in the 1880s and 1890s to filter and convert waste with bacteria to harmless substances. Debate over the most efficient and sanitary plumbing systems and fixtures extended beyond the professional journals of civil engineers, plumbers, and public health officials; women both wrote and read such debates, as *Good Housekeeping*'s "Domestic Sanitary Appliances" series illustrates.

Cast-Iron Stove   The cast-iron stove was widely purchased during the industrial era and made cooking a less arduous and safer task for women. Previously, women had cooked over open hearths. The open hearth used fuel far less efficiently, requir-

This cast-iron stove, made by Ransom Stove Works in 1878, was likely used both to heat and to decorate a parlor. Cooking stoves resembled the parlor stoves, but they had a flat surface on top for cooking. (Courtesy Strong Museum, Rochester, NY 2004)

ing many more trips to gather wood. Moreover, the fire needed constant poking and tending to keep it burning steadily. The open hearth also required special equipment for suspending pots over the fire, equipment that could tip over, causing injury to anyone nearby. The kitchen fireplace was a constant hazard to young children who might be attracted to the fire and to women whose long skirts dragged on the ground where stray embers could drop.

The cast-iron stove with its vent and fuel efficiency reduced the amount of smoke in the home. The interior oven could also be heated to a hotter temperature. Because the fire was enclosed, it posed less of a risk to the family. Ornate stoves also provided a decorative addition to the kitchen, though some domestic advice columnists inveighed against decorative embellishments that were hard to keep clean.

Ironically, the increased efficiency of the cast-iron stove led to other hazards. Closing off the chimneys and heating the home with an airtight stove led to concentrations of carbon monoxide. In their efforts to conserve heat, people insulated their homes as well as they could, creating a poisonous atmosphere for the family and especially for women and babies who went outdoors less than other family members.

WOMEN'S RESPONSIBILITIES: A TYPICAL WEEK

To a contemporary American, the housework of a typical woman in the industrial era likely seems overwhelming. It may be tempting to see her role as an unrewarding one, full of drudgery. There were, however, compensations for her round of toil. Many women felt a great deal of pride in their household crafts. At a time when the division of labor increasingly robbed men of the satisfactions they had at one time taken in creating a finished product, women still designed elaborate clothing, specialty cakes, and decorations for the home. With the exception of domestic servants, women in the home also had more control over their work schedules than men who reported to supervisors. Their work more closely followed the natural rhythms of days and seasons than did factory work. Finally, much of their work took place in a social atmosphere. Women might take their sewing over to a neighbor's home for a sewing circle. They likely cooked alongside other women in the home. If they hung laundry outside or gardened in a small, urban lot they found occasions to socialize with their neighbors. Generally, they were surrounded by their young children, which, while it may have complicated their round of tasks, also enlivened them.

The following schedule illustrates the tasks of women who did not work outside of their own homes. For women who labored in the factories, these tasks would fall to another member of the family or would have to be abbreviated to fit into the little time a factory woman would have at home. For those in domestic service, only Sundays and one evening per week would likely be available for time with their families. Consequently, few married women went into domestic service. Women fortunate enough to have older daughters in the home might share these tasks with them.

Monday—
Washing
Day
Washing a family's clothes and bed linen was a physically onerous task and most women set aside one day a week just for laundry. Because people generally wore fresh, clean clothes on Sunday, Monday was typically the day for washing.

Wood or coal had to be gathered for heating water, and in homes without indoor plumbing, water also had to be carried from outdoor wells. Susan Strasser estimates that one family's laundry, using just one wash, one boiling, and one rinse, required about four hundred pounds of water, which usually had to be carried in from outside in buckets weighing as much as 40 or 50 pounds (*Never Done* 105). The bathtub or a smaller tub would be set up in the kitchen, though some wealthy homes had a special

Standard equipment for washing clothes in the industrial era included a hand wringer, pictured on the right, for squeezing out excess water from clothes, and several irons of different weights and shapes for different clothes. Irons were heated in a fireplace or stove and rotated regularly so that they could be reheated. (Courtesy Library of Congress)

room set aside for laundry. The laundry would be soaked in separate tubs depending upon the color of the fabric and the amount of dirt. During the soaking, women used little if any soap. Most soaked clothes over night; others started the soaking stage early in the morning. While the laundry soaked, a woman would tend to her other daily chores—child care, cooking, fueling fires, and the like. At the end of the soaking stage, women would add soap and wash each item by rubbing it across a wash board. After wringing out each item by hand or in a wringer, she would set it aside for the boiling stage. She might rub soap on persistent stains.

During the boiling stage, women would cut up bar soap and dissolve it in boiling water. One domestic advice book recommended adding concentrated ammonia and powdered borax (bleach) to the boiling water, a mixture that would sting and severely dry women's hands (Mrs. H.W. Beecher 220). Women then transferred the heavy, damp clothes to the kettle of boiling water. After a quick boiling, during which they stirred the clothes with a heavy stick, they removed the clothes into a rinse of plain water. Some recommended a second rinse with bluing, a preparation meant to counteract the yellow stains common to sweat-stained clothes, and another wringing.

Then the laundry had to be hung, generally outside, even in winter weather. Pioneer Mary Dodge Woodward had a special room built for hanging laundry in the winter, commenting, "Everybody in Dakota should have a covered place in which to hang clothes in winter. It would pay a man as well as anything he could build. It would save the wear and tear on the clothes, besides the health of the ones who hang them out" (Culley 171). If possible, women would do laundry outside; but in inclement weather, they had to do it indoors. Without the ventilation pipes contemporary washing machines have, the smell of boiling, soaking, soiled clothes would fill the home. On laundry day, women had to stand next to a hot stove or outdoor fire for most of the day, heaving heavy, damp clothes between basins of water and hoisting them onto laundry lines to dry. It's no wonder it was commonly referred to as the most dreaded of women's household chores.

Because laundry was so physically onerous, and because it easily could be done outside of the individual house and yard (as, for example, cooking, cleaning, and gardening could not), it was one of the first tasks to be hired out when a family became more prosperous. Even the working class commonly took men's collars and cuffs to individual laundry women or commercial laundries. Wealthier families might either drop off all of their wash or have a laundry woman come weekly to pick it up. For working-class women, laundry service provided a way for them to earn money while staying at home. Toward the close of the nineteenth century, however, commercial laundries, benefiting from large equipment and economies of scale, drove individual laundry women out of business (Strasser, *Never Done* 111–12).

**Tuesday—
Ironing**

Most clothing and table linens had to be pressed on the day after laundry day because Americans did not have the blends and synthetic fabrics we have today that hold their press. To press clothes, women placed three to six flat irons on a cast iron stove or on a hot piece of sheet iron set in the hearth. Before each use, each iron had to be wiped with beeswax to keep it from sticking to fabrics and then tested on a piece of scrap material to make sure it would not scorch the clothing. Women dipped cuffs, collars, and shirt fronts into starch. The rest they sprinkled with water. They used towels or pot holders to grasp a heavy iron and used it until it began to cool, when they exchanged the iron for another. It was heavy labor and a dangerous job during which many women were burned (Strasser, *Never Done* 105–08).

**Thursday and
Saturday—
Baking**

Bread took a full 24 hours to bake and was, consequently, one of the first prepared foods Americans purchased outside of the home. Nonetheless, by 1900 75 percent of American families still baked their own bread because good, home-made bread was a source of pride for many women (Green 61). On the day before baking white bread, women mixed up the flour, yeast, sugar, and water, and left this "sponge" to rise. The next day, they divided this into loaves and left it to rise more. They might also chop fruits or mince meats for pies the night before baking. On baking day, they finally baked the white bread as well as brown bread, biscuits, cakes, and pastries for the next few days. Faster-acting yeast, developed during the industrial era, ultimately made it possible to abbreviate the process of making white bread. Women generally baked on Saturdays in preparation for the Sunday Sabbath and one other day during the week, usually Tuesday or Thursday (Green 60).

In general, the most time-consuming housework was cooking. In an era before most Americans could afford to purchase canned goods or prepared foods, and at a time when they expected to eat three large meals per day, preparing food consumed hours every day. Breakfast, for example, likely consisted of bread, fried or baked potatoes, cooked or raw fruit, and beef, ham, or fish (Green 60). Many women, however, found this work comparatively enjoyable since a good cook often received much appreciation from her family. Moreover, nutritious, tasty food was considered an expression of a woman's love for her family.

Every Day— Cooking

Tending to the open hearth or the cast-iron stove was a central task for women. Both had to be carefully fueled and ashes removed regularly. In the winter, the kitchen might be the only heated room in the house; consequently, the family generally gathered in the kitchen to conserve on fuel. Cooking could be a highly social activity for women and one that often involved all of the family's capable females.

Most foods were either grown on the property—even urban families commonly kept vegetable gardens to defray costs—or brought from the marketplace unprepared. Cooks ground their own spices, roasted and ground their own coffee, and sifted their own flour, which was purchased in an impure form. Because refrigeration was still relatively rare, urban families brought live chickens home from market and then killed and plucked the chickens themselves.

The frequency of cleaning chores varied depending on the chore. Daily tasks included sweeping the kitchen, washing the dishes, making beds, and tending lamps (Green 76). Washing dishes in houses without running water meant hauling a great deal of water by hand from an outdoor pump. Even making beds was a more complex task than it is today. Feather beds had to be fluffed, adjusted, and frequently flipped to keep them from becoming uncomfortably lumpy.

Every Day— Cleaning

Tending kerosene lamps could also be a time-consuming job. It meant wiping the top chimneys, replacing or trimming the wicks, and filling the lamp with oil. Despite the time it took to maintain kerosene lamps, they were a big improvement over the candles people had used earlier in the century. The kerosene lamps produced a brighter, steadier light than candles. Still, improperly tended, they presented some drawbacks. A dirty chimney would result in dimmer light and sootier stains on the walls above the lamp. An over-filled lamp would overflow when lit, resulting in grimy oil stains beneath the lamp. Even well-tended lamps, along with the cast iron stoves or hearths, left soot and grime throughout the home (Strasser, *Never Done* 60).

Because of all of this grime, as well as the dust, mud, and horse manure that drifted in the house from unpaved streets, the well-kept home required not only daily but weekly and seasonal cleaning. Rugs had to be pulled up, hung outside, and beaten to remove loose dirt. The introduction of the carpet sweeper, which became popular in the 1880s, made the weekly task of sweeping rugs far easier (Strasser, *Never Done* 78). The carpet sweeper consisted of two brushes wrapped around the axle between two wheels on the base of the sweeper. The rest of the base was enclosed to retain whatever debris was picked up from the rug.

Each spring, women thoroughly cleaned their homes, beginning by taking up their heavy carpets and drapery and washing them, a physically arduous chore. Typically, they also washed windows and floors, polished their wood furniture, scrubbed walls, repainted the kitchen, cleaned the furnace if they had one, put away extra heating stoves, and replaced or refurbished the ticks on beds. Ticks were fabric covered pillows or mattresses commonly filled with feathers or hay. Women sometimes sewed new covers or more simply replaced the stuffing inside of the ticks. Blankets and comforters were also washed at this time (Green 77).

Seasonal— Gardening Most Americans, even those living in urban areas, maintained vegetable gardens during the era to supplement their home's food purchases. Urban families even kept chickens and the occasional goat, cow, or pig to supply fresh milk and meat. Families grew tubers and root vegetables (beets, carrots, turnips, potatoes, and parsnips), winter squashes, celery, and cabbages for storage in a root cellar. Since few families canned food, these vegetables as well as dried apples were the only fruits and vegetables they were likely to eat over the winter (Strasser, *Never Done* 28–29).

The urban garden was especially prevalent among the poor. It helped families to fill the gap between their food budgets and their family's nutritional needs. Food purchases consumed a greater percentage of a working-class family's income than they do today. When Katharine Davis designed a model workingman's home for the 1893 Chicago World's Fair, she estimated that a family would spend 40 percent of its income on food. Even with an annual income of $500, which was approximately $40 more than the average workingman made, Davis struggled to put together ample, nutritious food for the family. She was heard to comment, "you could feed a workingman's family on fifty-four cents a day but it was a grave question whether you ought to do so" (Barnes 15). The small children in her model family failed to gain weight and the slight, 100 pound mother of the family had actually lost three-quarters of a pound at the end of a month.

Undoubtedly echoing the sentiments of many working-class women who were charged with stretching the meager earnings of their families, Davis lamented the limitations of her work. She claimed that there were only two ways to increase the value of a fraction. She believed working families should increase their income, the numerator, through fair wages and labor organizations, but it was her job to try to reduce household expenses, the denominator (Barnes 16). To meet the challenge of feeding a family, many chose to send their children into the factories to work. Even the small income of a child could make the difference between starvation and adequate nutrition.

It fell to women to care for the ill, who generally recuperated at home rather than in hospitals. Whereas doctors administered medicines and specialized treatments, protracted illnesses required more constant care and attention than a doctor could provide. In *American Woman's Home*, Catherine Beecher described women as especially suited to nursing as an extension of their maternal natures. Quoting a female physician, she wrote:

Episodic— Caring for the Ill

God himself made and commissioned one set of nurses; and in doing this and adapting them to utter helplessness and weakness, what did he do? He made them to love the dependence and to see something to admire in the very perversities of their charge. He made them to humor the caprices and regard both reasonable and unreasonable complainings. He made them to bend tenderly over the disturbed and irritated, and fold them to quiet assurance in arms made soft with love; in a word, he made *mothers!* (342–43)

According to Beecher, nursing a sick person—whether through cold-like symptoms, dyspepsia (an upset stomach), or nervous ailments—required a well-run sick room. She advised covering the patient for warmth and then opening all of the windows to ventilate the room twice a day. To remove impurities in the bedding, it too was to be aired and washed frequently and the patient was to be given periodic sponge baths.

Beecher stressed the calming effects of a neat and well-ordered sick room. "A sick person has nothing to do but look about the room; and when every thing is neat and in order, a feeling of comfort is induced…" (340). To relieve the discomfort of fever, she recommended "cooling the pillows, sponging the hands with water,…and swabbing the mouth with a clean linen rag on the end of a stick" (341). Medication should be given only with a physician's directions because, Beecher believed, illness generally stemmed from the disruption of natural physical rhythms. Improperly administered, medicines could easily complicate rather than cure an illness.

WORKING OUT AND MANAGING DOMESTIC SERVANTS

According to historian Faye Dudden, two separate models for domestic service existed in the North and the West during the nineteenth century. The hired girl, often referred to as "help," bore a fairly egalitarian relationship to her employer. She was generally of the same ethnicity as the mistress of the home and sometimes a younger relative such as a sister or cousin. She likely worked alongside the mistress, sharing the same tasks. She also ate with the family and received the same care as family members if she fell ill. She may have helped the mistress of the home for only a short and particularly busy time, such as after the birth of a child or during harvest season. Finally, she may have been informally compensated, through room and board, access to educational opportunities, or with the understanding that she would be similarly helped at a later point in her life (Dudden 5, 36–38).

The second model for domestic service was the "domestic," a woman who was likely to be of a different ethnicity and class from the mistress of the home. The domestic generally performed distinct tasks, the most physically arduous and least prestigious tasks in the home. Her position as a servant was reinforced through customs many found insulting; a domestic did not eat with the rest of the family, she was liable for her own medical care and she was seldom permitted to entertain callers in the home. She was likely to be hired on a more long-term basis than "help" and to be paid wages in addition to room and board.

The model of hired help prevailed prior to 1870 for several reasons. First, American-born women had few employment options—sewing paid poorly, teaching was largely a man's occupation, taking in laundry was only feasible in urban settings and was considered degrading work, and factory work was seldom available to women. Domestic work, on the other hand, was readily available. By some estimates, 15 to 30 percent of all urban households employed live-in domestic help in 1850 (Dudden 1). Second, prior to the industrial era, immigrants comprised a relatively small percentage of Americans and most of these immigrants came from England, Scotland, and Wales, the same countries from which the American-born women traced their ancestry. The effect was to minimize perceived differences between employer and employed. Finally, the boundaries between family and marketplace were less strictly policed in the early 1800s. Hired girls shared more personal relations with their employers; they were often familiar as neighbors or relatives prior to their employment.

After 1870, middle-class ideals of the private home encouraged the middle class to see the home as an arena separate from work. The "angel in the home" was increasingly seen as a spiritual presence who did little physical labor. Domestic servants made it possible for middle-class women to escape heavy housework. At the same time, an influx of immigrants, as well as the domestic migration of African Americans from the South to the North, contributed to the changing character of domestic service. Freed African Americans and immigrants, especially Irish women, took the domestic work American-born women increasingly rejected. The transience of Americans during the period also served to break down the personal bonds between employer and employed. Accustomed to layoffs when a middle-class family left the city for the summer, domestics in increasingly anonymous cities felt little need to give notice when they intended to leave. A middle-class woman might awake to find a cold stove and an absent servant.

Advising middle-class women on how to retain their domestic help, Catherine Beecher first described her perception of the difference between hired help and the domestic:

A lady living in one of our obscure New-England towns, where there were no servants to be hired, at last, by sending to a distant city, succeeded in procuring a raw Irish maid-of-all-work, a creature of immense bone and muscle, but of heavy, unawakened brain. In one fortnight she established such a reign of Chaos and old Night in the kitchen and through the house that her mistress, a delicate woman, encumbered with the care of young children, began seriously to think that she made more work each day than she performed, and dismissed her. What was now to be done? Fortunately, the daughter of a neighboring farmer was going to be married in six months, and wanted a little ready money for her trousseau. The lady was informed that Miss So-and-so would come to her, not as a servant, but as hired "help." She was fain to accept any help with gladness. (311)

As Beecher relates the story, the American-born "help" is efficient, neat, polite, and significantly, treated as a member of the family circle. Beecher's description of the Irish immigrant conforms to the stereotype of the new "domestic" that abounded in middle-class magazines. The domestic was considered ignorant of middle-class housekeeping standards, slow, and frequently resentful of her employers.

GOING OUT TO SERVICE

Louisa May Alcott, writing of her experience going "out to service," reveals many reasons for domestics to resent their employers. She describes a position quite different from the one she was told she would fill. Far from performing the home's "light tasks," she is expected to split logs, haul water and fuel, scrub the hearth, and minister to the whims of the lazy, intrusive preacher who hired her. A domestic servant's tasks and hours were often vaguely defined and she could find herself constantly at the beck and call of one or another family members in the home. Without private space or free time, Alcott begins to feel like a "galley slave."

At first I innocently accepted the fraternal invitations to visit the study, feeling that when my day's work was done I earned a right to rest and read. But I soon found that this was not the idea. I was not to read; but to be read to. I was not to enjoy the flowers, pictures, fire, and books; but to keep them in order for my lord to enjoy. I was also to be a passive bucket, into which he was to pour all manner of philosophic, metaphysical, and sentimental rubbish. I was to serve his needs, soothe his sufferings, and sympathize with all his sorrows—be a galley slave, in fact. (358)

Among working women, domestic service was frequently compared with slavery and considered far more degrading than factory work. The worst imposition of service, according to Louisa May Alcott, is the condescension of employers toward their employees, and their desire to control the dress, companionship, and thoughts of their domestics. Beecher acknowledges this in her description of domestic service.

[T]he girls of New-England, with one consent, preferred the factory, and left the whole business of domestic service to a foreign population; and they did it mainly because they would not take positions in families as an inferior laboring-class by the side of others of their own age who assumed as their prerogative to live without labor. (320)

The servant problem seemed endemic to a society in which no one saw herself as part of a servant class. Women saw domestic service as a short-term occupation until they could run their own households. Yet ideals of womanhood and desires to escape the drudgery of housework impelled many to seek domestic help. Beecher advised middle-class women to be more respectful of domestics and to provide more detailed, formal employment contracts. But she also recommended that middle-class women dispense with domestics if at all possible. She advised them to do their own household work scientifically and to value their work as a respected profession.

CONCLUSION: WORKING "IN"

Despite the availability of wage work outside of the home, most adult women continued to work inside their own homes for a variety of reasons. The stigma of factory work and the low wages paid for most so-called women's work was sufficient to keep most middle-class women at home. Orestes Brownson, a reformer of the 1840s, called female factory workers "white slaves of the North." He claimed female factory workers of his generation were virtually unmarriageable because such work was mentally stultifying, physically unhealthy, and morally ruinous. Presumably, factory work was morally degrading because bosses might sexually harass their female workers and because factory workers had greater freedom to move about the city, possibly leading to promiscuous behavior. Such views continued to prejudice many families against factory work in the industrial era. Those native-born, white women who did "work out" generally took jobs as teachers and nurses.

Factory work was likely to be less stigmatized in working-class, immigrant communities and some women, especially those without children, took on factory work, domestic service, and commercial laundry work. Still, many working-class women remained in their homes because of the sheer volume of work nineteenth-century homes required. Many avoided working out in order to care for children or other dependents in the home. Working-class women creatively combined the housework described above with other types of work that could be done in the home—cooking for boarders, taking in laundry, or sewing piecework for clothing manufacturers. While the ideal home of domestic writers was a place of repose, for women, especially working-class women, the home was a center for nearly constant work. Nonetheless, work inside the home was more akin to the craft work of artisans than the regimented tasks of factory operatives. Women controlled the pace of their work and could take pride in particular crafts such as cooking and sewing.

Women's domestic responsibilities extended beyond washing clothes, preparing food, and cleaning the home. Women also cared for children and coordinated family rituals and social obligations. The patterns and rituals of family life will be discussed in the next chapter.

5

Childhood and Family Life

INTRODUCTION: THE CREATION OF CHILDHOOD

Prior to the middle of the nineteenth century, children were understood to be miniature adults. To a people schooled in the severe, Protestant theology of Calvinism, children were not only "innately depraved," they also lacked the restraints more fully socialized adults had. Eighteenth-century Americans understood aging to be an improving process as the sinful, impulsive child became the self-controlled adult. Consequently, most Americans believed children required frequent, stern punishment; Calvinists believed the motto "spare the rod and spoil the child."

By 1870, childhood had come to be recognized as a distinct stage of human development, and with this recognition women came to be viewed as crucial to the formation of a well-educated, democratic citizenry. Women's supposedly patient natures were expected to discover the innate qualities of a child's nature, and their gentle influence was supposed to draw out and shape these undeveloped elements into the child's character. No longer did the child require the stern discipline of a vigilant patriarch to suppress his or her sinful nature; the child required the loving guidance of a mother.

One might say that childhood itself was invented in the middle of the nineteenth century. Many believed human culture corrupted the innate innocence and positive impulses of the child. Consequently, a person's life was not characterized by the steady progression from sinful ignorance to god-fearing obedience. Instead, one was born in an exalted state and it was the duty of parents, especially mothers, to nurture the child's natural gifts. The child was no longer a blank slate upon which to impress social and religious rules, but a complex, endearing, malleable nature to groom. Parents hoped to foster what was good in their children.

Family life increasingly revolved around the needs of children in the home. Americans reshaped their holidays to center on family feasts and child-centered activities rather than public revelries or church rituals. The increasing sentimentality found in holidays spilled over into other family-centered rituals, including marriages and funerals, which became more elaborate, less somber affairs.

This chapter will describe family life of the late nineteenth century. It will describe the rituals and major events that shaped family life as well as the cultures that shaped children of different classes, ethnicities, and genders.

"CALLING HER WOMEN TOGETHER": LABOR AND DELIVERY IN THE HOME

Most children were born in their family homes in the industrial era. As pregnant women grew near to their delivery dates, their mothers, sisters, or female friends who lived at a distance frequently came to stay with them. Those who lived nearby might be called as a woman went into labor. Surrounded by her female relatives and often her closest female friends, a laboring woman usually faced "the shadow of maternity," as many nineteenth-century women called childbirth, with the support of a strong women's community (Leavitt, "Under the Shadow" 253).

Childbirth was often a fearful as well as painful event which women regarded with dread as well as anticipation. In New York City, nearly 13 women died for every 1,000 live births in 1880 (Emerson and Hughes qtd. in Leavitt, "Under the Shadow" 258). According to the uniform standard for reporting such figures today, that is 1,300 of every 100,000 live births. In comparison, only 7.7 women across the United States died per 100,000 live births between 1987 and 1997 ("State-Specific Maternal Mortality"). Given the large families common in the industrial era, particularly in immigrant and African American communities, most women knew of another woman who had died as a result of childbirth (Leavitt, "Under the Shadow" 259). Women reasonably entered childbirth with great trepidation.

For some, the risk of injury was more frightening than the risk of death. Injuries incurred during delivery could render a woman bed-ridden for the rest of her life. Tears in the perineal tissues, the tissues between the vagina and rectum, were the most common. Midwives did not carry surgical equipment and male doctors, still uncommon among all but the wealthy, seldom sewed tears. They were left to heal themselves, and some never did. The most serious tears, called fistulas, were holes between the vagina and rectum or bladder. Fistulas allowed urine and feces to constantly leak through the vaginal opening, leaks a woman could not control. Suffering from embarrassing stains and odors, some women isolated themselves as a result of childbirth injuries.

A prolonged or difficult delivery could also lead to tears in the vaginal wall or cervix, a condition that could cause a prolapsed uterus. A prolapsed uterus is a uterus that has fallen and presses down on the vagina. In severe cases, the uterus could actually fall into the vaginal opening, making sexual intercourse painful and future pregnancies difficult. Even activities like walking and sitting upright could become painful with a prolapsed uterus. Because corsets applied downward pressure on the abdomen, wearing a corset could aggravate the condition. Women frequently treated a "fallen womb" by wearing a pessary. The pessary came in many shapes and was inserted into the vagina to lift up the uterus. Unfortunately, pessaries could cause severe infections and even ulcers within a woman's vagina.

BRINGING UP BABY IN THE UPPER-MIDDLE-CLASS HOME

Physicians and the authors of a growing number of advice columns and books on infant and child care urged mothers to breastfeed their babies. Diseases were a major concern given the impurities common to well water, poorly cleaned bottles, and makeshift nipples. Moreover, bottle-fed infants drank a variety of mixtures, most of which were based upon cow's milk—something to which many infants had allergic reactions. It was believed at the time that breastfeeding depleted a woman's energy, so some wealthier women chose to hire wet nurses to breastfeed their infants. One pediatrician estimated that "at least three children out of every four born into the homes of the well-to-do classes" were not breastfed by their mothers (Luther Emmett Holt qtd. in Formanek-Brunell 114). The practice of hiring a wet nurse to breastfeed was widespread enough to incur the disapproval of many advice columnists who believed some wealthy women chose European tours and socializing over the care of their infants.

Just like today, when a baby cried, his or her caregiver checked to make sure the baby was not hungry, tired, or wet. Moreover, the industrial era caregiver also checked to be sure that the baby was not stuck by a pin—before the development of safety pins, baby diapers were fastened with straight pins that could prick a child.

Much, however, improved during the last thirty years of the nineteenth century for children's comfort. Whereas early nineteenth-century parents had regarded creeping as animalistic and degrading, the appearance of pictures celebrating the creeping baby suggests that creeping was increasingly regarded as part of the baby's winsome nature (Calvert 44). In the earlier period, tightly laced clothes, long skirts, and walking stools had forced babies into an upright posture and had restricted their movements. By the industrial era, however, most parents had discarded these in favor of creeping blankets and rompers that left babies more free to move (Calvert 42).

Middle-class parents placed a high priority on fostering independence and self-reliance in their children. Advice columnists in women's magazines and in childrearing manuals discouraged parents from the widespread practice of sleeping with their infants. Many went further and discouraged unnecessary holding or rocking. One manual advised, "When an infant is washed, dressed, and well fed at proper intervals, one may think of it till the heart is satisfied; but the less noticeable care it has, over and above that, the better for the comfort of the family by-and-by, and a thousand-fold better for the child itself, from its birth and all the way up to maturity" (Mrs. H.W. Beecher 223). Beecher recommended placing the baby in his or her crib for the bulk of the day where the baby "will lie cooing and smiling, watching the shadows on the wall, or the waving leaves and branches seen from the window—anything that is in motion—till the eyes grow small, and at last the white lids close over them, and the baby is asleep" (224). This regimen of minimal holding was believed to free the mother to "attend to other duties" and strengthen the baby who would be free to "roll" and "stretch" and develop "stronger muscles" (224, 225).

As part of this effort to allow children to romp and play without restraint, upper-middle-class parents often reserved a space in the house just for the children. The nursery, complete with children's toys and often linked to a nanny's room, separated children from the fragile, luxurious items decorating wealthy, Victorian homes. The separate children's sphere catered to the child's specific needs but also isolated children from their parents' worlds of work and social formalities. Upper-middle-class fathers left for the office and mothers spent their days shopping, visiting, or entertaining in the parlor—activities to which children were not invited.

FLOWER CHILDREN AND PLAY

Physical freedom was deemed essential for children. Mary Lynn Stevens Heininger notes that children in the last half of the nineteenth century were frequently associated with flowers and cuddly animals. In popular poetry and art and in personal diaries, children were referred to as "flower-bud," "kitten," "bunny," "lamb," and "pup." Such images suggest that children were regarded as part of an Edenic, natural innocence. Heininger adds, "They were at what many considered the most attractive stage of their lives, doing little but playing and sleeping, happily ignorant of what would be required of them in the future" (15).

Play, by extension, was increasingly considered a valuable activity for children in its own right. Intellectual and moral instruction was no longer the primary goal of play, though it was often incorporated into the board games and toys of older children.

One of the social graces middle-class girls were encouraged to develop was a musical talent with which to foster a harmonious home in the future. (Courtesy Library of Congress)

Toys encouraged an early identification with expected gender roles. Late nineteenth-century girls are frequently pictured with elegantly dressed and coifed "lady dolls" as well as baby dolls. These dolls differ dramatically from the simple, cloth dolls antebellum American girls were given. The cloth dolls were less a focus for little girls' affection than a focus for her industry. Girls were expected to train for their future roles in life by sewing clothes for the doll and practicing their "mechanical skills" (Beecher and Stowe qtd. in Formanek-Brunell 109). In an age before sewing machines and before the rapid expansion of consumer goods, women were expected to defray household expenses by sewing the family's clothes. In keeping with other changing expectations of play among the middle-class, however, dolls took on an alternative function in the industrial era. Expensive wax, china, or bisque dolls, which often came with extensive wardrobes, helped to train girls in proper social etiquette. Girls held tea parties and were given dolls dressed in elegant visiting costumes (Formanek-Brunell 115, 116).

Parents encouraged girls to hold doll funerals as a means of socializing them into their later roles. Dolls could be purchased with mourning clothes, and fathers constructed doll coffins. The frequencies of death in a household made the ritual of a doll funeral seem practical rather than morbid. As part of their nurturing role and as part of their social obligations, women were expected to care for the sick and visit the bereaved. Learning the etiquette of mourning formed an essential part of a young girl's education (Formanek-Brunell 117).

Girls, however, did not always play with dolls in the ways their elders anticipated. While adults prized expensive, ornate dolls, their daughters often preferred homely, cloth dolls. Doll funerals, moreover, could become doll executions as physically active girls refused the sedate, demure behaviors expected at funerals. According to historian Miriam Formanek-Brunell, some girls expressed "aggressive feelings and hostile fantasies" through their dolls, intentionally breaking, crucifying, dismembering, and cutting them (123).

Parents attempted to enforce gender distinctions through the toys they purchased for children and through the toys they encouraged children to hold in portraits. The most common toys girls hold in portraits are dolls, while the most common toys held by boys are pony whips followed by toys of a military nature. Yet the diaries of boys and girls as well as surveys indicate boys' and girls' tastes converged in their real play. In an 1898 survey of 1,000 girls and 1,000 boys in Massachusetts, both girls and boys listed the hoop and stick as their favorite toy. Large hoops were made from casks and could be rolled on the ground by revolving a stick inside of the hoop. Both boys and girls preferred toys that permitted active forms of play (Calvert 110–19).

PLAY AND WORK AMONG URBAN, WORKING-CLASS CHILDREN

During the industrial era, the middle classes invented childhood as a distinct phase when children should be protected from the cares of a competitive world. They believed children should play and romp freely, not only for their pleasure, but for their full emotional and physical development. Working-class children, however, were often compelled to work to help to support their families. The difference between malnutrition and eating enough, for many families, was bridged through a child's wages. Karen Sanchez-Eppler comments on the industrial era, "Thus to the extent that childhood means leisure, having a childhood is in itself one of the most decisive features of class formation" (819). The working child was, in many ways, deprived of the primary activity defining childhood—play.

Employment for children—and adult attitudes toward child labor—ranged widely during the industrial era. Many children worked in traditional settings, on family farms alongside their parents. Farm work was often regarded as wholesome and character-building. Juvenile delinquents and orphaned or abandoned children, in fact, were frequently sent to the countryside as workers on family farms. Many children, however, experienced farm work far differently than those who extolled it imagined. Some worked long hours as itinerant laborers, picking sugar beets or dragging heavy bags of cotton. Stooping for twelve-hour days under a hot sun could result in heat exhaustion or back injuries. Carrying bags or boxes of produce to weighing stations, children were expected to lift enormous loads for their sizes. A report from the Children's Bureau revealed that 70 percent of children working in Colorado's beet fields were physically deformed "apparently due to strain" (Trattner 151).

Street peddlers—the children who sold newspapers, matchbooks, and gum or who scavenged for junk—comprised another class of child laborers who were often viewed romantically. These "street merchants" seemed, by some accounts, to turn work into play, roaming the streets with a familiarity and élan many adults admired. They frequented bars, gambling houses, and theaters. They gave some of their earnings to their parents, but often kept some for candy and other treats (Sanchez-Eppler 827; Nasaw, *Children* x).

While street peddlers had more control over their hours and work conditions than did children working in other distinctly industrial occupations such as mining and factory labor, newsboys commonly lived on the street rather than with families. They slept in boxes, under fire escapes, and in alleys. Some were orphans, others were abandoned by their parents, and others fled overcrowded or abusive homes in the rapidly growing cities. Starting in New York, reformer Charles Loring Brace founded the Newsboy's Lodging Houses in cities across the United States. Already well established by 1870, the Lodging Houses provided beds and baths for newsboys and encouraged literacy with their small libraries. (Sanchez-Eppler 826–27).

Street peddlers who did live at home commonly played in the streets where, to middle-class observers, they appeared to be unsupervised. Henry James described the crowds of children in the streets of New York's Lower East Side as a "swarming that had begun to thicken, infinitely...Here was multiplication with a vengeance" (in Nasaw, *Children* 17). Street children, however, recalled adults being within easy reach. Mothers looked down from tenement windows to watch children play. Shop owners and peddlers, familiar with neighborhood families, looked on from their shops and carts (Nasaw, *Children* 20).

Children working in cotton mills, factories, and mines where they were likely not accompanied by parents and subjected to highly structured, demanding work schedules were most easily recognized as victims of industrialization. Such children commonly worked 12- to 16-hour days. Some descended into dark mines where their small bodies could squeeze

These three "breaker boys" separated slate from coal once it came out of the mineshafts in a Kingston, Pennsylvania, coal mine. Breaker boys often worked 14-to-16-hour days and grew up illiterate. (Courtesy Library of Congress)

into narrow tunnels. Others replaced bobbins in cotton mills, where supervisors threw cold water on the faces of tired children to keep them awake (Trattner 41). The 1890 census, which likely underestimated the number, revealed that 1,500,000 children aged 10 to 15 were employed, more than 18 percent of the demographic group (Trattner 36). Children employed for long hours seldom attended school, virtually assuring a lifetime of hard, poorly paid, physical labor.

By 1900, despite the well-organized work of groups such as the National Consumers League, little had been done to curb the problem. Twenty-eight states had instituted some forms of protective measures, but they were so limited and infrequently enforced as to be largely ineffective. Typically, only children employed in mining or manufacturing were covered. Legislation generally established a minimum age for workers of 10 or 12, a maximum number of 10 or more work hours, and some limited literacy or school attendance requirements (Trattner 41). None of the southern states, where child labor grew rapidly in the proliferating textile mills, established child labor laws. Moreover, labor unions were unable to get much of a foothold in the South and thus were unable to negotiate agreements with individual companies to limit child labor.

WORKING-CLASS CHILDREN AND SOCIAL CONTROL

Overcrowded, working-class homes in the city provided little to no space for children to play. Consequently, children flocked to the streets, some to become the "little merchants" hawking newspapers or collecting junk ("junking"), and some to play improvised games. With no other place to go, these children appropriated the streets as their own, but police officers saw such public space quite differently. Children in New York and Chicago were arrested for so-called crimes as various as playing baseball in the street, shooting craps, throwing snowballs, and "loafing on the docks" (Nasaw, *Children* 23). Children who were found gambling were likely to be sternly rebuked by police and to have their change seized. Some, in fact, hypothesized that such petty graft was the motive for such interference (Nasaw, *Children* 23). Penalties for more serious offenses, however, differed dramatically for boys and girls.

A boy found "sleeping out" might be taken to one of the Newsboy's Lodging Houses, where his stay was voluntary. But a girl accused by officials or parents of sleeping out was viewed as a far greater social threat, someone likely to become a prostitute. If she was under 16 and deemed vulnerable but not yet corrupted, she was likely to be sentenced in probate court to a reform school.

The first such state reform school for girls, the State **The Beginning of** Industrial School for Girls in Lancaster, Massachusetts, **the Trend toward** was opened in 1856 and became the model for similar **Reform Schools:** schools. Lancaster took in girls from 7 to 16 who had **Lancaster**

One of many "street children" selling newspapers. She poses before a saloon; the exposure of street children to saloons, tobacco, swearing, and gambling alarmed many reformers. (Courtesy Library of Congress)

been sent by a state appointed judge or commissioner as a result of being homeless or "leading an idle, vagrant and vicious life" (Massachusetts House Document in Brenzel 70). About one-fifth of the girls sent to Lancaster were sent for petty thievery; the rest were sent for behavioral, rather than property, crimes (Brenzel 123). The institution primarily sought to save girls from promiscuity or prostitution; consequently, homeless girls, girls exposed to sexually illicit behavior in the home, and "stubborn" girls were all eligible for Lancaster. "Stubborn" was the catch-all term applied to girls who frequented taverns or brothels, ran away from home, or befriended "low" men and women. Between 1856 and 1905, an average of 55 percent of girls admitted to Lancaster were admitted for being stubborn (123).

Initially, the institution offered a common school education to girls as well as moral guidance from a male superintendent and a matron living in one of several 30-student cottages. The education and food offered were so valued by poor parents that some had their daughters labeled stubborn to be relieved of the burden of feeding another mouth.

By 1870, however, the focus of Lancaster and similar institutions had shifted. The death of over half a million men in the Civil War left many children fatherless. Moreover, rapid industrialization, poverty, and the breakdown of more local forms of social welfare and discipline in cities resulted in a large population of girls considered delinquent. Lancaster became part of a larger bureaucracy in Massachusetts that processed delinquent girls. Younger girls deemed more innocent were placed directly with foster families, while only the older girls and those considered morally questionable by orphan asylums were referred to Lancaster. With many more girls in the system, it became the goal of the reform school to quickly train girls in domestic service and to move them into placements. The Lancaster trustees increasingly paid little attention to the girls' common schooling.

The story of one girl illustrates the danger of being caught in the state's web of institutions. Mary R. was sent to Lancaster for promiscuity. At admission she was described as having "average intellect." In four years she was placed with five different families and had a child out of wedlock. Though she reportedly cared for the child well, she was sentenced to the Massachusetts Home for the Feeble-Minded, an apparently common sentence for Lancaster women who persistently transgressed sexual mores. Her child was sent to the Infants Asylum. Other women with similar stories were labeled "moral imbeciles," a charge having little to do with their intellectual capabilities but justifying a transference to the Massachusetts Home for the Feeble-Minded. Once institutionalized, a girl could lose all of her rights, even into adulthood (156).

Lancaster became the model for managing "wayward girls" in cities across the United States. In addition, Lancaster was part of a changing conception of the role of education in the United States. The girls of Lancaster were once offered a comprehensive education, but by 1869 were encouraged to acquire only basic literacy and simple arithmetic (142). As historian Barbara Brenzel notes, "The aim of education became not equality but the assurance of socially appropriate economic opportunity" (147).

FAMILY HOLIDAYS

Compared to both the years before and after the industrial revolution, family life in the industrial era was particularly intensive. Native-born white women were having fewer children than previous generations, leaving more time for parenting each child. Marriage ideals shifted to stress affective ties between partners rather than their duties to community and God. Religious holidays were becoming increasingly secularized and were more elaborately celebrated in the home. Holidays that had been celebrated as outdoor carnivals, times for raucous parades, heavy drinking, and masked revelry, were transformed by 1870 into sentimental holidays centered around children and nurturing mothers. These changes in rituals, in particular, were an important measure of changes in family life more generally.

In the midst of the Civil War, Abraham Lincoln adopted Sarah Josepha Hale's proposal for a new national holiday of Thanksgiving. It would be a family feast commemorating the harvest feast of the Pilgrims in 1621, a founding

The Invention of Thanksgiving

event of the nation. The new Thanksgiving holiday would affirm family values by providing an occasion for widely dispersed family members to return home. It also would celebrate "American exceptionalism," the belief that Americans shared a unique destiny in the New World. This non-sectarian, but nevertheless spiritual, civic religion portrayed the United States as a "city on a hill," an example of an enlightened democracy to be emulated by the rest of the world. Thanksgiving was intended to reaffirm the North's position in the Civil War as defender of the Union.

Thanksgiving celebrations during the industrial era took on an added significance as an initiation into the American civic culture. Schoolteachers transformed the image of Native Americans welcoming the "first immigrants," into an icon representing the nation's general position toward the new immigrants. All immigrants who pledged to become citizens and patriots were symbolically welcomed into the fold on Thanksgiving.

The Thanksgiving holiday emphasized gender distinctions. While the women in an extended family worked together (and in rivalry with one another) to cook their most impressive dishes, the men chopped wood for the fire, picked up relatives at the train station, or played football, a new Thanksgiving tradition in the industrial era. Women served the abundant food—including what has become the traditional turkey and pies with elaborately designed crusts, sometimes in the shape of the Mayflower—while men sat at the head of the table and were likely to say the grace. Women taught children to observe proper etiquette, using their napkins, greeting their relatives respectfully, and thanking those who gave them gifts. Older women in the family, who were likely to have spent more time than their male counterparts with relatives, were also the most likely to regale children with family legends as they sat around the table. In other words, women were primarily responsible for organizing family rituals and fostering a sense of intimacy among family members (Pleck 15–17, 24–25).

By 1900, most Americans in the northeast and the Mid-Atlantic states celebrated Thanksgiving, but it was seen as a Yankee holiday by many Southerners, and a Protestant one by many Catholics. Still other rural people had their own harvest celebration at different times and saw no need for a separate Thanksgiving celebration. For many living in industrializing cities, however, Thanksgiving became an important ritual for drawing together family and reaffirming bonds strained by the movement of men's work outside of the home.

A Melting Pot of Christmas Traditions   Christmas became a national holiday in the United States in 1870. Until the beginning of the nineteenth century, Protestant churches in New England viewed the celebration of Christmas as a profaning of the Bible, which made no mention of Jesus' actual date of the birth. Moreover, the Anglican tradition of celebrating Christmas as a raucous carnival "commemorate[d] any thing and every thing but Christ," charged New England minister Horace Bushnell in 1847 (qtd. in Restad 35). Still, Anglicans in the South and the new wave of Catholic immigrants in the Northeast celebrated the holiday in a variety of ways. Some celebrated with boisterous parades, feasts with free-flowing liquor, and, in rural areas, the shooting of guns. Such displays could become destructive to property, as roaming bands of young men visited the homes of the wealthy to carol and demand free food and drink. Others celebrated with beautiful music such as "The Messiah" and bountiful family feasts. It was both the threat that rowdy festivals posed to property and the attraction of a sentimentalized family feast that ultimately encouraged upper- and middle-class cultural leaders to recognize Christmas and shape it to their own ends.

The legend of Santa Claus as we know it today emerged at this time and helped to reorient Christmas around children and ritualized gift giving. Santa Claus emerged from two traditions: the German and Dutch legend of Christkindel, which translates as "Christ child," and the true story of St. Nicholas, a fourth-century Bishop living in what has become present-day Turkey.

Christkindel, later called Kriss Kringle, dressed as a medieval jester, left nuts, fruits, and cakes for deserving children, and carried a stick to punish misbehaving children. Dutch-American children hung up their stockings to receive Christkindel's gifts, although the child who had skipped school or teased a younger sibling might very well find nothing but a stick. With his absurd dress and his stick, Christkindel underwent a significant transformation to become the American Santa Claus of the industrial era (Restad 50).

The American Santa Claus drew more directly from the ancient story of St. Nicholas. As a bishop, Nicholas learned that an impoverished nobleman intended to sell his three daughters into prostitution or slavery. Nicholas secretly threw bags of money into the daughters' windows so that each would have a dowry and, thus, would be saved from being sold. When the father caught him, Nicholas swore him to secrecy. However, the story slipped out and St. Nicholas became famous for his many acts of charity toward children (45). Clement Clarke Moore's famous poem, "A Christmas Visit," first printed in 1823, combined these stories. Printed in beautifully illustrated volumes throughout the nineteenth and twentieth centuries, Moore's poem cemented the present-day notion of Santa Claus as a kind and generous gift-giver.

THE NIGHT BEFORE CHRISTMAS

'Twas the night before Christmas,
When all through the house
Not a creature was stirring, not even a mouse;
The stockings were hung by the chimney with care,

In the hopes that St. Nicholas soon would be there;
The children were nestled all snug in their beds,
While visions of sugar-plums danced in their heads;

[. . .]

As I drew in my head, and was turning around,
Down the chimney St. Nicholas came with a bound.
He was dressed all in fur, from his head to his foot,
And his clothes were all tarnished with ashes and soot;
A bundle of toys he had flung on his back,
And he looked like a peddler just opening his pack.

His eyes—how they twinkled! His dimples how merry!
His cheeks were like roses, his nose like a cherry!
His droll little mouth was drawn up like a bow,
And the beard on his chin was as white as the snow;
The stump of a pipe he held tight in his teeth,
And the smoke it encircled his head like a wreath;

He had a broad face and a little round belly,
That shook when he laughed, like a bowlful of jelly.
He was chubby and plump, a right jolly old elf,
And I laughed when I saw him, in spite of myself;
A wink of his eye and a twist of his head
Soon gave me to know I had nothing to dread.

He spoke not a word, but went straight to his work.
And filled all the stockings; then turned with a jerk,
And laying a finger aside of his nose,
And giving a nod, up the chimney he rose;
He sprang to his sleigh, to his team gave a whistle,
And away they all flew like the down of a thistle.
But I heard him exclaim, ere he drove out of sight,
"Happy Christmas to all and to all a good night!"

—Clement Clarke Moore

The image of a jolly Dutch gift-giver was significantly embellished throughout the nineteenth century. In Thomas Nast's famous 1870 sketch, a gilded watch dangles from Santa's vest, and the portly man becomes a familiar image of the captain of industry, keeping production on schedule. Penne Restad speculates that the invention of elves in the last half of the century reinforced the connection between Santa and the benevolent captain of industry. She writes, "These North Pole elves were not unlike immigrants working in the nation's sweatshops. Unassimilated, isolated from the rest of society, and undifferentiated by individual name or character, the best of them worked hard, long, and unselfishly" (149). They constituted a model workforce presented by a nervous capitalist class to the more demanding workers laboring in American factories.

CAUGHT!

One of many sketches of Santa Claus, the genial bearer of gifts to children, by cartoonist Thomas Nast. (Courtesy Library of Congress)

Americans also adopted the German tradition of decorating an evergreen or fir bough with small, lighted candles. By the end of the century, the bough became a full tree and Americans added small ornaments as well as lights. In many families the mother and perhaps an older sister decorated the parlor in secret. Once they had arranged the Christmas tree and presents, they grandly admitted the rest of the family to the delight of surprised children. In wealthy neighborhoods, it became customary to open the drapes and sometimes even admit visitors to admire the decorated parlor. Some homes added elaborate displays of train sets and miniature villages to their Christmas decorations. The danger of small candles on a dry fir tree did not escape the notice of insurance companies, many of which altered policies to exclude liability for fires caused by Christmas trees (Restad 112–15).

Imported from Britain, the custom of sending Christmas greeting cards served several purposes. For women tired from the elaborate preparations for the Christmas feast and gift giving, Christmas greeting cards could substitute for traditional holiday visits. For businessmen, the greeting cards could reinforce business relationships. Improvements in printing processes made elaborate, beautifully crafted drawings readily available to most consumers and provided a substitute for the cheap knickknacks purchased for casual friends in the 1870s and 1880s.

By 1900 most of the traditions we associate with contemporary American celebrations of Christmas were in place. The roving bands of threatening young men demanding food and drink from their neighbors became jovial and harmless groups singing Christmas carols. The mischievous Dutch Christkindel had become kind and generous Santa Claus. The German Christmas bough had become the more elaborate Christmas tree. The custom of giving small treats to children and small gifts to employees had grown into a much more lavish gift exchange, though still focused on children. Christmas cards had become a way of formalizing ties to a larger group of friends, relatives, and business acquaintances.

The Jewish Passover— An Ancient Tradition Meets New American Needs
Between 1882 and 1924, 2.3 million Jews immigrated to the United States, most fleeing persecution in Eastern Europe and Russia (Pleck 96). Famine in Lithuania and the assassination of Czar Alexander the II in 1881 led to the forced resettlement of Jews outside of Russian villages, onerous taxes on kosher (ritually pure) foods, and efforts to undermine Jewish culture. Denied access to many professions, forced to live in the Pale of Settlement, pressured to convert to Christianity, subject to violence, and impoverished, Eastern European Jews immigrating to the United States felt a close affinity to the Biblical Jews fleeing slavery in Egypt. It is not surprising that among the many festivals of Judaism, Passover, which commemorated this exodus, became the most frequently observed Jewish holiday in the United States (95).

The new Jewish immigrants stood in stark contrast to the comparatively secular and assimilated German Jewish population already settled in the United States. The new immigrants were more orthodox and more concerned with preserving Jewish customs and culture. One Jewish writer, describing to a Christian audience the traditional rules governing the preparation of Jewish food, explained the feeling of many Eastern European Jews in this way:

Grown up, perhaps in lands where there was a wide gulf—prejudice and gross civil inequality—between them and their Christian neighbors, their natures, as a matter of course, have become hardened against the influences of the Gentile world, and over their ways and habits no change can be expected to come. For them to eat buttered bread with meat would, I imagine, be more than merely improper—more than sin; I have no doubt that the habit of a life time would create, beyond the mere question of right or wrong, an unconquerable physical aversion. (Rosenblatt 677)

For many Jews arriving in the United States in the industrial era, being able to openly observe Jewish customs, such as the traditional dietary rules, without discrimination or scorn, was the very definition of freedom.

These new immigrants and the more assimilated immigrants of earlier generations, together, redefined the Passover ritual. Passover celebrations in the United States commemorated the exodus of the Israelites from Egypt, the "House of Bondage," but they also commemorated the delivery of contemporary Jews from their persecution in Europe. Passover celebrated the creation of the Jewish people in ancient times, as well as the melding of two distinct Jewish traditions in the United States. As Morris Joseph wrote in 1903:

Passover is, above everything, the commemoration of the great deliverance—a deliverance that transformed a horde of slaves into a people. It is, then, Israel's birthday. From one point of view it is the greatest of all the historical festivals. No other brings the Israelite into such close touch with his people's past. No other so powerfully appeals to his historic sympathies. He is one, for the moment, with his ransomed fathers; he shares with them the proud consciousness of the free, the dignified sense of nationality that is beginning to stir in their hearts. (189)

The Passover celebration became a means of feeling connected to Jewish history and Jewish identity amid strong forces urging assimilation in the United States. Moreover, Passover reinforced a sense of solidarity among American Jews from different European origins.

Passover commemorates several events besides the deliverance of Jews from Egypt. It recalls the sparing of Jewish sons who were "passed over" when the angel of death punished the Egyptians by killing their first-born sons. The family feast, also known as the seder, celebrates the survival of Jewish culture following the Roman destruction of the second temple in Jerusalem. In the United States, it was this family feast which became the most prominent part of the Passover period.

At the seder, families follow a written script called the Haggadah (Hebrew for "telling the tale") which includes parts for all family members, especially children. It is comprised of prayers and stories explaining the significance of the holiday and the meaning of each element of the traditional seder meal. The matzah, unleavened flat bread, symbolizes the haste of the Jews leaving Egypt who could not wait for their bread to rise.

Bitter herbs are meant to remind celebrants of the suffering of the Jews. The front door was to be left open so the prophet Elijah, as well as the poor and hungry, could join the feast. Families who did not ordinarily observe kashruth, orthodox Jewish dietary laws, often tried to observe these rules during the seven-day Passover festival. This meant that they ate only kosher meat, meat ceremonially slaughtered under the supervision of a rabbi. They ate no leavened bread, "hametz," and ate from no dishes that may have absorbed leavened bread. Moreover, they did not eat dairy and meat products together, or even allow the same bowls, serving dishes, or utensils to touch both.

The week before Passover was characterized by some as the "Jewish Matrons' week of trial" because of the intense work expected of house-wives in preparation for the feast. Women were expected to do a thorough spring cleaning. Added to the usual tasks of washing down walls, beating rugs, and airing furniture, Jewish women were expected to hold utensils over a fire and boil glasses for three days in order to purify the dishes from any hametz contamination. In wealthy homes, the everyday dishes were even packed up and stored away, while the traditional Passover dishes— which never touched hametz—were brought down from the attic.

New immigrants carried over social conventions typical of the Eastern European shtetl. According to custom, prosperous Jews were expected to provide the poor with Sabbath feasts, not just during Passover, but on each Sabbath, which extended from Friday sundown until Saturday sun-down. This custom led to a strong belief in the right of the poor to food and the obligation of the wealthy to provide that food. In the United States, Jewish organizations sponsored public seders, often held on the third night of Passover, after the family feasts on the two prior nights. Eventually, these third seders became celebrations of Jewish socialism (H. R. Diner, *Hungering for America* 172–77; Pleck 102).

COURTSHIP AND MARRIAGE

One of the central passages of life in most societies is marriage; mar-riages traditionally extend the kinship network through which property is passed from parents to children and through which family dependents are nurtured. Kinship networks convey status, and they often provide access to employment or privileged positions. In the very mobile society of the industrial era United States, nuclear families often moved away from extended kinship networks. While this mobility may have diminished the importance of a mate's family ties, it made the personal compatibility of one's mate all the more crucial.

For all of these reasons, American marriages in the late nineteenth cen-tury were central social events. In fact, for a woman of the industrial era, the choice of a mate was considered the single most significant decision of her life. A woman's future social circle, her material comfort, and even her physical health all hinged upon her husband. Middle-class women who had advanced educations or careers almost always gave up their careers once they married. Working-class women who earned wages generally ceased to work, or shifted to forms of paid work that kept them in the home, such as taking in boarders or sewing. A woman's public identity after marriage stemmed from her husband's identity. Privately, husbands could make sexual demands their wives were obligated to satisfy, regardless of their health or their desire for more children. At a time when divorce was highly censured—there were fewer than 2 divorces per 1,000 marriages in 1870—and when divorce settlements heavily favored men, women could be trapped in very unhappy marriages (Cott, *Public Vows* 107).

Men, too, had much to lose by a poor marriage. With so much work to be done in the home, a sickly, irresponsible, or extravagant wife could make home life very stressful. Moreover, men were obligated to support their families, and as the standard for what was considered a middle-class lifestyle rose in the industrial era, this proved to be an anxiety-provoking task for many men. As an increasing number of farmers became urban wage earners, children became more burdensome for working-class men. Whereas children in rural areas cost little to feed and housing was relatively cheap, children in the industrializing cities could place an enormous burden on families. Consequently, men approached marriage with almost as much trepidation as women did.

Despite such concerns, men and women looked forward to marriage as the primary means through which they established their position in society and fulfilled their emotional needs. From a pragmatic point of view, men who moved to cities to start their careers and lived in boarding houses gained a home upon marriage. Similarly, many working-class women who supported themselves through factory work or teaching looked forward to "settling down" and having a home of their own.

The model of a companionate marriage took hold during this era, influencing the nature of courtship and marital interactions. The language of marriage vows traditionally stressed the "duty" of women to "obey" their husbands and the reciprocal expectation that men will "cherish" their wives. These vows not only reflected an understanding that men would make the family's decisions, but also that they could command their wives to perform their "wifely duties" in the bedroom. The model of companionate marriage challenged this understanding and, for some women, gave them more control over their bodies and the size of their families. The companionate ideal emphasized gender equality, mutual respect, and emotional intimacy.

Regulating Class Boundaries through Courtship

Single adolescents and adults generally met one another through social institutions that brought together people of the same class, religion, and ethnic background. They met their future spouses in church, school, or the homes of their family and friends. In these environments older relatives or trusted community leaders, knowing the personal and family histories of individuals, would encourage matches deemed appropriate or thwart those deemed inappropriate. The increasing mobility of American society, consequently, posed challenges to the regulation of kinship networks and marriages. When, for example, a substantial number of women began working in factories employing men, many became concerned that they would be seduced by disreputable men. The factory made it possible for men with bad reputations to circulate among unsuspecting women who would not recognize the wolf in sheep's clothing. The popular dime novels of the day depicted lecherous factory supervisors pursuing and intimidating the women who worked for them.

Even the very wealthy feared the "promiscuity" of the city, where theaters and public parks might permit marriages and courtships across class boundaries. In the 1870s and 1880s, they developed elaborate social mechanisms to preserve the exclusivity of the upper class. The elite, upper-middle-class girl who was to be introduced to society "came out" under the careful guidance of her mother or nearest female guardian. She began by calling on other women of the same class or, perhaps, of the class to which she aspired. A mistake here could be devastating, however. The social climber calling on families who did not accept her was likely to experience the humiliation of unreciprocated visits and to develop a reputation for "ill-breeding."

A fundamental part of this ritual of female visiting was the complex system of exchanging calling cards. Upper-middle-class women called on some homes expecting to stay and visit, but called on others expecting only to leave cards with servants. The expectations depended on the purpose of the call and the status of the caller and recipient. Those of higher status could initiate a call, but those of lower status could only make a personal call if they were reciprocating an earlier visit to their home (Ames 41). The ornate cards women left were often decorated with flowers or birds and contained the elaborately printed name of the woman. If a mother circulated with a daughter who was just emerging into society, the daughter's name would be printed beneath her mother's on the card. When a mother intended to announce a girl's upcoming debut, she and her daughter would personally deliver these calling cards, visiting as many as 14 homes in a day (Montgomery). These cards were central to the female ritual of visiting and special card receivers were located in the front halls of elite homes to collect the cards of visitors.

Such visits were crucial to maintaining contacts among families of the same class. When in the 1899 novel *The Awakening*, Edna Pontellier leaves home during her visiting hours, her husband reminds her of the importance of the visiting ritual:

Why, my dear, I should think you'd understand by this time that people don't do such things; we've got to observe *les convenances* if we ever expect to get on and keep up with the procession.... I tell you what it is, Edna; you can't afford to snub Mrs. Belthrop. Why, Belthrop could buy and sell us ten times over. His business is worth a good, round sum to me. (73)

In the book, Edna facilitates her husband's business success by building social connections to other families of the same or higher class.

The female convention of calling became especially crucial as families prepared their daughters for marriage. A girl's debut signaled her availability for marriage. In the 1870s and 1880s a debut generally consisted of a supper with dancing afterward at a girl's home (Montgomery). Later in the century, afternoon teas became more common. The debutante dressed in a stylish, white gown symbolizing her purity and generally wore her hair in an elaborate up-sweep. Like the debut, wearing the hair up signaled a transition from girlhood to womanhood. Following the debut, a marriageable girl attended subscription dances in which men signed her dance card for the privilege of sharing a dance with her. For the sake of propriety, each man was permitted only one dance.

Maureen Montgomery notes the centrality of women in policing the borders between upper-middle-class society and the less privileged through the rituals of female visiting, private and semi-public gatherings, and debuts. Montgomery notes that aspiring newcomers to society had to be sponsored by "insiders" and introduced to other established insiders. If the newcomers passed the initial round of visits, they would be invited to larger forms of entertainment involving the men of the family. Only marriage into the inner circle would cement the family's acceptance, however.

Courtship among the Middle and Working Classes

While the initial meetings tended to be closely supervised among the working and middle classes—without a formal introduction, a polite woman did not permit a strange man to speak with her—couples of these classes generally had many opportunities to see each other privately after that. Studying the private diaries and correspondence of couples, Ellen Rothman concludes that there was "a strong bias in the culture against parental interference in courtship. Young people had the autonomy and privacy to develop relationships that were sexually and emotionally intimate, and they did" (122).

One reason couples may have been permitted such privacy in a society that so vehemently condemned sexual activity among unwed women is because of the training women received. Women were encouraged to consider themselves passionless, and were trained to view sexually active women as "fallen" and unmarriageable. Consequently, women and the men who cared for them had a strong incentive to preserve the woman's reputation. Moreover, women sometimes struggled to reconcile their feelings of attraction for their paramour with their culture's perception of women as passionless. One woman wrote to her fiancé, "True,... I learned to hunger for your tender words & caresses, the shelter of your arms &

pressure of your lips, but I never wanted extremes. When your magnetism tempted me into a responsive condition there was no real sweetness in it (except that you were more tender afterwards)" (Burlingame qtd. in Rothman 136). For this woman, and many like her, the understanding that women were naturally less passionate, even passionless, could enhance their purity and spirituality in the eyes of their loved one and larger culture. On the other hand, they often felt a sexual attraction for their partner they found unnerving and dangerous, something to be later denied. Women could claim to be passionless, moreover, as a tool to control the sexual overtures of their partners and thus preserve their reputation before marriage and their fertility after marriage.

Weddings   The white wedding and honeymoon are traditions stemming from the 1840 marriage of Queen Victoria and Prince Albert and the subsequent marriage ceremonies among British royalty. By mid-century, etiquette books instructed American women to dress in pure white with a white veil and a crown of artificial flowers. Protestant and Catholic weddings in urban areas generally took place in churches, while Jewish weddings took place at catering halls, hotels, or restaurants. Up until the twentieth century, it was considered a sacrilege to marry in a Jewish temple (Rothman 171; Pleck 209–10).

As weddings became more formal affairs, middle-class expectations regarding gifts and post-wedding trips changed. Where close relatives at a wedding might formerly have given strictly useful items to a bride, in the industrial era relatives and friends increasingly gave luxury items. By giving lavish items such as silver and china, they signaled their confidence in the husband's ability to provide the necessaries in life for his family. They also demonstrated their adherence to the ideal of a sumptuous domestic life. The bride and groom now commonly took a honeymoon trip to the new and burgeoning cities or to natural wonders like Niagara Falls. Unlike earlier in the century, however, these trips were no longer thought of as an opportunity to reaffirm family ties; the new couple usually did not stay with relatives or travel with friends; they traveled alone for the express purpose of enjoying a private, romantic excursion.

While most urban Americans had elaborate church weddings with music and formal processions, a significant number of them had more casual civil ceremonies. Pregnant brides, people getting married for the second time, interracial couples, interfaith couples, and the poor often were married by justices of the peace in homes or courthouses. Still others chose to just live together, including same-sex couples. Over time, cohabiting heterosexual couples were considered legally wed in common-law marriages. By the end of the century, reformers and ministers had launched a campaign to discourage such marriages in an attempt to strengthen the institution of marriage as well as the social and financial obligations that flowed from it.

Two demographic shifts during the American industrial era speak volumes about changing attitudes toward mar- **Marriage and** riage, sex, and children during this time. Fully 11 percent of **Sexuality** women born between 1860 and 1880 never married, the highest figure throughout American history (Rothman 249). Moreover, birth rates for native-born, white women plummeted from 7.04 children in 1800 to 3.56 children in 1900 (Rothman 115, 265). Both of these figures demonstrate women's increasing reluctance to be defined solely by marriage and motherhood.

Marriage rates dropped especially steeply among upper-middle-class women. College educations were newly available to such women; following the Civil War, many new women's colleges began to train women to take leadership positions in the growing array of social service agencies and government bureaus. Women entered the medical and legal professions for the first time. Many became social reformers. More than half of the college-educated women of the industrial era did not marry (Smith-Rosenberg 253, 281). Instead, they developed demanding careers not compatible with the contemporaneous expectations of women in marriage. Their most intense relationships were often with women similarly committed to more public lives. Ellen Rothman argues that the drop in the marriage rate should not indicate a more negative attitude toward marriage compared with earlier women. On the contrary, it was "a sign that marriage represented a woman's choice rather than her destiny—one, rather than the only option available" (283). The later increase in marriage rates, Rothman argues, indicates that women began to believe they could combine marriage with other pursuits outside of the home.

While working-class women married more often than these college-educated women, there was one group among the working-class women who married at rates comparable to the college-educated women: Irish immigrant women. Irish women came in larger numbers than Irish men, unlike other immigrant groups. They came to the growing cities of the northeast and to Chicago to find work and send money home to their impoverished families. Large numbers of them never married. With marriage came responsibilities to a husband and children, responsibilities that would interfere with their abilities to send money home. For example, only 44.2 percent of Irish immigrant women aged 30–39 in Cohoes, New York, a mill town, were married as compared with 83.3 percent of English immigrant women (Diner, *Erin's Daughters* 47–48). Studies of other mill towns and large cities prove that these numbers are typical. As a result of their parents' and grandparents' experience of the Irish Famine of the 1840s and 1850s, Irish men and women entered marriage reluctantly, afraid to have dependent children they may not be able to support (43–69).

Historians generally agree that, in the absence of effective birth control methods, married couples limited their families through abstinence or abortion. According to an 1898 estimate by the Michigan Board of Health, one-third of all pregnancies in the state ended in abortion and 70–80 percent of the women seeking these abortions were financially secure (Smith-Rosenberg 221). In the early nineteenth century, Americans generally accepted abortion before quickening, a term for when a woman begins to quickly grow larger at about four months into a pregnancy. However, industrial era journalists and male doctors increasingly criticized abortion. These critics portrayed the women who sought abortions as selfish socialites who preferred dances and European tours to children. This perception of women's selfishness led to the passage of the Comstock Law in 1873, outlawing the dissemination of drugs, medicines, instruments, or information used for contraception or abortion through the mail. The number of women seeking abortions indicates that it was not merely the selfish socialite, but the financially strapped, working-class matron who sought abortions.

Middle- and upper-class couples took other measures to limit their family size. They married later than their parents did, waiting until their mid- to late twenties, and it appears that some practiced abstinence to avoid having children. Under the model of the companionate marriage a husband, according to one advocate of the ideal, "has no 'marital rights'…except to take what is granted to him freely and lovingly" (qtd. in Battan 166).

As Jesse F. Battan argues, this widely disseminated ideal "provide[s] insights into the tensions and conflicts that permeated the married lives of men and women in nineteenth-century America" (166). In one of the first surveys of its kind, Mary Roberts Coolidge, a professor of history and economics at Wellesley College, researched sexual practices and attitudes in the 1890s. She concluded that newly married couples often found they possessed radically different feelings toward sex:

> To many a man there must have been a shock of astonishment, if not of dismay, on discovering that his wife was afraid of him, and had only the vaguest notion of their inevitable marital relation. The convention of absolute ignorance in which the young girl had usually been brought up, made of the sex relation an experience scarcely less terrible than bodily assault. (qtd. in Battan 176)

Coolidge's conclusions seem to be borne out by the private letters and diaries of women.

Northern, urban, middle-class men and women appear to have more frequently adopted the companionate ideal. In comparison, most working-class, immigrant, southern and western couples continued to live according to patriarchal notions of a husband's rights and a wife's duties. Margaret Sanger, a nurse and early birth control advocate, recorded her impressions of visiting the Lower East Side. In this working-class and immigrant section of New York she was brought gifts of food while she tended to women in childbirth:

Always back of the little gift was the question, "I am pregnant (or my daughter, or my sister is). Tell me something to keep from having another baby. We cannot afford another yet."

I tried to explain the only two methods I had ever heard of among the middle classes [withdrawal and abstinence], both of which were invariably brushed aside as unacceptable. They were of no certain avail to the wife because they placed the burden of responsibility solely upon the husband—a burden which he seldom assumed. What she was seeking was self-protection she could herself use, and there was none. (87)

Advocating the companionate ideal, Sanger was confronted by looks of despair. These women felt their communities supported their husbands in the husbands' perception that sex was a fundamental right, even the purpose, of marriage. Sanger describes the many botched abortions and dead women and babies she witnesses as a nurse in the early 1900s. By 1913, she resolved to challenge the Comstock laws and disseminate birth control information.

In some ways, Sanger represents the culmination of two trends in the nineteenth century. Doctors and journalists, almost exclusively men, decried the selfishness of middle-class, native-born women who were depressing the birthrate and committing "race suicide." One doctor, H. R. Storer, questioned who would populate the newly opened territory of the Great Plains, "Shall they be filled with our children or by those of aliens? This is the question that our own women must answer, upon their loins depends the future destiny of the nation" (qtd. in Smith-Rosenberg 238). Sanger began her fight for birth control to empower poor women in the way that "self-possessed" women of the middle and upper classes had empowered themselves. But eventually, her campaign focused on limiting population growth among the poor, many of whom she considered genetically inferior. She combined the efforts of industrial era women to control the size of their families with the efforts of industrial era conservatives to foster an Anglo-American nation.

LIFE IN DEATH AND DEATH IN LIFE: MOURNING AND FUNERALS

The most important ritual of industrial era life in the United States, measured in terms of expense and intensity of observance, was the elaborate mourning ritual. The funeral and attendant period of mourning for a loved one cost much more than a wedding and required extensive changes to a family's clothing, habits, and home. In part, this was because having a death in the family was a more common experience than marriage in industrial American life. There were several especially vulnerable periods in a person's life—childhood, when infectious diseases and home accidents claimed the lives of many, the years of childbirth for a woman, and, of course, old age. For industrial era Americans, then, loved ones often passed away suddenly during their youth. Moreover, they usually died at home, attended to by their relatives. Death was a regular and intimate experience.

At the same time, religious skepticism in the wake of Charles Darwin's theories of evolution caused many to fear death more intensely than previous generations. If humans were not created in God's image, if indeed, they evolved from lower animal forms, then perhaps humans were not, as one writer speculated, the "measure and explanation of the world" (Alden qtd. in "A Study of Death" 847). Perhaps people "were a fragment of the world, appearing suddenly upon the ocean of existence, moved this way and that by varying winds and currents and by the whims of [their] own variable and near-sighted intelligence, and then as suddenly submerged beneath the waves" (847). To ward off such skepticism, Americans developed elaborate funeral customs that preserved the body in a posture of sleep and promoted a more detailed vision of heaven as a meeting place for loved ones.

The ritual of mourning began at the deathbed. Family members living at a distance often returned home to sit with a dying parent or sibling suffering an extended illness such as tuberculosis, pneumonia, or the many other infectious diseases plaguing nineteenth-century Americans. Bedrooms often featured minimal furniture—a bed, dresser, washing stand, and then several chairs for family members sitting with the dying relative. Witnesses frequently described the trials of suffering relatives—their labored breathing, their groans, their feverish delusions.

Children, who were especially vulnerable to infectious disease and kitchen accidents, made especially poignant victims. One of the most familiar scenes in Victorian literature is the death of a child and the family's subsequent mourning. In one poem, the narrator initially finds comfort in imagining her son sleeping, but ultimately turns to religious faith:

The Teaching of Death

I SAW my darling in calm slumber lying,
His still, pale face so beautiful in death;
So like sweet sleep, that, hushed from tears and sighing,
I looked and listened for his gentle breath.
. . . . .
And in that room of death my soul drew nearer
To the great presence of the things unseen;
The deep, dark mystery of life grew clearer,
Until on life and death I looked serene.

And looked serene upon that lovely sleeper;
Kissed the pale face, which silently had taught
That death and sorrow bring us knowledge deeper,
And deeper joy than his dear life had brought.

So I gave up my babe's sweet, warm caresses,
And laid him from my breast beneath the sod;
My arms are empty, but my soul he blesses,
And when I long for him I trust in God. (652)

To ease the fear of death and the pain of such enormous losses, Americans began to blur the line between life and death by consciously creating an image of peaceful slumber and by retaining mementos of the deceased.

Undertakers began using embalming techniques more widely during the Civil War as families paid enormous sums to have their fallen soldiers returned home rather than buried on the battlefield. President Lincoln's embalmed body, displayed on a long, slow train ride from Washington, D.C., to Springfield, Illinois, also popularized embalming. Bodies could be preserved and displayed longer. Undertakers applied make-up to give corpses a more lifelike appearance and to heighten the perception that the corpse was sleeping. The corpse often rested in a silk-lined, mahogany or bronze coffin, newly named a "casket" to suggest that its contents were treasured. Americans began investing more heavily in flowers, especially lilies and roses, symbols of immortality (Pleck 187–88; Habenstein and Lamers 95).

Whereas it had been common in the eighteenth century to re-use the first name of a dead child for a subsequent child, it became much more uncommon among late nineteenth-century Americans. Some believe this is because children were earlier individualized and mourned more extensively when they died by the late nineteenth century. Families strove to remember their loved ones by saving a lock of their hair and, sometimes, having a daguerreotype, an early form of a photograph, taken of the newly deceased. For the mother or father who may have had no other picture of the child, the funeral daguerreotype likely provided an enormous comfort (Pleck 187).

Not only did mourning rituals offer comfort to a family, but they also signaled to the rest of the community that the family should be treated with special consideration. Families hung black crepe from the front door and often draped it about the parlor where the body was laid out for viewing. Parlors frequently had a separate door to the outside so caskets could be easily moved in and out of the room. During the first six months after the death of a parent, husband, or child, a woman wore a dress of dull, black fabric with a funeral bonnet that had black streamers hanging below her waist. During this period of deep mourning, a man would be expected to wear a black suit of dull material with a white shirt and have a black crepe mourning band wrapped around his hat. Because most men had to re-enter the world of work before the period of deep mourning was over, customs regarding their dress were not as strictly enforced. For women, after the period of deep mourning, they could wear black silk or crepe-de-chine, shinier fabrics, for the next six months. During the second year, they could wear white or violet and then after two years resume their normal dress (Habenstein and Lamers 92).

Social affairs for wealthy women were also seriously curtailed during mourning. During the first six months, these women were to have no social affairs and for the remainder of the year they could not attend weddings or other festive occasions. Women's stationery also reflected their mourning. Their writing paper was to be white or gray with a black border that steadily narrowed over the two-year mourning period. Even a woman's handwriting was to be small and contained to convey her diminished capacity for joy and self-expression.

By 1870, rural cemeteries, designed to look like Edenic gardens, largely replaced town graveyards or home burial plots in the industrializing Northeast. This was for both practical and ideological reasons. Burying the dead in the center of town could lead to cholera and other infectious diseases as decomposing bodies affected the town's water supply. For families burying their dead on their property, not only was the family's water supply endangered, but the family necessarily had to leave their family graveyard behind when they sold their land. Ideologically, the rural cemetery movement encouraged the bereaved to think of their loved ones lingering in an idyllic, inspiring environment, abiding with God in Nature and remaining near their loved ones. Visiting the rural gravesite gave surviving family members the feeling that they were communing with their dead and coming near God. Rural cemeteries did away with foreboding symbols such as the skull and crossbones and encouraged simpler designs for grave markers. They replaced the elaborate statuary of older graveyards with trees and flowers, considering "Nature superior to art as a symbol of Spirit" (Harris 107).

CONCLUSION

American family life during the industrial era was characterized by a new commitment to an idealized childhood. Children were increasingly viewed as naturally good and innocent, leading many parents, social critics, and writers to value children's playtime more and to become increasingly critical of child labor. At the same time, children became more of an economic burden to urban families, many of which necessarily relied upon the extra income children could contribute to the family budget. Increasingly, a family's class position determined whether a child had the privilege of enjoying the idealized childhood promoted by industrial era culture.

As children became more of an economic burden, adults sought to limit their family sizes or to avoid having children altogether. Adults married later in life, abortions became more common, and the dynamics between husbands and wives shifted to give some women more control over their sexuality. Childless, college-educated women found new opportunities in social institutions serving the poor and educational institutions serving young women.

Many of the rituals Americans observe today were popularized during the industrial era. Holidays centered increasingly on children and the family feast rather than the carnivalesque. Marriages and funerals marked important transitions and were made into more elaborate, more public rituals showcasing the class status and kinship connections of families. The wealthiest Americans invented new customs to protect their wealth and make it difficult for ambitious newcomers to break into the social and business networks of the elite. Even as industrializing America became a geographically and economically more mobile society, individuals and families designed rituals to draw kinship networks together and preserve their status.

6

Consumer Culture

INTRODUCTION

Consumers, those who purchased goods and services, had always been vital in the American economy. During the colonial period, many manufactured goods had been imported from England. Trade, both internationally and regionally, had long been a part of American life. But in the latter part of the 1800s, there were unprecedented changes in the nature and scope of consumption in the United States. As Richard Ohmann aptly puts it, "the way people made what they needed in our society changed utterly in the last half of the century" (48). Prior to industrialism, the home was a site of both consumption and work. People tended to live where they worked, be that on a farm, next to a workshop, or near an attached storefront. Even within a household, most products, from soap to clothing, had to be made by hand. With the rise of industry, work increasingly became something people left the home to do. That left less time for producing items for personal consumption, requiring additional purchases of goods. Then, of course, much of the work being done in factories was to produce the very items now being sold to consumers. While this brief summary addresses a major change in the period, it should not gloss over the diverse experiences of Americans. By 1900, 39 percent of Americans still worked on farms. Even in urban households there was still plenty of work being done, including the labor performed by paid domestic workers, the unpaid work of cleaning and childcare carried out by homemakers, and the paid piecework or small businesses women ran from their homes (Ohmann 48).

That said, during the industrial era, across classes, Americans began to purchase items that once had been made at home, including food, clothing, and soap. Even products that had long been part of American culture, such as alcohol and patent medicines, were experienced differently by consumers who now bought national brands. To get these items, consumers turned to a new array of sellers, from department stores to mail-order catalogs. A new industry, advertising, emerged to facilitate (or, as some would say, manipulate) these transactions. To this day, historians and critics argue over whether these changes were good or bad for Americans. The conclusion of this chapter considers the question of the political impact of consumer culture through an examination of Edward Bellamy's best-selling 1888 novel, *Looking Backward: 2000–1887.*

FOOD

Before industrialism, most people ate what we today would consider a restricted diet, varying primarily by region and season. People's food consumption was largely limited to what they grew or what could be grown near them. For many Americans, this led to diets with little variety, particularly in the winter months, and a host of medical maladies associated with monotonous eating habits from constipation to rickets. Harvey Levenstein describes the dominant eating habits prior to industrialism as part of "the British-American Culinary Heritage." The typical food regimen was high in meat, with vegetables used primarily for sauce or boiled beyond recognition (4). Though we may now look at this diet with disdain, for many Americans, especially those who recently immigrated, the United States was notable for having relatively few food shortages.

With the rise of industrialism, there were astonishing changes in how some, though not all, Americans ate. Railroad shipping, industrial food processing, and new nutritional ideas began to transform the American culinary landscape. At the beginning of this period, many Americans raised much of their own food and cooked on open hearths, even in urban areas. But by the end of the century, a variety of stoves were common, and familiar brands of packaged food were increasingly popular. Additionally, a range of household innovations were either introduced or perfected during this period including the ice box (a forerunner to the refrigerator), the Mason jar, the pressure cooker, the eggbeater, and the apple corer (McIntosh 89; Hooker 212).

As notable as these advances were, it is important to remember that a relatively limited group of Americans, stratified by class and region, experienced these innovations. As Richard J. Hooker notes,

Neither the new knowledge of nutrition nor any consequent improvement in health affected a great part of the country's population. Northern slum dwellers, southern sharecroppers, small farmers on the Great Plains, the recently freed slaves, and the underprivileged everywhere were, as always, concerned only with getting enough to eat. An appreciable portion of the country's population was regularly hungry and a larger part was badly nourished. (218)

Class made a significant difference in how people ate. This is partly due to the fact that people with more money could afford to buy more food and food of a different quality. But the difference was not only financial. Food was also a way in which social classes distinguished themselves from each other. Though this is not what is meant by the phrase, "you are what you eat," that cliché takes on new significance when applied to eating during this period.

Commentators had long remarked that the American diet was unique in the amount of meat people consumed, a trend that only escalated from 1870 to 1900. Existing evidence suggests that most Americans of this period ate as much meat as they could, at every meal if they could afford it. Of course, the kinds and qualities of meat people ate varied greatly across social class and region (Levenstein 23–24; Hooker 220; McIntosh 93). **Americans and Meat**

Beef was the meat of choice among most Americans, and foreign commentators were often aghast at the amount of meat Americans could consume at a sitting. However, Americans tended to celebrate this carnivorousness. "We are essentially a hungry beef-eating people, who live by eating," wrote one newspaper (qtd. in Jones 123). On average, as Americans became wealthier, they ate more beef. One study estimates that families with per capita incomes of over $800 consumed over twice as much beef than those earning under $400. However, since most Americans were not wealthy, beef was not the most frequently eaten form of meat. Pork, a less expensive meat, was consumed at an even greater rate. Not surprisingly, this distinction soon took on social dimensions, as middle- and upper-class cooks looked down upon pork as a lesser or crude meat (Hooker 221; Levenstein 218; McIntosh 92).

In 1879, Gustavas Swift revolutionized the meat industry by introducing refrigerated railroad cars. Prior to this time, grass-fed cattle had to be shipped cross-country directly to markets where they would be slaughtered. But now, cattle only needed to be sent for slaughter to Chicago or Kansas City. Refrigerated carcasses then made the journey to the Eastern seaboard. As a result, throughout the 1880s beef prices for consumers dropped, and the amount of beef purchased rose (Levenstein 31–32).

Food products were among the earliest and most successful products to be branded (sold under a specific title). These products were sold nationally and supported by, what were for the time, elaborate advertising campaigns. **Food and Brands**

Most of these new brands involved processed food, and by the end of the century, processed food had become a huge industry. By 1900, 20 percent of U.S. manufacturing involved food processing. A partial list of popular brands from this era include many that are still with us today: Chase and Sanborn coffee, Golden Cottonlene cooking fat, Knox's gelatine, Lion coffee, Pillsbury flour, Quaker oats, Price baking powder, Postum, Uneeda biscuit, Swan's Down flour, and Van Camp's beans (Hooker 213; Sutherland 70).

In many cases, the companies that owned these brands simply created a national market for types of food that were already popular throughout the country. In other instances, entirely new markets were created, transforming the ways in which people ate. The first breakfast cereals appeared in the 1870s as innovations offered by food reformers such as those by Kellogg's, made on behalf of a vegetarian, Seventh-Day Adventist organization. Brands that are familiar today such as Kellogg's Toasted Corn Flakes, Post Grape Nuts, Post Shredded Wheat, and Post Toasties soon made inroads on the American breakfast table. Part of the appeal of these cereals was the speed and convenience they offered, particularly to the majority of Americans who lived in homes without servants. However, these cereals also were promoted by advertisements in national magazines aimed at middle-class homemakers concerned about providing sanitary, healthy food for families. Ads for breakfast cereal typically made use of children and posited that it was a matter of maternal care to serve cereal rather than the more traditional breakfast of the previous night's meat and potatoes (Hooker 213; Levenstein 34; Norris 108).

Though different branded foods made all kinds of claims to being unique, what most shared in common is that they were standardized. A branded product should have been the same no matter where in the country or in what kind of store you bought it. For customers used to purchasing generic items of varying quality, standardization was seen as an advance that guaranteed a uniform condition. For example, one 1876 magazine article giving advice for planting a vegetable garden noted, "send to some responsible seed merchant, and don't depend on the kind of stock found in small boxes in the country grocery stores" (P. T. Q. 137). However, the rise of national brands also disrupted many traditional consumer practices. Once national brands began to dominate store shelves, familiar, regional foods became harder to purchase.

Food Adulteration
The industrial production of food in the nineteenth century was unregulated. Sanitation and quality control in food processing plants varied widely, but few facilities would have met standards considered acceptable today. It was also common practice to adulterate processed food. Adulteration added chemicals or other foreign matter to products to improve color and taste, to make them less expensive to produce, or to act as a preservative. Unregulated adulteration could, and often did, result in hazardous substances being added to food. Government studies conducted at the end of the 1800s found food adulteration was widespread. For example, formaldehyde was used to disguise rotten eggs; currant jam was actually flavored

with a coal tar derivative; flour contained ground rice, sand, and plaster of paris; lard was made with lime, alum, and starch; cayenne pepper contained lead, rice flour, and iron oxide; vinegar included sulfuric, hydrochloric, and pyroligneous acids. None of these ingredients were listed on labels and most people were unaware of the dangers to be found in everyday foods (Hooker 298–99; Goodwin 42–44).

The appeal of canned goods varied by region, but they gained rapidly in popularity during this time. From 1860 to 1870, there was a six-fold increase in the number of canned goods sold nationwide, 5 million to 30 million cans (Hooker 214). Canned goods such as beans, vegetables, and fruit found a ready market in the western and Plains states, where they often provided the only alternative to the limited diet of rural regions. However, in the East, the situation was different. The poor were unable to afford canned goods, and the middle and upper classes initially were suspicious of canned goods' ability to spoil. It was also a matter of pride for many housewives to use fresh ingredients in cooking. Also, as refrigerated railroad cars had made fresh produce available for much of the year, such ingredients were often preferred. Despite some initial resistance though, canned food did become popular, particularly in middle-class households. Nevertheless, causes for concern did remain. The ingredients in prepared foods were not always obvious, and in some cases they could be hazardous. Though canned goods were by no means the only adulterated food, in government studies they were found to contain foreign matter including copper and tin (Goodwin 43).

Canned Goods

The conditions of meat packing plants and the state of canned meat became particularly notorious. A large number of canned meats contained spoiled or parasite-infested products that were adulterated with a range of chemicals. Leftover scraps were shoveled directly off floors into preparation vats where they were ground up with pigskin, rope, dead rats, and garbage off the floors. "Potted chicken" did not contain any chicken; "deviled ham" was minced tripe with red dye. Though consumer groups and health professionals had long railed against these conditions, they did not become a public controversy until 1906 when revelations in Upton Sinclair's novel *The Jungle* led to nationwide outrage over the condition of food in beef packing plants (though, unfortunately, less outrage over the treatment of packing plant workers). Soon after, the passage of the Pure Food and Drug Act began the process of establishing standards for the food processing industry (Goodwin 43; Hooker 300).

Among the urban rich—those with the most income to spend on food and the most access to food shipped by railroad—French cooking reigned supreme, and it was associated with distinction and sophistication. Though French cooking was not new to America, before this time it had not been part of mainstream tastes. Elaborate dinner parties became the rage in elite soci-

Upper-Class Eating

ety, requiring chefs trained in French cooking and a number of servants to assist. These meals also tended to be gastronomical events, with multiple courses and an enormous amount of food served at one sitting. Excess was common, and it was seen to reflect the wealth of the host. Levenstein notes that the menu for one 1880 dinner party honoring General Winfield Hancock, the Democratic candidate for President that year, included raw oysters, soup, fish, a saddle of lamb, a filet of beef, chicken wings with green peas, lamb chops with beans, mushroom-stuffed artichokes, a terrapin casserole, roast duck, and quail. Dessert included ice cream, banana mousse, and fruit (11–12).

Even for daily meals, the rich tended to rely on hired personnel to do their cooking (employing a trained French cook was considered a sign of distinction). It should come as no surprise that clothing manufacturers during this period had to increase clothing sizes to account for the newly expanded waistlines of prosperous Americans. Girth became a symbol of affluence, and books such as *How to be Plump* recommended high fat and starch diets to achieve a desired stout appearance (Hooker 218; Levenstein 12–13).

Middle-Class Eating   Middle-class families, who typically had only one or two servants, could not afford to employ a trained chef. Nevertheless, some middle-class households attempted to mirror the food consumption patterns of the upper class, reproducing scaled-down elegant banquets. Other middle-class homemakers cooked in a more traditional manner, remaining suspicious of "fancy French cooking," and attempting to set a competent if not elaborate table.

Almost all middle-class households had at least one servant, but even if that servant assisted with food preparation, there was no guarantee that that servant had been trained as a cook. As a result, Levenstein writes, most cooking in middle-class homes retained British-American culinary tastes. "Roast meats, scalloped dishes, thick gravies—simple recipes that could be mastered by the succession of immigrant cooks under the watchful eye of the housewife remained the backbone of the cuisine" (18).

Books addressed to middle-class homemakers often encouraged them to view cooking as an essential household task. Catherine E. Beecher and Harriet Beecher Stowe, writing in the 1869 *American Woman's Home*, stated "The person who decides what shall be the food and drink of a family, and the modes of its preparation, is the one who decides, to a greater or less extent, what shall be the health of the family" (119). The Beecher sisters were critical of some traditional means of American cooking, finding that Americans, taking for granted the surplus and variety of food grown in the United States, tended to prepare meals sloppily and wastefully. They called for cooks to emulate the economy of traditional French cooking.

Yet, it was not the economy of French cooking that appealed to many middle-class Americans, but rather its suggestion of elegance. Inspired by the development of Home Economics (a movement that aimed to elevate and professionalize homemaking, often by employing scientific concepts), new cooking schools instructed women who aspired to prepare more elaborate meals. Middle-class dinner parties still involved a substantial outlay of funds for detailed menus. The finest cuts of beef, seafood, and fresh fruits, all served in large quantities, came to be expected. Faced with higher expectations for variety, the urban middle-class cook increasingly was drawn to the convenience of canned food (Levenstein 19).

While some middle-class families put on dinner parties, their everyday meals were far simpler. A breakfast might include bread, mush, ham and eggs, or cold cereal, all with coffee. During this time, urban families began to transition away from a large midday meal (such a meal remained typical in rural households). Lunch may have consisted of a hot or cold dish with fruit or cake with tea. Dinner would involve soup, meat or fish, vegetables, and perhaps cheese (Plante 120).

The best sources for information on middle-class meals are the myriad of cookbooks that catered to the middle-class reader. Though some detailed elaborate dishes that few readers were likely to prepare, many others list the kind of meals that people often ate. As cooking became the purview of middle-class homemakers rather than servants, a greater variety of meals undoubtedly became part of the middle-class palate. Recipes also began to incorporate canned food and prepared ingredients.

RECIPES

Contemporary cooks will notice that animal fat was used frequently in cooking. Also, no precise oven temperature or cooking time could be recommended, considering the variety of stoves and the imprecision of their heating at this time. These recipes were collected in Ellen Plante's *The American Kitchen, 1700 to the Present* (155–59).

Beef or Mutton Pudding

Boil some good potatoes until they are ready to fall to pieces; drain well in a sieve, clear them of all impurities and specks, mash, and make into a smooth batter, with two eggs and a little milk. Then place a layer on rather thick slices of cold roast beef or mutton, seasoned with pepper and salt, at the bottom of a baking dish, cover them with the batter, and so on until the dish is full, adding a thin layer of butter at the top. Bake it till well browned.
—Alexander V. Hamilton, *The Household Cyclopaedia of Practical Recipes* (1873)

Fritters of Canned Corn

1 can sweet corn, drained in a cullender [*sic*], 3 eggs very light; 1 cup of milk; pepper and salt; 1 table-spoonful butter; flour for thin batter; dripping for frying; a pinch of soda. Beat up the batter well, stir in the corn and drop the mixture in spoonfuls into the boiling fat. Drain off all the grease in a cullender.
—Marion Harland, *Breakfast, Lunch and Tea* (1875)

Baking Powder Biscuits

Have the oven hot to begin with, then rub a piece of butter the size of an English walnut into a cup of flour and butter your baking tins. Next put a level teaspoon of salt, and two heaping teaspoons of baking powder in the flour and stir it well. Up to this time you can work leisurely, but from this onward, work as fast as you can "fly." Add a cup of sweet milk, stir it, and add enough more flour to make a soft dough; take it out onto the molding board, and form it quickly into a round mass; cut it in 2 parts, then 4, then 8; give the pieces just a roll in the floured hands, put it in the tin, and bake 8 to 10 minutes. The oven should brown them top and bottom in that time. Everybody likes them.

—Smiley Publishing Co., *Smiley's New and Complete Guide for Housekeepers* (1898)

Working-Class Eating There was no single working class diet. Some workers thrived in the cities and their nutrition reflected that fact. Many recent immigrants attempted (and were often able) to maintain traditional ways of eating despite being in a new country. However, many others did not eat better for being in the cities, particularly if they came from rural areas where they were used to growing their own food in gardens. While new large clothing sizes were being designed for larger, wealthy Americans, poor nutrition and living conditions led to an overall decline in the height and weight of Americans beginning in the 1830s and lasting into the 1870s (Levenstein 23).

Quality of food tended to be more of an issue for workers than quantity. While bread, potatoes, cabbage, and onions could be found in most workers' diets, skilled workers, typically of Anglo-Saxon and Northern European origin, tended to eat traditional British-American cuisine. Unskilled workers, who were often recent immigrants from Southern and Eastern Europe, would eat food prepared according to ethnic traditions. Stews and goulashes were typical (though middle-class food reformers frowned upon them, erroneously thinking they were less nutritious than foods prepared and served separately). Most working-class families could not afford canned foods, and they ate few fruits and vegetables out of season other than what they canned or "put up" themselves. Notably, all workers during this time were likely to live in rented housing, and so the introduction of kitchen gadgets had little impact on their lives. Many workers still continued to cook on open hearths into this period (Levenstein 23–26; McIntosh 102–05).

In the 1870s, Carroll D. Wright carried out the first statistical studies of workers' daily lives. Though by today's standards these studies were methodologically flawed (see D. Horowitz 13), they did provide a detailed glimpse into daily lives that would otherwise have gone unrecorded. For instance, an 1875 study Wright carried out for the Massachusetts Bureau of Statistics of Labor detailed how select working-class families spent their money. One typical mill laborer family of seven earned a total of $650 per year. Of that $650, $54.62 was spent on meat, $18.00 on dry goods, $13.50

on fish, $14.80 on milk, and $300.00 on assorted groceries. Rent and fuel for this same family amounted to $122.75 per year. This family spent more than three times as much on food than housing. In fact, food purchases made up more than 60 percent of this family's yearly expenditures (D. Horowitz 15).

Considering the cost of food, it is perhaps not surprising to see that the family ate a rather limited diet. The study recorded typical meals for this family as follows:

Breakfast: Bread, butter, sometimes fish, or the remains of the day before, coffee.
Dinner: Meat or fish, potatoes, bread, sometimes pie.
Supper: Bread, butter, gingerbread, molasses, tea. (D. Horowitz 15)

It is notable that breakfast was a small meal, often consisting of leftovers from the previous day and not including packaged cereals. The family's large meal was in the middle of the day, the typical pattern for families who lived close to their workplace and worked long hours. Supper was a light repast, thrown together quickly for often exhausted workers. Bread was served at every meal.

ALCOHOL AND DRUG CONSUMPTION

Whereas drinking had been customary for Americans of all classes in the early part of the century, by the 1880s most middle-class Americans disapproved of alcohol consumption. Drinking had become part of a larger cultural conflict between middle-class and working-class Americans. The working class in the industrializing North was comprised largely of new immigrants from Catholic countries such as **Saloons: A Source of Conflict between Classes** Ireland and the countries of southeastern Europe. The middle class was largely descended from Protestants who had immigrated from England or Scotland two or more generations earlier. They believed Catholicism was antidemocratic and many felt that the new immigrants lacked the education and self-control to succeed in a democratic society. The new immigrants' drinking patterns were seen to verify these perceptions (Rorabaugh 28).

It may at first seem baffling that temperance societies achieved record memberships in the industrial era. Alcohol consumption was much lower in the last third of the century than in the first third. Hard liquor, particularly whiskey and rum, were such common drinks in the early nineteenth century that they were used as currency; men received part of their salary in the form of liquor. Men of all classes, moreover, broke from work for periodic drams of whiskey. The prevalence of alcoholism, particularly among men, alarmed early reformers. Animated by the missionary zeal of Protestant evangelism, American temperance societies succeeded in the 1830s and 1840s in discouraging alcohol consumption.

Per capita alcohol consumption never again reached the levels it had in 1825 and, in fact, remained fairly constant throughout the last half of the century, but a change in the nature of drinking alarmed reformers. One of the most noticeable changes was in what people drank. Per capita beer consumption doubled between 1870 and 1890, in part because the Union army introduced soldiers to beer by providing it as part of their rations. Tax policy also contributed to the shift from hard liquor to beer. While beer was lightly taxed, taxes on hard liquor were exorbitant. Federal taxes more than doubled the price of whiskey and constituted nearly 20 percent of the federal government's revenues. As a result, many distillers evaded taxes by secretly producing and selling whiskey, dubbed "moonshine." German immigration brought new brewing techniques and new traditions to the United States, also contributing to the shift among American workers from the midday dram of whiskey to the stein of beer with lunch. Refrigerated railroad cars made it possible to transport beer longer distances to local grocery stores or tap rooms, where most people carried beer home in their own buckets. The most important changes, however, were in who drank and where they drank (Rorabaugh 29; Tice 57).

An advertisement touting the broad appeal of Lager Bier. From left to right, the captions read, "A National Drink," "A Healthy Drink," "A Family Drink," and "A Friendly Drink." (Courtesy Library of Congress)

A focal point for the middle-class Americans' campaign against drinking was the all-male saloon. Saloons became a predominant feature of towns and cities across America and they often drew violence, prostitution, and crime. Because there were so many saloons, they faced stiff price competition and some used gambling dens or prostitution to increase revenues. Some saloons also tried to increase their customer base by serving alcohol to teenagers and even children. To bring in hungry workers, they served complementary food—often salty items like pretzels, salted herring, sour pickles, and potato salad—to encourage workers to buy additional drinks. Middle-class Americans saw drinking as part of a larger clash of values between themselves and the new immigrants. By the end of the nineteenth century, as the reformers of the Women's Christian Temperance Union pointed out, Americans spent more than five times as much on alcohol as public education (Rorabaugh 32; Tice 61).

While "old stock" Protestant Americans often associated drinking with degradation, many of the new immigrants of the industrial era understood drinking as an important social ritual. Saloons and the Catholic Church were the only institutions working-class Americans controlled. Working men met at the saloon to exchange employment tips, secure loans, pawn items to make their rent payments, drum up political support for candidates, and sometimes sell their votes. The saloons were integral to big city political machines and to union activity.

Popular middle-class perceptions of the working class often blamed their poverty and family strife on alcohol consumption. Stephen Crane's 1893 novel *Maggie: Girl of the Streets*, for example, was sold as a realistic portrayal of a drunken, Irish American couple and their three children. The family's poverty is directly ascribed to their violent, household fights during which they routinely neglect or injure their children, break their furniture, and stop only when one or both pass out. The parents' workplaces are never shown and their wages never discussed in the novel, suggesting that alcoholism alone is the cause of their poverty. Upton Sinclair's later, proletarian novel, *The Jungle*, attempts to better understand working-class culture. Sinclair's main character, Jurgis Rudkus, immigrates to the United States as a sober, hardworking young man. He refuses to spend his meager earnings on alcohol initially, but free lunches, the company of other working-class men, and a search for relief from the harsh, dehumanizing conditions of the packinghouses eventually seduce him. He develops a drinking problem that exacerbates his family's poverty.

Middle-class women led reform efforts aimed at curbing alcohol consumption through the Women's Christian Temperance Union (WCTU). The WCTU was formed in 1874 and had 200,000 members by 1892. They initially agitated against alcohol, holding "pray-ins" at local saloons and publicly circulating the names of men seen drinking at saloons. Some saloonkeepers initially responded to these "Crusaders" by agreeing to stop selling liquor, but others rebelled. They locked their doors at the sight of women singing hymns and marching toward their saloons, or they threatened to have the women arrested. The WCTU's methods and goals soon became more varied; they educated people about the dangers of alcohol consumption, they lobbied for legislation restricting the sale of alcohol, and, under the banner "home protection," they agitated for women's suffrage. Their efforts, however, were often perceived by working-class men to be intrusive and condescending.

Americans of the era had a limited understanding of addiction. Many still believed that drinking and drug use were matters of will power, and they felt a habitual user could stop if he or she wanted to. However, familiarity with the alcoholic's delirium tremens (during which the sufferer shook uncontrollably) led to a growing consensus that chronic drunkenness was a disease requiring medical treatment. Unfortunately, medical treatments at the time frequently did more harm than good. Patricia Tice notes, "Wealthy and middle class people often consulted privately with doctors who frequently dosed addicted patients with opium, morphine or other drugs to treat withdrawal symptoms. In many cases, the treatment simply created another chemical dependency" (65). Working-class alcoholics may have tried any of a wide assortment of patent medicines based on quackery; many ultimately landed in prisons, poorhouses, hospitals, and insane asylums. The struggle between brewers and distillers on one side and temperance reformers on the other raged beyond the industrial era and culminated in the Eighteenth Amendment, which prohibited the sale of alcohol between 1920 and 1933.

Narcotics— Patent Medicines, Coca-Cola, and Gum

Without federal laws restricting the sale of drugs or patent medicines and without much knowledge of the properties of drugs, Americans of the industrial era used highly addictive substances on a casual basis. Patent medicines sold for infant colic, "feminine afflictions," morning sickness, consumption, diabetes, and a wide variety of other ills commonly contained opium, alkaloids of opium such as morphine, or cocaine. Private companies often sold such mixtures without revealing their contents and sometimes suggested they were made with completely fictitious items. Doctors prescribed opium and morphine freely, referring to it as "God's own medicine." As one index for the casual nature of drug consumption during the era, manufacturers made cigarettes and soda laced with cocaine and chewing gum laced with opium (Tice 49; Goodwin 106).

A variety of sodas and tonics containing cocaine were sold to "invigorate" consumers, but the most famous was Coca-Cola. Between 1886 and 1900 pharmacist John Pemberton openly advertised the cocaine base of his fountain drink, Coca-Cola. His first advertisement read:

It seems to be a law of nature that the more valuable and efficacious a drug is, the nastier and more unpleasant its taste. It is therefore quite a triumph over nature that the Coca-Cola Co. of Atlanta, Ga., have achieved in their success in robbing both coca leaves and the kola nut of the exceedingly nauseous and disagreeable taste while retaining their wonderful medicinal properties, and the power of restoring vitality and raising the spirits of the weary and debilitated [*sic*]. Not only have they done this, but by some subtle alchemy they have made them the basis of one of the most delightful, cheering, and invigorating of fountain drinks. (Spillane 21)

While the amounts of cocaine in tonics and fountain drinks remained small, patent medicines sold for "catarrh"—runny noses—sometimes contained nothing but cocaine and were prescribed for frequent use over a long period of time, leading to severe addictions. Their labels seldom revealed their contents.

The unregulated market in patent medicines led to many tragedies. Infants treated with a concoction like Mrs. Winslow's Soothing Syrup sometimes died of overdoses. Patients seeking relief from relatively trivial symptoms often found themselves addicted to narcotics as a result of patent medicines. In 1888, *Popular Science Monthly* reported this typical scenario:

One apothecary [a pharmacist] told me of an old lady who formerly came to him as often as four times a week and purchased a fifty-cent bottle of "cough-balsam."

A trade card for Mrs. Winslow's Soothing Syrup from 1887. Given to infants, this patent medicine contained narcotics. (Courtesy Strong Museum, Rochester, NY 2004)

She informed him that it "quieted her nerves" and afforded rest when everything else had failed. After she had made her regular visits for over a year, he told her one day that he had sold out of the medicine required, and suggested a substitute, which was a preparation containing about the same amount of morphine. On trial, the woman found the new mixture answered every purpose of the old. The druggist then told her she had acquired the morphine-habit, and from that time on she was a constant morphine-user. (Eaton 11)

As the above scenario suggests, women were often the victims of patent drug abuse. While drinking among women, particularly middle-class women, was frowned upon, there seemed to be nothing improper about the use of Lydia Pinkam's Tonic or a similar mixture of narcotics to quiet one's nerves. One doctor explained that women were more vulnerable to addiction because they were, "[d]oomed, often, to a life of disappointment, and, it may be, of physical and mental inaction, and in the smaller and more remote towns, not unfrequently, to utter seclusion, deprived of all wholesome social diversion" (Oliver 5). The doctor argued that women's passivity led to "nervous depression," which they could then "discretely" treat with opium.

Eugene O'Neill's autobiographical play, *Long Day's Journey into Night*, dramatizes his mother's morphine addiction that began in 1888 following the birth of her third child. O'Neill's mother had had a difficult delivery and recovery (and perhaps what would now be diagnosed as postpartum depression). A doctor prescribed morphine for her, and she soon developed an addiction that she struggled with for most of her life. Her addiction had a devastating effect on the O'Neill family.

Narcotics— Opium Dens
It was women's public consumption of opium in the opium dens of the West that provoked the strongest condemnation of, and some of the earliest legislative prohibitions against, mind-altering substances. British trade policy had forced the Chinese into opium production. Asian governments benefiting from the lucrative opium trade were slow to act against the spread of opium production, and Chinese culture developed a tolerance of opium smoking. Subsequently, Chinese immigrants in Denver, San Francisco, and other western boom towns opened opium dens where Americans of both sexes experimented with smoking opium, a drug that relaxed and sedated users. Lurid accounts of these opium dens depicted partially clad, white women lounging among Chinese men. These women, it was reported, became addicted to smoking opium, ran into debt to support their habits, and were then lured into prostitution. Anti-Chinese sentiment among white laborers who competed for jobs with the Chinese, and fear of racial miscegenation (relationships that produced biracial offspring), made this vision of Chinese men among sedated, vulnerable, white women especially inflammatory.

An opium den. (Courtesy Library of Congress)

OPIUM

Most Chinese immigrants to the United States were men. This was because of immigration rules that barred Chinese women, as well as Chinese cultural restraints on them. Chinese parents of immigrant sons hoped that their sons who came to the United States would send money home, and would one day return to their wives and families in China. By keeping a man's family in China, parents hoped to keep sons bound to the homeland. The U.S. government's immigration policy reflected a similar line of thinking. Chinese immigrants provided cheap labor for the railroads and other onerous industrial era work, but many Americans believed the Chinese could not assimilate into American culture. By barring women from immigrating, U.S. immigration policy was designed to ensure that Chinese workers did not settle permanently in the United States.

When Jacob Riis toured New York's Chinatown for his 1890 documentary photo essay, *How the Other Half Lives,* he expressed his culture's racist view of Chinese immigrants. He was particularly horrified by the effect of opium on white women and he attributed their willingness to marry Chinese men to their addiction to opium. He described the "conventional households of the Chinese quarter" as follows:

The men worshippers of Joss; the women, all white, girls hardly yet grown to womanhood, worshipping nothing save the pipe that has enslaved them body and soul. Easily tempted from homes that have no claim upon the name, they rarely or never return. Mott Street gives up its victims only to the Charity Hospital or the Potter's Field. Of the depth of their fall no one is more thoroughly aware than these girls themselves; no one less concerned about it. The calmness with which they discuss it, while insisting illogically upon the fiction of a marriage that deceives no one, is disheartening. Their misery is peculiarly fond of company, and an amount of visiting goes on in these households that makes it extremely difficult for the stranger to untangle them. I came across a company of them "hitting the pipe" together, on a tour through their dens one night with the police captain of the precinct. The girls knew him, called him by name, offered him a pipe, and chatted with him about the incidents of their acquaintance, how many times he had "sent them up," and their chances of "lasting" much longer. There was no shade of regret in their voices, nothing but utter indifference and surrender. (80)

Reformers Respond to Drug Abuse Frances Willard, the president of the National Women's Christian Temperance Union, toured the West in 1883 and significantly changed the mission of the WCTU. Willard decided to join forces with the anti-opium crusade in major, western cities. She became convinced that the WCTU should enlarge its mission to combat not only alcohol but all "enslaving substances" (Goodwin 31–34).

As a part of the WCTU's efforts to enlarge not only its mission but its methods, it incorporated Mary Hunt's campaign for scientific instruction. Hunt, a retired Massachusetts schoolteacher, emphasized prevention over rehabilitation. She believed the pressures of industrializing society led people to seek relief from overwork, anxiety, and isolation. Greedy patent medicine companies, doctors, and pharmacists took advantage of the ignorance of consumers to addict them to stimulants and narcotics. She proposed combating this greed and quackery by educating young people about physiology, hygiene, and substance abuse. She began the first drug prevention programs rooted in the public schools (Goodwin 23–27).

Hunt's message was an appealing one because it avoided the controversies the WCTU inspired over closing saloons or giving women the vote. Joining forces with the WCTU in 1882, Hunt generated a grassroots campaign to compel public schools to adopt "scientific instruction," a term that tapped into the era's cultural respect for science and de-emphasized the antidrug and alcohol nature of the curriculum. The organization had to overcome opposition from powerful brewers and from school boards reluctant to take a position on temperance. Inspired by WCTU lecturers, women collected petitions and wrote state legislators to pressure them to pass laws making scientific instruction mandatory. Between 1882 and 1901, they succeeded in passing laws in every state, Indian reservation, and federal district to make scientific instruction mandatory in public schools (Goodwin 103).

Agitation during this period also helped the passage of the Pure Food, Drink, and Drug Act of 1906. This act forced drug manufacturers to disclose the contents of patent medicines and the amount of specified dangerous drugs including alcohol, opium, and opium alkaloids. It provided for inspectors who could analyze the contents of products, and it called for the prosecution of dealers and manufacturers in cases of fraud. Still, it did not bar outright the sale of dangerous drugs, nor did it require manufacturers to disclose ingredients if they sold products in the same state where they were produced (such products were subject to state rather than federal regulations).

DEPARTMENT STORES AND MAIL-ORDER CATALOGS

With the rise of industrialism and cities, there were new products to be distributed and new places in which to sell them. Though general stores and door-to-door salesmen did not disappear from the retail scene, two very different modes of retailing emerged during this period, changing the ways in which people purchased goods: the department store and the mail-order catalog.

The first department stores predated the Civil War. A. T. Stewart had opened his "Marble Palace" in 1846 in New York. But it was in the industrial era that department stores came to dominate urban shopping. Department stores differed from specialty retailers in that they offered a vast assortment of factory-made goods under one roof. Department stores carried a range of merchandise previously sold in separate stores such as carpets, clothing, dry goods, furniture, phonographs, soap, and typewriters. While national chain stores or "five and dimes" such as Woolworth's also carried a range of products, department stores dwarfed chain stores in scale. Designed to draw in urban upper- and middle-class shoppers with disposable income, department stores of this period were lavishly designed, both inside and out.

Department Stores

Department stores of this period were located in central business districts of American cities and typically were placed along trolley lines. A. T. Stewart, Jordan Marsh, Lord & Taylor, Macy's, Marshall Field, and Wanamaker were some of the companies that spared little expense to lure people in from the street. Their buildings had elaborate doorways, attractive window displays, and impressive neoclassical facades that faced the passing potential shopper. During the time before electricity was readily available, department stores made use of available light by constructing a central rotunda covered by a tinted, glass dome. Shoppers would walk up a central staircase in this rotunda to visit different floors where goods were arranged into categories or departments. Inside, they would find items including expensive carpets, rich wood and glass fixtures, and decorative chandeliers (Ferry 12; Mohl 42; Trachtenberg 131).

What made the department store model work was turnover. Goods needed to sell quickly and regularly and be replaced by new merchandise. This led to a standardization of the ways in which items were sold. Department stores adopted one-price policies and forbid bickering over prices, a common practice in smaller specialty shops. This allowed them

An elaborate fountain in New York City's Siegel, Cooper and Co. Amenities such as this fountain became common in efforts to lure shoppers into department stores. (Courtesy Library of Congress)

to hire sales clerks who had less experience with the merchandise. In fact, a virtual army of sales clerks and office workers, consisting primarily of women, staffed department stores. In 1898, Macy's employed more than 3,000 people. In 1900, Jordan Marsh was the fourth largest employer in New England (Strasser, *Satisfaction* 207; Trachtenberg 134).

Department stores used a range of imaginative tactics to draw in customers. Marshall Field's installed electric lights in 1882 when electricity was still a new phenomenon. Restaurants and lunch rooms appeared in some department stores. Others added post offices, fountains, child care, beauty parlors, and even public library branches, often in an attempt to appeal to female shoppers, who were understood to be the primary purchasers. Department stores were among the leading advertisers in newspapers, inaugurating elaborate circulars that accompanied Sunday editions. They were also among the first businesses to employ advertising agencies (Strasser, *Satisfaction* 210; Trachtenberg 136).

Historians and cultural critics argue that while department stores literally changed the way people shopped, they also symbolically altered how individuals related to the goods they purchased. The process and pleasures of department store shopping involved ways of thinking and behaving that were completely opposed to the rationality and structure of the workplace. The irony, as Rachel Bowlby points out, is that "the department stores are organized like factories, with hundreds of workers, shareholding companies, vast turnovers, and careful calculation of continual strategies of expansion" (6). Nevertheless, the experience of shopping was meant to be as different as possible from the experience of working. Alan Trachtenberg notes that department stores did not just sell merchandise; they sold ways of using merchandise, "educating" customers as to the role a certain commodity could play in their lives (135). Carefully arranged window displays of, for example, the latest furniture designs, showed individuals how to use products as part of a good life, a life defined by what one bought. Even at the time, writers such as Theodore Dreiser, wondered about the effect of the spectacle of the department store on people, as he showed his 1900 novel, *Sister Carrie.*

CARRIE AND THE DEPARTMENT STORE

The nature of these vast retail combinations, should they ever permanently disappear, will form an interesting chapter in the commercial history of our nation. Such a flowering out of a modest trade principle the world had never witnessed up to that time. They were along the line of the most effective retail organisation, with hundreds of stores coordinated into one and laid out upon the most imposing and economic basis. They were handsome, bustling, successful affairs, with a host of clerks and a swarm of patrons. Carrie passed along the busy aisles, much affected by the remarkable displays of trinkets, dress goods, stationery, and jewelry. Each separate counter was a show place of dazzling interest and attraction. She could not help feeling the claim of each trinket and valuable upon her personally, and yet she did not stop. There was nothing there which she could not have used—nothing which she did not long to own. The dainty slippers and stockings, the delicately frilled skirts and petticoats, the laces, ribbons, hair-combs, purses, all touched her with individual desire, and she felt keenly the fact that not any of these things were in the range of her purchase. She was a work-seeker, an outcast without employment, one whom the average employee could tell at a glance was poor and in need of a situation.

—From Theodore Dreiser, *Sister Carrie* (1900), 16

Mail-Order Catalogs

The mail-order catalog rose to prominence alongside the department store. Although they tended to serve very different groups of consumers, the success of each was based on the capacity of large manufacturers to make standardized goods and the need to find people to buy those goods.

Most major department stores also had catalogs that allowed customers, particularly those in rural areas, to purchase products without visiting the urban centers. With the rise of the railroad, it became practical and quite profitable to ship items to rural areas that could not support a chain store. The arrival of new catalogs became a celebrated moment in rural and small-town life. It allowed people to purchase items once restricted to those in urban centers. As with advertisements of this period, the catalogs also allowed an individual to imagine him or herself as the owner of a product even if it was never purchased. More mundanely, catalogs became known as regular outhouse reading.

The success of mail-order retailing can be seen in the increasing size of catalogs during this period. Macy's began mail-order in 1874, had a 127-page catalog in 1881, and a 311-page catalog 10 years later. Montgomery Ward's 1884 catalog packed almost 10,000 products into 240 pages. Sears, the most prominent of the mail-order retailers, had a 786-page catalog in 1897. But the rise of the mail-order catalog also made life difficult for small town merchants who could not compete with the economies of scale of the department store chains (Strasser, *Satisfaction* 207–15).

ADVERTISING

Advertising played a crucial role in developing national markets for new commodities. Though national advertising was not new in the industrial era, Richard Ohmann notes that "As late as the 1880s, the practice of branding and nationally advertising products was one way of doing things among many, not a standard system of marketing" (82). However, by the turn of the century, advertising had become a formidable industry, and national brands had become the accepted way of doing business. As with department stores, advertisements of this period (in magazines, in newspapers, as trade cards) were less about describing a product than about illustrating a desired way of life and showing how a given product was part of that way of life. Though people purchased a product, that product had become enhanced with psychological significance through advertising.

The Case of Soap   The soap industry provides a telling example of how advertising changed the way people behaved. Although soap had been advertised in the United States as far back as the Colonial era, up until the Civil War most soap was produced in the home. Making soap was a difficult process, requiring someone to spend an entire day boiling and stirring a combination of ingredients including water, ashes, animal fat, salt, and even bacon rinds. While products like Ivory Soap were readily available after the Civil War, they were not widely in use (Norris 51).

But between 1880 and 1899, the amount of money spent on soap in the United States doubled. It's not that Americans were twice as dirty during this period; rather the demand for soap increased dramatically. National advertising led the way by tapping into a desire among middle- and upper-class Americans to fit in. Soap became more than just a tool for getting clean. In advertisements, it became associated with a range of appeal-

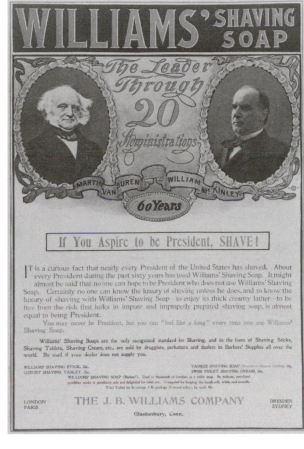

Portraits of Presidents Martin Van Buren and William McKinley are featured prominently in this advertisement for Williams' shaving soap. The accompanying text states, "It is a curious fact that nearly every President of the United States has shaved." (Courtesy Library of Congress)

ing qualities and individuals. B. T. Babbitt's soap used the slogan "Soap for all Nations: Cleanliness is the Scale of Civilization." Pears's Soap reprinted testimonials by Henry Ward Beecher and Sarah Bernhardt in an ad titled "Professional People Prefer Pears' Soap." One advertisement for Williams' Shaving Soap implied that being clean shaven was a prerequisite for becoming president, though it also noted that "You may never be President, but you can 'feel like a king' every time you use Williams' Shaving Soap." Cleanliness had long been considered a virtue, but now, through advertising, cleanliness and soap were associated with a certain stature or class position (Norris 53; Ohmann 188; Sutherland 67).

CLOTHING AND FASHION

During the industrial era there were two dominant innovations, which at first would seem to be contradictory: an increase in homemade garments made possible by inexpensive sewing machines and the rise of ready-to-wear clothing. Both advances happened simultaneously, but they affected different forms of clothing.

Sewing Machines and Patterns Making clothing by hand is a demanding task requiring a great deal of skill. It was not uncommon for a wealthy household during this time to maintain a full-time seamstress to keep up with the work required to outfit a family.

Those unable to afford professional services were forced to fend for themselves, which is one reason that the development of sewing skills was central to many women's upbringing. People in the nineteenth century tended to have far fewer clothes than is typical today, and they tended to wear them longer. Worn clothes would be repaired rather than discarded, leftover scraps of fabric would be reused in other garments, and, as Jenna Weissman Joselit notes, "The practice of hand-me-downs was as regular as the seasons and just as essential" (15). Any number of periodicals offered advice to women on how to economically make clothes for a family (Joselit 9–10; Ley 46).

In this context, two innovations of the period radically changed the experience of sewing. The first was the expiration of the patent on the sewing machine in 1876. As manufacturers introduced competing sewing machines, prices dropped and the machines began to make inroads into American households. The rise of the "graded paper pattern" also changed the nature of sewing. Prior to this time, making clothing involved an elaborate process of guessing the approximate size needed, then cutting, measuring, and re-cutting cloth until it fit the person for whom the garment was intended. In 1863, the first patterns appeared on paper (graded for different sizes) that allowed for cloth to be cut and sewn without an elaborate fitting process. In the 1870s, magazines appeared that reproduced patterns that women could buy for their own clothing, and the ready-to-wear industry quickly adopted paper pattern methods for its own production (Ley 7–8).

Ready-to-Wear The term "ready-to-wear" describes clothing that can be purchased without having to be individually designed, measured, and sewed for the person wearing it. The first ready-to-wear clothing success story in the United States was that of Levi Strauss, who designed rugged jeans originally created to outfit miners during the California Gold Rush in the 1850s. The industry as a whole came into its own after the Civil War; between 1860 and 1880, the number of ready-to-wear manufacturers increased from 96 to 562, and their business rose from 2 million to 32 million dollars during the same period. Early in the industrial era, the ready-to-wear industry focused primarily on clothing for men and children as well as accessories for women. Men's suits proved easier to make than women's dresses, very few of which were ready-to-wear during this period. Only at the end of the century, with the rise of the blouse (or "waists" as they were called) did ready-to-wear fashions begin to cut into the market for personally made dresses (Ley 4, 9, 29).

The lower cost of ready-to-wear garments attracted many working-class and immigrant customers, but it was not just saving money that drew these buyers in. As Jenna Weissman Joselit writes, "...the growing availability of attractive yet inexpensively produced hats, gloves, blouses, suits, shoes, and even jewelry—much of it produced by immigrant hands—made possible the promise of fitting in. Stylish clothes, once the exclusive preserve of the well-heeled and well-to-do, were now within everyone's reach" (3). For many immigrants seeking to acculturate or "Americanize" themselves, ready-to-wear clothing offered an affordable path toward acceptance.

Of course, as Joselit notes, the main reason these clothes were affordable is that they eliminated personal attention and the use of skilled seam-stresses. The ready-to-wear industry relied on a "homework" model of employment, giving their workers (who were mostly women) raw cloth and sending them elsewhere to do their sewing. Middlemen would act as go-betweens providing poor workers with materials and a place to sew. A "sweatshop" industry quickly arose in New York City and other areas, as garment workers often labored for excessive hours (60+ hour workweeks were not uncommon) and exploitative wages (Ley 29, 46).

Women's fashion followed a path related to, but never wholly dependent upon, developments in clothing manu-facturing. The most memorable fashion trend of this period was what has been dubbed "Victorian dresses." These full-length dresses were worn over corsets designed to mold women's bodies to a desired hourglass shape (corsets that tightly constricted the waist frequently caused women lasting physical damage). These dresses were very elaborate, and the many ribbons and ruffles to be found on them needed to be hand sewn. They also were extraordinarily heavy and voluminous. According to one study, from 1893–96, the average width of skirts was 13.5 feet and this outer skirt was made to stand out from a women's body by the use of several layers of petticoats worn underneath the dress. Physically, such dresses were difficult to wear; but their larger function was to provide women with something in which to be seen (as can be see in the except from Theodore Dreiser's *Sister Carrie*). Toward the end of the century women's dresses included large, padded sleeves, dubbed "leg-of-mutton" sleeves. The development of aniline dyes also allowed fabric to be dyed in very bright colors, such as royal blue and verdigris, previously unseen in clothing. Particular fabrics had specific connotations: silk was associated with upper-class evening wear, wool was common in less formal elite clothing and in dresses for the middle class, cotton was associated with working-class dresses (Ley 30–31, 47; Mosher qtd. in Schroeder 353).

Women's Fashion

THE BROADWAY PARADE

The walk down Broadway, then as now, was one of the remarkable features of the city. There gathered, before the matinée and afterwards, not only all the pretty women who love a showy parade, but the men who love to gaze upon and admire them. It was a very imposing procession of pretty faces and fine clothes. Women appeared in their very best hats, shoes, and gloves and walked arm in arm on their way to the fine shops or theatres strung along from Fourteenth to Thirty-fourth streets. Equally the men paraded with the very latest they could afford....

Men in flawless top-coats, high hats, and silver-headed walking sticks elbowed near and looked too often in to conscious eyes. Ladies rustled by in dresses of stiff cloth, shedding affected smiles and perfume.

—From Theodore Dreiser, *Sister Carrie*, 226–27

The industrial era saw a new wave of "dress reform," action taken by women to change the standards of clothing styles and fashions. Much of the reform of this period was tied to women's involvement in sports, particularly bicycling. Elaborate Victorian-style dresses were impractical for bike riding and most other athletic activities. As a result, "rational" garments such as skirts with baggy knickers (designed so as not to outline women's legs) emerged to provide viable clothing for women involved in sports. As many middle- and working-class women found employment in the department stores and service industries in cities, they also found the traditional Victorian dress too restrictive. "Man-suits"—tailored suits consisting of a jacket, skirt, and blouse—were designed for women who needed mobility, and they quickly became popular in urban areas (Fischer 171; Ley 38–39).

LOOKING BACKWARD AND CONSUMER CULTURE

The rise of consumer culture has been a much contested development in American history. Was it a triumph of democratic capitalism that provided people with pleasure and satisfaction on a national scale? Or, in becoming consumers did Americans give up their own capacity to create culture, sacrificing unique traditions and skills for the manufactured baubles of mass culture? One answer to these questions can be found in Edward Bellamy's utopian romance, *Looking Backward: 2000–1887*, the best selling American novel of the industrial era. Though little read today, *Looking Backward* was a phenomenon in the years following its publication in 1888 (selling more than a million copies within a decade), and aspects of the novel speak to the nature of consumer desires (Hart 171).

Bellamy's novel follows Julian West, a nineteenth-century Boston aristocrat who falls into a hypnotic trance and wakes up 113 years later in a world that has been transformed by a peaceful revolution. Led by his twenty-first century guides, Dr. Leete and his family, West is introduced to the utopian society that emerged from the turmoil of his own times. In the year 2000, competition has been replaced by cooperation, and the monopolies of the industrial era have evolved into "one big business" that is now under public control. Each citizen receives an equal share of the national output. In this utopian world, large, regional distribution centers have replaced small stores and they provide personally tailored goods and services. Neighborhood dining centers serve meals and most housework has been mechanized.

The vision of the future Bellamy offered was one that responded to and attempted to solve the problems of his own times, and it is in this context that his specific predictions prove most interesting. His prophecies were both utterly wrong and incredibly perceptive. His belief that greater industrial monopolization would lead to democratic nationalization of industry did not come to pass in the United States. However, many of Bellamy's predictions concerning consumer culture did come true. During Julian West's tour of the future, he is introduced to new consumer goods and services including credit cards, radio, doctor licensing, product labeling, alarm clock radios, covered walkways, and malls. What is important about these details is not the extent to which Bellamy did or did not predict the future, but rather that Bellamy was able to represent the desires of many people of the industrial era. These desires, or what could just as accurately be called the utopian impulse, had real implications even if the future did not unfold as Bellamy and many of his readers wished.

What Bellamy's novel provides is a way to think about the development of consumer culture as something other than just manipulation. One strain of thought, often associated with critics of the Frankfurt School such as Theodor Adorno, sees technology as compelling certain modes of consumption; people are conditioned as consumers to behave in certain ways. From this perspective, the emergence of consumer culture determined and limited people's actions. By becoming consumers, people traded away their own intellectual and cultural autonomy.

However, the problem with this way of thinking is that not all technological advances lead to new forms of consumption. People often reject new technology. To take one example, the technology to produce a videophone had been available for decades, but it remained undeveloped because research surveys showed that few people actually wanted to be seen talking on the phone at home. Consumer demands are more likely than not to precede the technologies that can satisfy them. As Antony Easthope notes, "The Victorians tried for fifty years to invent the cinema—with their 'Zoobiographs' and so on—but without success" (95). Successful consumer technology is less likely to manufacture desire than it is to fulfill an already existing want.

At one point in Bellamy's novel, Julian West fears an afternoon walk will have to be cancelled because rain has made the streets impassable. However, to his surprise, when the rain began, a public awning was let down and covered all sidewalks, making it possible to walk outside after all. West's host, Dr. Leete, noted that "in the nineteenth century, when it rained, the people of Boston put up three hundred thousand umbrellas over as many heads, and in the twentieth century they put up one umbrella over all the heads" (123). For Bellamy, and many of his readers, the rise of consumer culture held within it the promise of a general prosperity and a re-envisioned social landscape. They believed that just as one big awning could replace myriad umbrellas, so too could a more equitable economic and political structure be envisioned. The insights of *Looking Backward*, seen from this perspective, were not predictions but revelations. They revealed the consumerist wants of the nineteenth century, but they also revealed the democratic desires that did not come to pass. It is fair to say that many people did wish for more consumer goods and services, but that desire was of a piece with a willingness to reconsider the nature of work and government and to rethink some of the fundamental precepts of their society. It is important, when looking backward to consumerism in the industrial era, not to let the novelty of new stores and commodities keep us from appreciating the utopian impulses that were part of the rise of consumer culture.

7

Leisure and Entertainment

INTRODUCTION

In the industrial era, people took leisure seriously. It was an issue of public debate, the cause of strikes by workers, a subject of reform work, and seen by many as a necessary corrective to the rigidity of work in the new factories. A new entertainment industry arose to meet this demand for leisure, and the shape of that industry was defined by (and occasionally defied) class lines.

Concern with leisure initially would seem to be at odds with the "Protestant work ethic," a belief in the religiously inspired value of hard work for its own sake. Although there was a great deal of concern within some middle-class households over "proper" leisure activities, it would be wrong to see the Protestant work ethic as a universally shared belief at this time. As Michael Kelly writes, "Accounts of work conditions in the mill and mine of the early period of industrialization do not suggest that work was satisfying, central to life's meaning or personal identities, or an experience to be looked forward to" (163). For those who had little control over their working conditions, the sphere of leisure assumed much greater social importance than it had at earlier points in history.

This chapter first looks at how leisure was understood and experienced by members of different classes. Then it examines some of the notable leisure developments of the era in the areas of physical recreation, public amusements, and traveling shows, focusing on specific entertainments from the bicycle to vaudeville to Wild West shows to novels.

THE CLASS CONTOURS OF LEISURE AND ENTERTAINMENT

Leisure and the Eight-Hour Movement   Perhaps the most widely shared goal of the labor movement in the industrial era was the aspiration for working shorter hours. In industries where 6-day work weeks and 12-hour days were common, workers were receptive to the call for 8-hour days, as in the movement anthem on this page. Leisure, or "eight hours for what we will," assumed an importance that has to be understood in the context of the industrial workplace. Workers, particularly those who had migrated from farms or emigrated from rural areas of Europe, were no strangers to long hours and demanding work. However, in nonindustrial settings, laborers had had more control over the pace of their work. An individual artisan could choose to take a break during the course of a day. A farmer could stop plowing for lunch with his family. But, on an assembly line, breaks could only be taken when management chose to halt the line. When family members worked in a variety of urban locations, they only saw one another outside the workplace.

"EIGHT HOURS"

The 1878 song "Eight Hours," with words by I. G. Blanchard and music by Rev. Jesse H. Jones, arguably was the most popular labor song of the nineteenth century, and it became the official song of the eight-hour movement. The first verse, chorus, and fourth verse follow.

We mean to make things over,
we are tired of toil for naught,
With but bare enough to live upon,
and never an hour for thought;
We want to feel the sunshine,
and we want to smell the flowers,
We're sure that God has will'd it,
And we mean to have eight hours.
We're summoning our forces from
shipyard, shop and mill,

Chorus:
Eight hours for work, eight hours
for rest, eight hours for what we will.
Eight hours for work, eight hours
for rest, eight hours for what we will.

From factories and workshops,
in long and weary lines,
From all the sweltering forges,
and from out the sunless mines,
Wherever toil is wasting

the force of life to live,
There the bent and battered armies
come to claim what God doth give,
And the blazon on the banner doth
with hope the nations fill.

—From *American Labor Songs of the Nineteenth Century,* ed. Philip S. Foner, 224

Proponents of the eight-hour movement saw leisure not as simply "time off" but as essential to the development of character, to the well being of workers, and to the future of democracy. George Gunton of the American Federation of Labor argued in 1889 that "With increased leisure and less exhaustion, the laborer will be continually forced or attracted into new and more complex social relations, which is the first step toward education and culture in the broadest and deepest sense of the term" (13). Gunton, like many eight-hour supporters, felt that a diversity of leisure and entertainment was needed to counteract the monotonous conditions of most factory work.

Though the eight-hour movement had its greatest successes in the first half of the twentieth century, it did achieve limited victories during the industrial era on a state by state and industry by industry basis. By 1868, precedents for the eight-hour day had been set among federal employees in government jobs, and eight-hour legislation had been passed in eight states. On May 1, 1886, eight-hour day rallies drew as many as half a million workers into the streets. David Nasaw writes in *Going Out* that "The average manufacturing worker worked three and a half hours less in 1910 than in 1890; for many blue-collar workers, unionized employees, and white-collar workers, the decrease in the workweek was even more dramatic" (4). Victories for the eight-hour day movement were won through a combination of factors. Without workers' agitation, hours would not have been reduced. And, as neighborhoods became increasingly segregated by income, the upper and middle class became less concerned about what workers did in their off hours (Kelly 158; Roediger and Foner 101, 139, 146).

Some eight-hour day opponents feared that if workers had time off from work, they would simply drink and squander their money. However, though the saloon remained central to working-class culture, workers lacked the disposable income to patronize many of the new entertainment industries of the industrial era, and there is scant evidence that increased free time led to greater drinking. It was not until the first decade of the twentieth century that new entertainment industries like movies and amusement parks made significant inroads among workers. However, by the 1890s, the beginnings of new working-class cultural practices appeared. Young people began to form their own "social and pleasure clubs" and organized their own dances and plays (the precursors of the popular dance halls of the early twentieth century) rather than simply attending functions at their parents' institutions. For the most part, though, working-class leisure continued to center around ethnic associations, union halls, and neighborhoods. In these organizations, the line between entertainment and civic culture was blurred (McBee 53; Nasaw, *Going* 14).

New Entertainments for the New and Old Middle Class

The emerging entertainment industry, businesses that provided public amusements detailed later in this chapter, primarily served the urban white-collar workforce that expanded rapidly during the industrial era. Between 1880 and 1910, the number of typists in the United States increased from 5,000 to 300,000, and the number of people working as sales clerks grew from 160,000 to 1.7 million. Many of these workers were new to cities and a large number of them were women. Though white collar work could be as tedious as that in the new factories, these workers with disposable income and jobs that were not physically taxing were more likely to take advantage of all that "a night on the town" had to offer (Nasaw, *Going* 5).

Leisure also mattered to the traditional, Protestant middle class, though in a much different way. The hedonistic pursuit of pleasure was frowned upon by this largely Evangelical segment of the American population. In general, traditional middle-class families were more likely to socialize at home. When they went out for entertainment, it was typically for an "uplifting" purpose. Church-sponsored functions, lectures, and museums were popular. Vacations also became fashionable among the middle class during the industrial era. Inexpensive rail travel made pleasure trips possible, and a vacation became a marker of prestige as well as a welcome respite from the congestion of city life. In an attempt to assuage concerns that vacations would undermine a commitment to a virtuous life, religiously themed resorts, such as Ocean Grove, New Jersey, were opened to provide recreational opportunities that carefully conformed to the standards of middle-class morality (Aron 5; Nasaw, *Going* 15; Uminowicz 23).

The sphere of leisure also functioned as a space where class identity was formed. Richard Ohmann has argued that the new mass-circulation magazines of the 1890s were essential to the class identity of the nascent professional-managerial class (PMC). He writes that "Engineers sensed a kinship not just with other engineers, but with urban administrators, lawyers, managers, health workers…The PMC identified itself with the new, with progress, with the modern; it wanted a culture that privileged these ideals…" (220–21). Publications such as *Munsey's Magazine*, *McClure's*, *Cosmopolitan*, and *Ladies Home Journal*, found a successful formula in providing the low-cost, advertising-driven magazines that focused on vivid portrayals of the consumer culture to those who could afford to buy the products they saw and read about.

The issue of physical activity provoked much discussion and concern among middle-class professionals. Recreation, undertaken in moderation and in healthful settings, increasingly was considered a necessary release from the pressures of city life and the workplace. As middle-class work became increasingly industrialized and involved less bodily exertion, no less an authority than Herbert Spencer, the creator of Social Darwinism, began to speak of a "gospel of recreation," fearing that overwork was diminishing people's physical capacity and could lead to the ruin of "civilized" man (qtd. in Uminowicz 23). Many commentators recommended regular exercise for women as well, and many women soon became visible and avid proponents of such activities as bicycling and roller skating. Concern for physical fitness also played into what historians have marked as a "masculinity crisis" during the industrial era. What it meant to be a man became less clear to many Americans, as new forms of work and shifting family structures altered traditional ways. Recapturing the physical potential of men became a goal of much of the recreation of the industrial era (Hoover 66).

"BUILD UP THE BODY"

Cyrus Edson, the Chief Inspector of the New York Board of Health, expressed widely shared beliefs as to the necessity of exercise for the future of the United States in an excerpt from an 1892 article.

Outdoor sports and recreative pursuits should be judiciously encouraged. One month, at least, in every twelve, should be spent in rest. Sundays and other holidays should be observed as days of rest and recreation. Fresh air and exercise are of even greater importance for the girls than for the boys, if such a thing be possible. The girls will find their reward for the work when they become young ladies in society, in the bright eyes, clear complexions, stately carriage, graceful walk and perfect health which they will enjoy. More than that, when the time comes in their lives that they need all their strength they will find they have a reserve which will not fail them, and their children will be healthy and strong. Build up the body, build up the body! In our modern life, this should be dinned into the ears of all until it is obeyed, for, verily, unless we build up the body, the strain on the brain will ruin the American people. The very elements in ourselves that have made us great, the push, the drive, the industry, the mental keenness, the ability and the willingness to labor, these contain in them the seeds of national death. No race may endure that has not the stamina and power of the healthy animal.

—From "Do We Live Too Fast?" 286

As the rich grew richer during the industrial era, their leisure and entertainment increasingly occurred apart from other segments of the population. Also, while new entertainment industries aimed to amuse, the goal of upper-class leisure activities like theaters, symphony orchestras, and formal museums was to refine tastes and mold audiences. Elite European standards prevailed in these settings. The "Grand Tour of the Continent" became a hallmark of upper-class status, and in 1893 more than 90,000 Americans vacationed in Europe. Beginning in the 1890s, elaborate theaters were built to cater to the rich, who themselves built expensive mansions in exclusive neighborhoods. This new opulence won the scorn of

Culture and the "Leisure Class"

many metropolitan newspapers and some moralists, though it came as little surprise to one of the foremost sociologists of the day, Thorstein Veblin (Braden 152; Hart 182).

Veblin's 1899 classic study, *The Theory of the Leisure Class*, introduced concepts, such as "conspicuous consumption" (making expensive purchases in order to flaunt one's wealth), that are still in common use today. Veblin argued that hypocrisy was at the heart of many industrial era standards of taste and culture. Rather than bespeaking an elevated character, Veblin claimed that elite ideals of dress, of deportment, and of education, were superficial indicators designed to reflect one's level of wealth. In their ostentatious displays, the rich of the industrial era were judged as little different than tribal chieftains by Veblin.

Conspicuous consumption of valuable goods is a means of reputability to the gentleman of leisure. As wealth accumulates on his hands, his own unaided effort will not avail to sufficiently put his opulence in evidence...Costly entertainments, such as the potlatch [a ceremony among the Kwakiutl tribe in which gifts were lavishly distributed to highlight the status and wealth of a chief] or the ball, are peculiarly adapted to serve this end. (47)

Veblin's contentious claims have remained controversial, but they point to a crisis at the time over what the proper relation of work and leisure was and what role leisure was to play in American society.

PHYSICAL RECREATION

The recreation movement of the late nineteenth century emerged in response to urban conditions. As cities became increasingly industrialized and crowded, opportunities for healthy physical activities declined, especially for poor families that could not afford to travel out of the city. Reformers such as Jacob Riis, Jane Addams, and Joseph Lee made substantial efforts to improve urban recreation, pushing for the establishment of playgrounds and parks (as is detailed in this book in the chapter, "The City"). However, other means of physical recreation, including roller skating, bicycling, and baseball, also became quite popular during the industrial era among those who had the money and time needed to participate (Kelly 159).

Roller Skating   Prior to the 1880s, roller skate wheels had been made out of wood and proved both slow and difficult to use. However, roller skating became one of the biggest fads of the 1880s due a combination of growing interest in exercise and the technological advance of metal skate wheels with pin bearings. Indoor roller rinks opened up in towns and cities throughout the country and proved popular among men, women, and children. As a sport that could be undertaken in a supervised setting where liquor was not allowed, roller skating was thought of as an appropriately moral form of recreation. At the peak of the fad, roller skating had become a 20 million dollar business. Rinks became more commercialized and lured in customers with vaudeville acts, professional trick skating exhibitions, and the team sport, "roller polo." However, after the initial enthusiasm of roller skating wore off, interest waned and other forms of entertainment (particularly the bicycle) superceded it. By the turn of the century, most of the roller rinks from the 1880s boom had closed (Braden 240; Hoover 65, 72–74).

The biggest fad of the 1890s, and of the industrial era as a whole, was bicycling. Two technological innovations made the rise of bicycling possible: the safety bicycle—the rear **Bicycling** wheel chain driven bike that allowed for both wheels on a bike to be of a uniform size and closer to the ground than earlier models—and the pneumatic tire—the rubber, air-filled tire that made for a less bumpy ride. However, new technology alone did not make the craze. Bicycling caught on because it addressed a desire among many Americans, both men and women, for greater mobility and freedom of movement (Dodge 94, 109).

During the 1890s, what has become known as the "Golden Age of Bicycling," interest in bicycling increased exponentially. Membership in the League of American Wheelmen grew from 44 members in 1880 to 141,532 members by 1898. As an industry, bicycle manufacturing employed just 1,800 workers in 1890 but had over 17,000 employees by 1900. At the peak of the craze in 1896, there were as many as four million American bicyclists (Braden 243, Dodge 116).

Bicycles provided a source of exercise, but, in an era predating the automobile, they also offered a means of transportation previously unavailable to most city residents. The cost of bicycles initially placed them out of reach for all but the rich. In 1884 a bicycle cost $150, about one-third of a year's wages for most Americans. Prices began to decline to $100 in 1890, and went as low as $22 after the collapse of the bicycling boom in the late 1890s. As a result, bicycle riding became less a pastime for the rich than a hobby enjoyed across classes. In 1898 there was even a Socialist Wheelmen's Club that rode from Boston to New York City distributing pamphlets. Bicycles became a common sight on city streets. Amateur and professional bike races were a regular feature of the entertainment landscape. The bicycle craze had a domino effect on other industries and institutions. In New York City, piano sales were cut in half, theater attendance dipped, cigar consumption fell, and a drop in church attendance was even blamed on the bicycle (Dodge 120, 162; Smith 30, 36, 111, 119).

Women made up one-third of the market for bicycles during the 1890s, and the bicycle came to play a surprising role in women's rights struggles toward the end of the century. Victorian dresses with their restrictive corsets and long, heavy skirts were impractical for bicycle riding. The types of clothing that made sense for women bicyclists were uncorseted skirts or the controversial "bloomers," a combination of loose trousers and

Championship bicyclist William Martin on a large-wheel bicycle of the type made obsolete by the introduction of the safety bicycle. (Courtesy Library of Congress)

a short shirt worn by dress reformers since the middle of the century. Wearing bloomers or other reform clothing immediately put women in the center of controversy. In fact, language used to describe the clothing women wore to bicycle became entwined with understandings of women's sexuality. The terms "loose" and "straight-laced" initially referred to women's bicycling wear, but they are still with us today as slang used to describe women's sexual behavior (Dodge 122, 132).

Many moralists were concerned about the social effect of bicycling. When Sunday bicycle riding cut into church attendance, one clergyman prophesied that cyclists were heading down a metaphorical hill, without brakes, toward "a place where there is no mud on the streets because of the high temperatures [i.e. hell]" (qtd. in Smith 72). But in the case of women, conservative moralists feared that cycling would tax women's "delicate constitutions" and, if they rode without chaperons, could lead them to further temptations (Larrabee 84).

However, advocates of women's rights were quick to seize upon the liberating potential of the bicycle. Suffragist Susan B. Anthony stated that bicycling "has done more to emancipate women than anything else in the world...It gives women a feeling of freedom and self reliance" (qtd. in Dodge 130). Francis Willard, the long-time leader of the Women's Christian Temperance Union, was so enamored of the bicycle that she endeavored to learn to ride at the age of 53. In her 1895 account, Willard writes not only of her struggles to master her bike with the help of a series of instructors (and of one crashing fall), but she argues that the bicycle would lead to more equitable gender relationships. "We saw with satisfaction the great advantage in good fellowship and mutual understanding between men and women who take the road together, sharing its hardships and rejoicing in the poetry of motion..." (45). In the 1890s, the bicycle was not just a toy or even just a sport; it was a means through which changing conceptions of exercise, freedom, and femininity were realized.

Baseball in the industrial era began as a middle-class, urban recreation. Amateur teams at this time drew their **Baseball** players primarily from men who could choose to leave work in mid-afternoon to take to the field. Baseball was celebrated as a genteel sport. However, baseball differed from other forms of middle-class leisure and commercial amusements in that it tended to be undertaken solely by men, and, like the male-only concert saloons, it was a space where drinking and gambling were common. Amateur baseball teams really were "clubs," and the players were themselves members of the clubs rather than employees. The first truly professional team, the Cincinnati Red Stockings, made their debut in 1869 and posted a perfect 65-0 record. In the space of two years the team lost fan support and left town to become the Boston Red Stockings. Making "America's Pastime" a professional sport was a gradual and erratic process. During the industrial era there were many conflicts between amateur and professional approaches to baseball, in addition to controversies over race and class on the diamond (Nasaw, *Going* 102; G. Ward 22).

The success of amateur league baseball was in many ways its undoing. As baseball grew in popularity and clubs began charging admission to games (as much as 50 cents per ticket), a transition to professional play began. Part-time players found themselves unable to compete with full-time paid professionals. Skilled pro players soon began moving from team to team in search of better pay and working conditions. In an era before professional leagues established geographical monopolies, teams of "barnstormers" would travel from city to city taking on the local club (Goldstein 99; G. Ward 20).

Early baseball did not formally discriminate against African American players, though plenty of informal discrimination was to be found. There were black barnstorming teams like the Philadelphia Pythians and the Cuban Giants. More than fifty black players played openly in organized baseball in the 1870s and 1880s and some, like Frank Grant of the Buffalo Bisons, proved to be stars. It was not until 1887, when rising racial animosity (and the refusal of Cap Anson, then the game's most popular

African American baseball players from Morris Brown College in Atlanta, Georgia, in 1899 or 1900. (Courtesy Library of Congress)

player, to play alongside African Americans) led to the formal segregation of black players from baseball. Until Jackie Robinson broke baseball's "color line" in 1947, the only opportunities African Americans had to play in the main professional leagues were by passing as Cuban or Native American. There were also Negro Leagues which operated from 1920 to 1948 (Malloy lii; G. Ward 40–43).

With the founding of the main professional leagues (the National League in 1876 and the American Base Ball Association in 1882) baseball became an established professional sport, though barnstorming teams and assorted smaller leagues still played a prominent role. Baseball became a notably rough game in the 1890s. Dirty tricks such as spiking players were common. Umpires were harassed and occasionally beaten up. An 1894 brawl between players in Boston spilled out into the stands and escalated into a fire that burned down the stadium. While amateur clubs declined in prominence, playing baseball remained a popular pastime, spreading beyond its early base among urban, middle-class men to include working-class immigrants, players in small towns, and women. Hometown ball was a rowdy recreation, and it was not unusual for games to include the "German Disturber," a keg of beer next to third base with a dipper for any player who made it to third (G. Ward 46, 51).

PUBLIC AMUSEMENTS

As American cities grew exponentially during the industrial era, so too did the entertainment they provided. Consider that in 1870 San Francisco had had just two dramatic theaters and one opera house. By 1912, San Francisco was home to 5 dramatic theaters, 11 vaudeville houses, and 69 movie theaters. By 1900, New York City had more theaters than any other city in the world. San Francisco and New York's experiences were by no means unique. At the beginning of the industrial era, only the wealthy were likely to devote substantial time and money to the few public amusements that were available. But by the turn of the century the landscape of most American cities had been transformed into a "world of phonograph and kinetoscope parlors; of vaudeville halls and ten-twenty-thirty melodrama theaters; of world's fair midways; of amusement parks, ballparks, dance halls, and picture palaces (Nasaw, *Going* 2–3).

Though the majority of workers could not afford these leisure activities, and the traditional middle class looked down on hedonistic pleasures, new white-collar workers readily took advantage of the entertainments of the new city. Perhaps the most significant social development represented by public amusements was their break with standard forms of family and community leisure. As David Nasaw writes, " 'Going out' meant laughing, dancing, cheering, and weeping with strangers with whom one might—or might not—have anything in common. The 'crowd' replaced the select circle of acquaintances as the setting in which one sought and found amusement" (2). For the most part, these new amusements did not take place in the home, church, lodge, or ethnic club.

Theaters, Concert Saloons, and Vaudeville

Urban theaters of the early 1800s were notably class-inclusive. Lawrence Levine writes that theaters housed, "under one roof a microcosm of American society" (25). Rich, middle class, and poor all attended the same theater, sitting in different sections according to what they were willing to pay. Those with money could purchase cushioned chairs in reserved boxes. Workers tended to stand in the "pit" right below the stage. Cheap upper-balcony seats were also available, and, in most theaters, African American patrons (no matter what they were able to pay) and prostitutes were restricted to this section (Nasaw, *Going* 10–11).

This diverse audience was typically treated to a wide ranging lineup of entertainment designed to provide something for everyone. Shakespearean recitations would alternate with jugglers and trained monkey acts; it was not uncommon to see Italian opera performed alongside contemporary sentimental ballads like "Home Sweet Home." Nor was it entirely clear that people's tastes divided along predictable class lines at this time. Both Italian opera and Shakespeare were part of an early nineteenth-century culture that was shared across social classes (Levine 21–23, 71, 90).

However, beginning around mid-century, and continuing into the industrial era, cities grew in prosperity and new theaters were built that catered to the upper class. The cost of a theater ticket in the mid-1880s was a dollar, two-thirds of an average worker's daily wage. David Nasaw writes that "Balcony seats at Boston's Globe Theater in 1886 were priced at seventy-five cents to one dollar, with second balcony and gallery seats at fifty cents, this at a time when the average hourly wage in manufacturing was twenty cents and the average daily wage for unskilled laborers was under one dollar and fifty cents" (*Going* 13). Workers and much of the middle class found themselves priced out of most legitimate theaters and turned instead to the cheaper concert saloons and vaudeville. As a result, Shakespeare and opera, which were once part of a shared culture, became almost the exclusive domain of elite society. The diversity of early theatrical and musical performances disappeared as well, and gone were the days when Shakespeare was performed alongside trained monkeys (Levine 33; Nasaw, *Going* 13).

Concert saloons varied in the amount of theatrical entertainment they provided, but most had some kind of musical stage show. These were exclusively male establishments (with the exception of prostitutes and female dancers), and while they drew patrons from a range of class positions, they tended to be too expensive for most workers. In the end, the vacuum left by the decline of theaters for the middle class was filled by vaudeville (Nasaw, *Going* 13–14).

The innovation of vaudeville in the 1880s came with the realization that selling the same theater seat four times a day for 25 cents made as much money as selling a one dollar seat for a daily performance. By offering low cost, continuous performances of variety acts, a whole new audience was found among middle-class and, to a lesser degree, working-class patrons. Benjamin Franklin Keith, the most famous of the vaudeville impresarios, established successful vaudeville theaters in a number of U.S. cities with a rotating schedule of performers. Most theaters were open 12 hours a day, 6 days a week. Anyone with a quarter could stop in for an hour or stay for a whole evening. Vaudeville theaters made a point of distinguishing themselves from saloon theaters by attracting female customers. Special advertisements and matinees were set up to bring in women shoppers. Smoking and drinking were prohibited or tightly controlled (Nasaw, *Going* 19–27).

The diversity of audiences and performances that Lawrence Levine laments had disappeared from now-elite theaters reappeared in vaudeville. While a headline act would be featured on a vaudeville theater's marquee, a given night's bill might include as many as 30 short acts including ballad singers, magicians, blackface minstrels, acrobats, opera singers, one-act plays, and sports stars, each taking the stage for 15 to 30 minutes. Vaudeville aimed to attract the largest possible audience by providing an assortment of acts. By the end of the century, vaudeville had still only made limited inroads into the urban working class (it offered little for immigrants with marginal English language skills), but it did bring in droves of middle-class men, women, and children. Some vaudeville houses even began to attract wealthy patrons by building new, elaborate theaters and including symphony performances as part of their bill of fare (Braden 138; Nasaw, *Going* 27–32).

Peep Shows, Early Movies, and Photography

In the 1920s, movies were truly mass entertainment, attracting an average of 50 million customers (equal to half the U.S. population) per week. However, though forerunners of movies were popular in the 1890s, the first recognized feature film, *The Great Train Robbery*, was not made until 1903. In the 1890s, cinema consisted of a range of primitive machines and films shown in a variety of settings and formats. Following Thomas Edison's invention of the Kinetoscope in 1893, new Kinetoscope or peep show parlors appeared in the United States. These parlors offered row after row of Kinetoscopes (and similar machines made by Edison's competitors) that allowed a viewer to look through a peep hole and see a short film, perhaps a minute in length, of a man flexing muscles or a slapstick routine or a circus act. Kinetoscope parlors charged a quarter for admission, keeping them out of the price range of the majority of the population. It was not until early in the next century that prices dropped and workers and children became patrons of these parlors, which then were renamed "nickelodeons," and later "penny arcades" (Nasaw, *Going* 130–33; Rosenweig 191).

Edison's Vitascope, introduced in 1895, marked another innovation. It was the first successful movie projector, allowing projection of short silent films. The Vitascope proved to be a novelty, appearing in vaudeville theaters and as part of lecture-hall performances. Entrepreneurs would travel with Vitascopes to small towns, finding eager audiences, particularly in the west, that had never before seen moving pictures. Storefront theaters solely devoted to Vitascope screenings appeared in cities and proved popular with immigrant populations that did not need to speak English to be entertained by silent films (Braden 162–63; Nasaw, *Going* 138–48).

However, film technology remained primitive through the turn of the century. Early projectors played as little as sixteen seconds of film at a time (though the film could be looped for continuous play) and a lack of new films also contributed to a gradual decline in audiences and the temporary disappearance of films from vaudeville bills. However, the coming of the Spanish-American war in 1898 created new interest in "war films," and fledgling studios were quick to produce documentary war footage (or to stage their own battles in makeshift studios) for vaudeville. Still, it was not until the first decade of the 1900s, as technology and filmmaking improved, that movie theaters truly became popular. By 1910, movies were a huge industry, with 10,000 movie theaters in the United States drawing 25 million customers per week, a figure that would exceed the combined audiences of "all legitimate dramatic performances, variety shows, dime museums, lecture programs, concerts, circuses, and street carnivals" (Braden 163; Nasaw, *Going* 147–50).

Still photography also underwent a transformation in the industrial era. Although cameras had long been available for professionals and hobbyists, in 1888 George Eastman introduced the first camera made for a mass audience, the Kodak. The Kodak was designed for ease of use in shooting, and more important, Eastman's company developed completed film for photographers (prior to this time, photographers had to have their own dark rooms). "You press the button—We do the rest" was an early advertising slogan that captured the novelty of the product (Collins 56–59).

The Kodak, which initially sold for $25, was an immediate success, selling 2,500 units in its first six months and over 13,000 in its first year. It proved popular with travelers, particularly those traveling by train to new vacation spots, but many families also used Kodaks to visually record for the first time family events such as birthdays, christenings, and reunions. The success of the Kodak led Eastman to produce a number of modified versions, including the Folding Kodak, the Pocket Kodak, and the Brownie. The Brownie camera was designed to be so simple to operate that a child could use it. When the Brownie was released in 1900, it sold for only $1. Within two years, almost a quarter of a million Brownies had been sold (Collins 65, 76, 97).

TRAVELING SHOWS

With the rise of rail travel and other improvements in transportation, it became economically feasible to take entertainments usually restricted to urban locations on the road. Theatrical companies would often begin a show in a major city and then take advantage of the publicity it received to launch a regional tour of smaller cities and towns. Other traveling shows developed in unique ways that took advantage of the logistics of rail travel and one-night-only appearances. While the best known form of this type of entertainment was the circus, other popular traveling shows of the period include Wild West shows, *Uncle Tom's Cabin* shows, and the traveling lectures that became known as Chautauquas.

The cultural form that in many ways set the standard for traveling shows was the World's Fairs. Though World's Fairs were not exactly traveling shows (like the present day Olympics, they rotated regularly among different cities), they proved hugely successful in bringing together a range of entertainments, educational exhibits, and technological displays into one location. The World's Fairs drew unprecedented numbers of people—the 1876 Centennial Exhibition in Philadelphia attracted nearly 10 million people, almost one-fifth of the U.S. population at the time, and the 1893 World's Columbian Exposition in Chicago had over 27 million visitors. Robert Rydell argues that the Fairs' greatest importance was in organizing and explaining a changing social world in a way that promoted the beliefs of the nation's ruling class. Educational exhibits and displays of manufacturing technology were central to the Fairs, but the Fairs were huge and decentered experiences. A visitor could stroll the grounds of Chicago's "White City" (the central fair ground designed in a neoclassical style) or visit the Midway Plaisance, the accompanying side show venue that featured pseudoscientific ethnographic displays (often featuring stereotypical and racist presentations of foreign peoples) and a range of popular entertainments. As Rydell notes, "Exposition promoters drew upon and reshaped such sources of entertainment as the zoological garden, the minstrel show, the circus, the museum of curiosities, the dime novel, and the Wild West show" (6). However, in addition, these Fairs gave back to the realm of popular entertainments a model for the spectacular. Traveling shows of the period learned from the Fairs and increasingly grew in size, in scope, and in the level of technology used to dazzle customers. These shows addressed a desire for entertainment in the most remote sections of the expanding United States. However, in the end, they also put forward lessons about the place of the United States in the world and about the role of racial hierarchies, lessons that paved the way for overseas imperialism and domestic racial segregation (O'Loughlin 77; Rydell 3, 10, 40).

The last decades of the nineteenth century and the first of the twentieth are known as the "Golden Age of the Circus." **The Circus** At least 40 different traveling circuses wound their way

through the United States, playing large cities as well as isolated rural locations. Though circuses had long traveled by horse-drawn wagons, major
circuses were quick to see the advantages rail travel provided. Dan
Castello's Circus and Menagerie made its way west by rail just two months
after the transcontinental railroad was completed in 1869. P. T. Barnum was
a showman who was already well known for his museums and concerts
when he formed his first traveling circus in 1871. Over time Barnum's circus grew in size and scope; its 1873 incarnation took the unwieldy title of
"P. T. Barnum's Great Traveling World's Fair Consisting of Museum,
Menagerie, Caravan, Hippodrome, Gallery of Statuary and Fine Arts, Poly-
technic Institute, Zoological Garden, and 100,000 Curiousities, Combined
with Dan Castello's Sig. Sebastian's and Mr. D'Atelie's Grand Triple Eques-
trian and Hippodromatic Exposition." It is worth noting that the name
"circus" does not appear in that title. For many in the middle class, the circus at this time had connotations of immorality. In an effort to appeal to a
family audience, Barnum initially claimed that his extravaganza was not a
circus, and he included educationally focused exhibits designed to assuage
moralists (Adams 172–73; Braden 145; Chindahl 89–94).

Nevertheless, Barnum's circus, like many, provided a grab bag of attractions designed to appeal across generations, genders, and classes. The circus business was highly competitive, and new novelties were constantly
introduced in an effort to draw in customers. Though clowns, animals,

"The Grand Lay-Out." An 1874 lithograph of a circus parade prior to a performance. Note that the circus site is directly beside a railroad line. (Courtesy
Library of Congress)

and acrobats were to be found in most circuses, one of the features Barnum was known for was exhibiting people who were either physically malformed or who were from "exotic" locations or cultures. The makeup of these exhibits illustrated the then-prevalent beliefs of Social Darwinism, a belief that the "survival of the fittest" explained the current social order and that the power held by white, Anglo-Saxon men was natural and even scientifically ordained. Non-white people would be displayed in their "primitive" states, cast in a role designed to contrast as much as possible with that of white audience members (Adams 188).

When major circuses began traveling by rail and bypassing small towns, scaled down circuses, called dog and pony shows, sprung up to fill the void. Regardless of size, when the circus came to town, it usually held a parade down the Main Street in an effort to drum up business for that day's performance. Animals and performers, accompanied by music, would march through town, stopping traffic and business in its wake. The success and scope of the circus set the standard for other traveling shows of the period (Braden 149).

In 1883, when "Buffalo Bill" Cody launched his first Wild West show, he was already a famous man. As a military **Wild West** scout and frontiersman, Cody had been in the frontlines of **Shows** efforts by the U.S. government to pacify and remove native Indian tribes. His adventures had been celebrated (and augmented) in a series of dime novels, and he even starred in a play dramatizing his western experiences. But with the enormous success of the Wild West shows, Cody became perhaps the foremost American celebrity of the late nineteenth century. His Wild West show at the 1893 World's Columbian Exposition in Chicago drew an estimated six million visitors. By 1900, over 100 imitators were touring the United States with their own Wild West shows (Braden 149; Kasson 5; Reddin 56–57).

Wild West shows were a hybrid form of entertainment. Part circus, part rodeo, part shooting exhibition, and part historical pageant, they offered a combination of spectacles that proved hugely popular in tours throughout the United States and Europe, despite having high admission costs (50 cents for adults and 25 cents for children at a time when the average worker earned between a dollar and a dollar fifty per day). A typical show would be publicized in advance with four-color promotional posters and extensive newspaper advertising. When the troupe came into town, they would have a circus-style parade through the center of a town to drum up interest. The show itself began later that same day with a procession in which the troupe raced around the arena on horseback to the roar of the crowd. What then followed varied from season to season, but the show usually included horse races and riding tricks, displays of marksmanship (some featured the popular female sharpshooter, Annie Oakley), staged scenes of reenacted historical battles between cowboys and Indians, and rodeo style roping and bronco riding (Reddin 65–71).

An 1899 poster for Buffalo Bill's Wild West show. The scene purports to picture American Indians attacking pioneers in a caravan of covered wagons. The inset picture shows Buffalo Bill Cody on horseback. (Courtesy Library of Congress)

The cowboy's entry into American mythology can be traced back to the popularity of Wild West shows. So, too, can many traditional understandings of the settlement of the West. The stories of the Wild West shows were tales of Manifest Destiny about a savage wilderness needing to be tamed and about the frontiersmen who settled the West by battling Indians. In its reenactments of famous conflicts such as the Battle of Little Big Horn, the Wild West shows claimed to be representing history and portraying the ways of an uncivilized West that was quickly vanishing. Though Native Americans were a vital part of the Wild West show, they played a supporting role and their stories were not told, even when famous Native leaders, such as Sitting Bull and Geronimo, appeared as part of Cody's troupe (Reddin 69, 80).

Wild West shows can now help to illustrate the connection between the U.S. government's Indian removal policies and its entry into imperialism. The beliefs of Manifest Destiny and racial superiority that governed the settlement of the West appeared on a global stage during the Spanish-American War in 1898, and Cody's Wild West shows were quick to capitalize on the connection. In 1899, Cody reenacted the Rough Riders' charge up San Juan Hill in Cuba with actors who had once played Indians now portraying Spaniards. In 1901, the show's finale was "The Battle of Tien-Tsin," a reenactment of a pivotal moment in the Boxer Rebellion in

China when a group of European nations quelled an uprising of Chinese nationalists (again the defeated rebels were played by Native Americans, this time wearing traditional Chinese clothing). Such scenes proved popular with crowds but drew criticism from opponents of imperialism. The author Mark Twain had once been a big fan of Cody's shows, but during a 1901 performance in Madison Square Garden he responded to a reenactment of a scene from the Boer War by openly cheering for the Boers (the "bad guys" in Cody's version) and walking out during "The Battle of Tien-Tsin" (Kasson 62; Reddin 125, 135–36).

The Chautauqua Movement

The traditional middle-class version of the traveling show was the Chautauqua. It began in 1874 when an assembly of Sunday school teachers met at Chautauqua Lake, New York, for a two-week course of religious instruction, recreation, lectures, and study in music, art, and foreign languages. The success of these early assemblies led Chautauqua's founder, Rev. John Heyl Vincent, to establish in 1878 a guided reading program, the Chautauqua Literary and Scientific Circle. Though Vincent had hoped to form perhaps 10 study groups as part of the Circle, 8,400 people signed up and 10 years later as many as 100,000 people were enrolled in the Circle. Circle members formed their own assemblies, taking the name "Chautauqua" and bringing together, in Joseph E. Gould's celebratory words, "Healthy fun, wholesome recreation, religious reverence, good taste, and honest inquiry" (10). By 1890 there were as many as 200 independent, permanent Chautauquas that held summer retreats in idyllic settings, and even more "tent Chautauquas" circled the country during summer months in the early twentieth century. (Braden 144; Gould 5, 8; Schultz 1).

By 1900, the Chautauqua movement had become the nation's unofficial adult summer school. As Donna R. Braden writes, the Chautauquas, "combining elements of vaudeville, dramatic 'entertainments,' lectures, and musical performance, provided an acceptable and highly anticipated diversion for many Americans living in small towns and rural areas... [T]hese shows subtly combined the highly moral and religious atmosphere of a camp meeting, and elements of the lyceum lectures, with the entertainment aspect of a county fair" (144–145). The Chautauqua movement was particularly successful in the Great Plains states, where homesteaders found themselves in newly settled regions without established cultural institutions. Chautauquas offered "appropriate" recreation and instruction with many of the entertainments usually only available in the industrialized East, and the movement's summer festivals, book clubs, and musical events still can be found throughout the United States today (Gould 11).

Uncle Tom's Cabin Shows

The most popular play of the industrial era was *Uncle Tom's Cabin*. This may come as a surprise to those who think of *Uncle Tom's Cabin* primarily as a novel (written by Harriet Beecher Stowe in 1851) and associate it with conflicts over slavery before the Civil War. While Stowe's book was the best selling novel of the nineteenth century, for every person who read the book perhaps 50 saw a dramatized version of it. In 1879, there were 49 traveling troupes performing *Uncle Tom's Cabin,* sometimes exclusively, and by the turn of the century there may have been almost 10 times that many troupes. One reviewer predicted that in 1902, 1 out of every 35 Americans would see a performance of *Uncle Tom's Cabin* (Birdoff 257; Gossett 260, 371).

The "Tom troupes" took many liberties with the details of Stowe's novel, and some of the permutations of the play make more sense when considered, not in light of the novel, but in terms of the competition a traveling Tom troupe was likely to face on the road. Like circuses, Tom troupes would advertise appearances with a parade of the cast down small-town Main Streets, and some performances of the play even attempted to compete with circuses by including elephants and alligators. Horses and trained bloodhounds also were added to the play, most likely in response to the success of Wild West shows. In the 1880s "Double Mammouth" shows became popular. These shows brought the novelty of a two or three ring circus to the stage by "doubling" the most popular characters of the play. In a Double Mammouth performance there would be two Uncle Tom's, two Topsys, and two Marks (the latter was a minor character in Stowe's novel that became a substantial comedic role in the play) (Birdoff 297–98; Davis 358).

The popularity of *Uncle Tom's Cabin* at this time is a complex issue to account for. The play did not aim to arouse people over current events the way Stowe's novel did in the 1850s, but it did provide a range of pleasures for its audiences. Tracing its lineage back to Stowe, producers of the play offered it up as morally appropriate entertainment (an approach very similar to that of the Chautauquas) and sometimes recommended it as a lesson in history (much like Wild West shows). Yet at the same time the play constantly changed to offer new, spectacular features. Some versions featured electric lights as special effects. Others incorporated brass bands or choruses of African American "jubilee singers." Many simply replayed routines that had earlier become popular in Minstrel shows (with rare exceptions, black characters in the play were performed by white actors in blackface). During this period, *Uncle Tom's Cabin* told what had become a familiar, acceptable story that rarely made its largely white, Northern audience question itself. But it told that old story in a new way, bringing novelty to the city stage and the far reaches of rural America.

CONCLUSION: NOVELS OF THE INDUSTRIAL ERA

By the end of the nineteenth century, novels had become the most popular form of reading for Americans, accounting for more than a quarter of all books published in the United States. The invention of linotype in 1885, and falling paper and ink prices, brought down the price of books. High literacy rates, public investment in libraries, and increased education in the United States, all contributed to a growing audience for fiction. Throughout much of the industrial era, novels were still sold primarily through "subscription," a means of distribution that stretched back to the colonial period. Book agents would canvass door-to-door, bringing the latest novels, biographies, and their biggest sellers, Civil War histories. Book stores were not even allowed to sell copies of many books until subscription sales had been exhausted. European novels by writers such as Charles Dickens, Sir Walter Scott, and Charlotte Brontë remained popular, particularly in pirated editions that could be sold legally in the United States before the International Copyright Act was passed in 1891. American novelists often lamented the difficulty of making a living through fiction when they had to compete with cheap, pirated editions for which no author royalties were paid. Significantly, with the passage of copyright protection, American authors did begin to dominate the new "best-seller" lists that appeared after 1895, when pirated editions and reprints became illegal (Borus 38; Hart 150–53; Wilson 66, 74, 79).

The majority of novel readers were women (as has been the case throughout most of American history). During the industrial era, women, particularly those of the middle class, formed what was called "the backbone of the reading public" and played a vital role in forming book clubs and supervising their children's reading. Novel reading also rose in popularity among traveling businessmen. Train station bookstalls grew steadily as more people traveled by rail on a regular basis.

Though a range of Americans regularly read novels during this period, they were not necessarily reading the same novels. As with other forms of leisure, the types of novels people read tended (but only tended) to correspond with their social class. Some critics, such as Henry Nash Smith, have labeled the different types of novels at this time as highbrow, middlebrow, and lowbrow. But those terms, in addition to their offensive elitism, do not do justice to the variety of readers and writers at this time. For while it does make sense to distinguish between realist literary novels, popular novels, and dime novels, those categories of fiction do not easily match up with a corresponding readership of the upper class, the middle class and the working class. For example, among the cultural elite, European literature continued to hold greater prestige than American literature. Dime novels were a notorious "guilty pleasure" for middle-class readers. Popular novels of the period that are little read today, such as George du Maurier's *Trilby* or Kate Wiggin's *Rebecca of Sunnybrook Farm*, included among their enthusiastic readers, respectively, the writers Willa Cather and Jack London. Some realist novels, such as Edith Wharton's *The House of Mirth* and Frank Norris's *The Pit*, were popular enough to achieve best-seller status (Borus 105, 110–11; Denning 28; Hart 183; Hochman 7, 143n1).

The best known novels of the industrial era, those that are
Realist   still in print and are regularly taught in schools, are those
Novels   that are classified under the heading "realism" and include
Charles Chesnutt's *The Marrow of Tradition*, Stephen Crane's
The Red Badge of Courage, Henry James's *Portrait of a Lady*, and Mark
Twain's *Adventures of Huckleberry Finn*. Realism is in some ways an unfor-
tunate term, because it suggests that this type of novel simply sought to
show what was "really" going on in the world. The aim of realists was
more specific than that. Realist writers broke with the earlier romantic
view that people had essential, unchanging personalities (sometimes
called archetypes). Realists believed that physical and environmental conditions shaped people's characters and actions. The details of everyday
life mattered to realists not simply because they were "real," but because
they believed that those details conditioned people's specific personalities. It should come as no surprise that the rise of realism coincided with
the rise of sociology and the rapid growth of cities. Both the novels and
sociological studies of the period struggled to account for the effect of a
rapidly changing social landscape on Americans.

The major realist writers—including Chesnutt, Crane, Hamlin Garland,
William Dean Howells, James, Jack London, Frank Norris, Edith Wharton,
and Twain—also distinguished themselves in believing that the goal of
the novel was mimetic rather than moral; that is to say, they aimed to
show and explain the world they saw rather than the world as they
wished it could be. As Barbara Hochman notes, "Realist texts tended to
thrust their readers, unaccompanied, into a chaotic, sometimes violent
space, generally that of a contemporary American city, where an increasingly diverse population struggled for equilibrium" (50). Realist writers
focused almost exclusively on the time in which they lived and, though
they were rarely the most popular writers of the day, they have proved the
longest lasting (Borus 14; Wilson 11).

The most popular novels of the industrial era included
Popular   works that are little known today such as Winston
Novels   Churchill's *Richard Carvel*, Francis Marion Crawford's *A
Roman Singer*, and George du Maurier's *Trilby* (though the
central character of *Trilby*, the mesmerist Svengali, remains an iconic figure). Many popular writers confronted the same social problems that the
realists did, but offered different solutions. Some works harkened back to
what seemed easier times, as in the southern plantation of Joel Chandler
Harris's *Uncle Remus* collections and the old West in Helen Hunt Jackson's
historical romance *Ramona*. Other writers responded to religious skepticism by reaffirming Christian beliefs as in Henryk Sienkeiwicz's *Quo
Vadis?* and Lew Wallace's *Ben-Hur*. In general, popular writers assumed a
more personal tone with readers than did realists. Rather than document
rising social fragmentation, popular novelists tended to celebrate tight-
knit families and communities (Hart 163–68, 194–203; Hochman 50).

Dime novels, inexpensive mass market books that focused on exciting or sensational stories, have long been the black sheep of literature. Not atypically, James D. Hart has described them as "addressed to simple-minded people, **Dime Novels**

and therefore soon to become the property of children" (153). More recently, particularly in the work of Michael Denning, dime novels have been given greater consideration. The subjects of dime novels ranged from westerns to detective stories to tales of factory life and millionaires. Some were similar to television "movies of the week" in that they took on current events in fictionalized form. The trial of the Pennsylvania coal miners known as the Molly Maguires served as the subject of many dime novels. Train robbers and the men who pursued them were written about in books like *Frank Reade, The Inventor, Chasing the James Boys With His Steam Team.* Some characters spawned their own serials such as the 33 novels Edward L. Wheeler wrote about the cowboy Deadwood Dick between 1877 and 1884. Ninety-seven more novels about Deadwood Dick, Jr. were published between 1885 and 1894, though the authorship of these books remains unclear since Wheeler apparently died in 1885 (Brown 269–70; Denning 118).

Dime novels became increasingly popular in the industrial era, particularly as rising wages and falling production costs provided literate workers with disposable income for small purchases. Not all workers read dime novels, however. Many new immigrants did not have the facility with English to be dime novel readers. Denning argues that the main dime novel audience was young workers, particularly of Irish or German ethnicity, who lived in the cities and mill towns of the industrialized North and West. While dime novels rarely attempted to faithfully reproduce working-class life (as some realist novels did), they did often represent the concerns of their working-class readers, albeit in an allegorical form. Denning writes "What we find are less depictions of social classes than figures of social cleavage, less portraits of life in the factory than mythic landscapes of tramps and millionaires. Moreover, the dime novels that seem furthest from working-class life—from the 'legends of the Revolution' to the tales of western outlaws—are often told in accents of mechanics and laborers" (79–80). Dime novels appealed to their largely working-class readers because they presented a fantastic world in which contemporary social situations could be understood and often resolved more easily than in the actual world (Denning 45).

Mark Twain, the pen name taken by Samuel Clemens, is perhaps the most widely recognized author of the industrial era. His best known works today include *The Adventures of* **The Case of Mark Twain**

Tom Sawyer, Adventures of Huckleberry Finn, The Prince and the Pauper, and *A Connecticut Yankee in King Arthur's Court.* However, Twain was not a typical writer for the period. Raised in the Mississippi river town of Hannibal, Missouri, Twain worked in a variety of jobs before establishing himself as a newspaperman and, later, as a novelist and lecturer. He was a humorist as well as a cynic, a writer who celebrated traditional American ideals but was horrified by American imperialism, and, as an author, he sought to find success within an elite culture that he also frequently satirized. Twain was known during his lifetime primarily as a humorist, though he was respected as a realist by critics such as William Dean Howells. In works like *Adventures of Huckleberry Finn* (1884), Twain broke new boundaries by tackling questions of race and slavery little dealt with in fiction since the 1850s. He was also the first writer to successfully use a narrator who spoke colloquial American English in mainstream fiction. Many other writers had used characters who spoke non-standard dialects, but such speech usually marked these characters as less intelligent and different from likely readers. With Huck Finn, as can be seen in the excerpt on this page, American slang became part of literary culture.

"A MONSTROUS BIG RIVER DOWN THERE"

In the following excerpt, from the beginning of Chapter 19 of Mark Twain's *Adventures of Huckleberry Finn*, Huck, in his trademark ungrammatical English, describes floating down the Mississippi River on a raft with a fugitive slave, Jim.

Two or three days and nights went by; I reckon I might say they swum by, they slid along so quiet and smooth and lovely. Here is the way we put in the time. It was a monstrous big river down there—sometimes a mile and half wide; we run nights, and laid up and hid day-times; soon as night was most gone, we stopped navigating and tied up—nearly always in the dead water under a towhead; and then cut young cotton-woods and willows and hid the raft with them. Then we set out the lines. Next we slid into the river and had a swim, so as to freshen up and cool off; then we set down on the sandy bottom where the water was about knee deep, and watched the daylight come. Not a sound, anywheres—perfectly still—just like the whole world was asleep, only sometimes the bull-frogs a-cluttering, maybe.

—From Mark Twain, *Adventures of Huckleberry Finn* (1884), 156

Twain was an anomaly for his ability to work successfully in different genres and to appeal to a wide range of readers. For instance, *Adventures of Huckleberry Finn* was serialized in the established elite journal *Century* and then sold via the less respectable method of subscription sales. James D. Hart writes "Among the distinguished men of letters, only Mark Twain could flavor a realistic analysis of society with such romance as the people wanted" (189). On the other hand, Michael Denning calls Twain "the classic American writer closest to the dime novel in practice, influence, and audience...Indeed almost uniquely, Twain bridged the gap between the audiences of the cultivated novel and the dime novel" (208). Twain's domain ran the gamut from literary fiction to the popular romances to the terrain of the dime novel. At a time when the class divisions separating forms of leisure were increasing, Twain proved adept at crossing the line.

8

Education and Health Care

INTRODUCTION: THE GROWTH OF PUBLIC
EDUCATION AND PUBLIC HEALTH PROGRAMS

In many ways the story of health care advancements in the industrial era
is a story of education. The development of germ theory, combined with
the growing sanitation movement, translated into public health policies
that saved many from infectious diseases. A public education campaign
directed at mothers taught them the value of hand washing, sterilizing
bottles, and, by 1900, drinking homogenized milk. The education and
accreditation of medical personnel also became increasingly important.
Male physicians, trained in medical schools approved by the newly
formed American Medical Association, gradually replaced midwives and
homeopathic doctors.

At the same time, education in the United States became increasingly
centralized as cities collected taxes to support school districts and for-
malized requirements for new teachers. Schools, moreover, became central institutions for the dissemination of health care, social services, and
American culture. Urban schools, in particular, were charged with the
task of unifying an increasingly diverse population by establishing
kindergartens for poor children, teaching respect for authority and gen-
erosity toward the less privileged, and "Americanizing" new immigrants.

THE RISE OF THE SCHOOLMARM AND PUBLIC EDUCATION SYSTEMS

Concern for the moral education of young people played a crucial role in fostering the transition from the one-room schoolhouse to the centralized school system in the mid-nineteenth century. Horace Mann, the foremost proponent of public education during this period, called for a longer school term; typically, children attended school for only a few months during the winter and a month in the summer. He also criticized the impoverished schoolhouses, poorly trained teachers, and large, heterogeneous classes that characterized mid-nineteenth century education. Arguing that the schools were uniquely positioned to counter the antisocial tendencies of urbanization and industrialization, Mann devoted his life to the expansion and centralization of public education.

By 1870, most northern states collected taxes for the support of public education, had centralized school systems, and required specific training for teachers. High schools devoted to the training of teachers, called Normal Schools, sprang up during this time. Enrollment in the common schools, which included first through eighth grade, shot up, in part because parents looked to the public schools to provide children with opportunities for upward mobility. Wealthy parents also turned away from the private, residential academies that had previously educated many. These were increasingly seen as expensive, religiously sectarian, and educationally inferior. In Atlanta, for example, the city's burgeoning public school system, which was designed to culminate in the finest high school education available, drove nearly two-thirds of the city's 35 private schools out of business between 1872 and 1874 (Strickland 253).

Some parents, especially those who depended on their children's earnings, resisted the compulsory student attendance laws enacted toward the end of the century, but labor unions and middle-class reformers pushed for these laws. The labor unions saw compulsory student attendance laws as a way of diminishing low-paid competition from children for factory work and as a way of developing a less easily exploited workforce. Middle-class parents feared downward mobility and looked to public education as a means of empowering their children in the marketplace. The middle-class reformers who were the most visible proponents of public education also feared the consequences of poorly supervised children whose parents were working in factories. Idle adolescents who no longer worked on family farms or as apprentices were also a concern. They looked to the common schools and high schools to transmit a positive work ethic, respect for authority, and national loyalty (Katz 107–8; Pawa 296–97).

The rapid increase in enrollments put an enormous pressure on taxpayers. In the extreme example of fast-growing Chicago, public school enrollment shot up from 1,919 students in 1850 to 130,000 in 1888 (Button and

Enrollments in urban school districts grew so rapidly that some schools lacked even the essentials, such as desks, for their students. Jacob Riis photographed the Essex Market School in 1890 to show the limited opportunities available to the children of the poor on New York City's east side. (Courtesy Library of Congress)

Provenzo 133, 135). One solution to this burden was to hire female teachers. While male high school teachers started at a salary of $2,000 in 1880, female high school teachers started at $850 (133). Women had few occupational alternatives. They could work as domestic servants, mill hands, seamstresses, clerks, or prostitutes. As the century drew to a close, nursing also became an option for some. Among these positions, teaching carried the highest status. Moreover, the mission of schools, increasingly understood by middle-class reformers to be one of moral instruction, seemed best accomplished by women. As "angels in the home," women were considered morally superior to men. Many saw teaching as an extension of women's maternal role (Button and Provenzo 133, 135; Katz 99).

A DAY IN THE LIFE OF A GRAMMAR SCHOOL STUDENT

Children in industrial era classrooms were likely to sit in desks that were bolted to the floor, arranged in neat rows, and facing the teacher and blackboard at the front of the room. Having desks bolted to the floor minimized the noise of shuffling desks and contributed, in the eyes of educators, to an orderly classroom. Class size in the common schools was likely to exceed fifty students for a single teacher and include students of many ages and abilities. Because of the high student-teacher ratio and bolted desks, teachers generally relied upon exercises in which students read aloud and drills in which students repeated the teachers' words. Psychological thinking at the time reaffirmed the notion that children learned good habits through drills and rewards that conditioned their behaviors (Spring 208, 215).

Manual Training
As an extension of this emphasis on establishing good work habits and ethics, educators increasingly advocated manual training courses. As proponents would carefully argue, however, these courses were to be distinguished from trade schools. Advocates wanted it understood that they were not recommending a separate course of study for the children of unskilled workers that would prepare them for factory work and another course of study for the children of skilled workers or professionals that would prepare them for better paying, higher status positions. A two-tiered educational system smacked of Old World elitism and seemed incompatible with American democracy to many. For example, an 1896 Hartford committee recommending manual training courses wrote:

[A] manual training school is not a trade school. It does not teach a child a trade. It teaches him the use of quite a range of tools, of a large number of mechanical operations applicable to a considerable variety of materials, and gives him considerable knowledge of the qualities of those materials themselves. (Greene 10)

Boys were introduced to woodworking and ironworking, while girls were expected to sew and cook. In some schools, especially the institutes opened specifically for the education of Native Americans and African Americans, students were expected to spend a substantial part of their day farming. Ideally, manual training integrated hand and head work; far from replacing academic training, it more fully engaged students' interests.

However, in its early application, manual training was specifically directed to "the heathen and the savage" and "the vicious and defective" (Samuel Dutton qtd. in Lazerson, *Origins* 94). Both Hampton Institute, a Virginia school founded for the education of Native American and African American students, and Tuskegee, an Alabama school founded for the education of African Americans, expected students to defray the expense of their education by raising crops for the market. Male students at Hampton also worked in a sawmill and in the dining hall, while female students cleaned, washed clothes, cooked, sewed, and plowed the fields (Spring 181).

Samuel Armstrong, the white founder of Hampton Institute, believed manual education would not only teach important skills to emancipated

African Americans but would also improve their morals. Hampton's non-white students would learn self-discipline and the virtues of hard work through manual training (Watkins 47–49). Armstrong and his protégé, Booker T. Washington, founder of Tuskegee, scorned the classical education that they viewed as a "vanity" for nonwhite students. White benefactors like Andrew Carnegie applauded this accommodating approach to the limited economic and political opportunities available to nonwhite Americans. Significantly, only nonwhite students and juvenile delinquents were expected to do such work as a component of their education in the period leading up to the industrial era.

By the 1880s, manual training was touted as a solution to the special problems associated with educating mill children. Compulsory student attendance laws and child labor laws increased the number of textile mill workers who sent their children to school. By 1884, children under 12 were prohibited from working in the mills and children under 14 were required to attend school for 20 weeks before they were eligible for mill employment. While many families and employers evaded these laws, school attendance did increase among mill children. Still, many of these children

Founder Booker T. Washington (third from left in front row) and benefactor Andrew Carnegie (fourth from left in front row) are pictured at Tuskegee Institute, an African American industrial school in the heart of the black belt. (Courtesy Library of Congress)

attended school less frequently than their more financially stable neighbors and many worked part-time, coming to school tired and sometimes resentful. Consequently, they posed a challenge to teachers. To reduce truancy, capture student interest, and inculcate the moral lessons many educators thought were not transmitted in factory homes, Massachusetts introduced manual training into its public school curriculum in the 1880s (Lazerson, *Origins* 92–96). Because of a strong feeling against separate programs of study for students of different socio-economic backgrounds, Massachusetts, and other states in the northeast, introduced manual training into all of their schools.

Challenges to Rote Learning and Manual Training   By the end of the century, however, some education reformers challenged these prevailing ideas about human psychology and teaching methods. The monthly opinion magazine, *Forum*, hired a prominent pediatrician and education critic, Joseph Mayer Rice, to tour schools throughout the United States and report on the conditions he found. His series of nine articles spanning 1892–93 showed students bored and alienated by rote learning. They read aloud from primers like *McGuffey's Reader* that taught the virtues of hard work and respect for others through short, didactic pieces. Rice complained, "In no single exercise is a child permitted to think. He is told just what to say, and he is drilled not only in what to say, but also in the manner in which he must say it" (qtd. in Kaestle 72).

MCGUFFEY'S READER

First published in 1836, the *McGuffey's Reader* quickly became the most popular reader for school-aged children in the United States. At the peak of its sales, between 1870 and 1890, 60 million copies were sold (Spring 146). Children read aloud one- to three-page passages that conveyed moral lessons, especially those showing models of charity, self-denial, thrift, and hard work. The following lesson came from the second reader and was introduced in 1879 when the reader was extensively revised. A list of vocabulary with pronunciation symbols prefaced the story:

Lesson XIV

Henry, the Boot-Black

1. Henry was a kind, good boy. His father was dead, and his mother was very poor. He had a little sister about two years old.
2. He wanted to help his mother, for she could not always earn enough to buy food for her little family.
3. One day, a man gave him a dollar for finding a pocket-book which he had lost.
4. Henry might have kept all the money, for no one saw him when he found it. But his mother had taught him to be honest, and never to keep what did not belong to him.
5. With the dollar he bought a box, three brushes, and some blacking. He then went to the corner of the street, and said to every one whose boots did not look nice, "Black your boots, sir, please?"

6. He was so polite that gentlemen soon began to notice him, and to let him black their boots. The first day he brought home fifty cents, which he gave to his mother to buy food with.

7. When he gave her the money, she said, as she dropped a tear of joy, "you are a dear, good boy, Henry. I did not know how I could earn enough to buy bread with, but now I think we can manage to get along quite well."

8. Henry worked all the day, and went to school in the evening. He earned almost enough to support his mother and his little sister.

—From the *Annotated McGuffey*, 60–62

Even as Rice condemned prevailing teaching methods, John Dewey and other progressive educators were theorizing alternative methods of educating young people. Dewey's new techniques were premised on the idea that intellectual and social learning did and should occur simultaneously. He argued that studying the social context within which skills, concepts, and facts were relevant inspired more interest and creativity in students. In the University of Chicago's laboratory school, which was under Dewey's control, children worked in groups toward a common goal; four- and five-year-olds worked together to make their mid-morning meal. Older children learned to read, write, and do arithmetic by pretending to operate a dry goods store. In the process of learning these traditional subjects, they also learned to cooperate and to be responsible for individual tasks. Dewey aimed to develop students' "social imagination," their understanding of the relationship between individual occupations and community goals. He encouraged students to explore the connection between a specific culture's ideas or industries and the social forces that shaped those ideas and industries. Bolted desks and high student-teacher ratios limited the widespread application of Dewey's educational theories during the industrial era, but future generations of teachers adopted many of Dewey's theories (Spring 211–12, 215; Kaestle 74).

PUBLIC EDUCATION AND IMMIGRATION

The major social institutions bringing urban, industrial workers together were the saloons and churches, especially Catholic churches in the case of the new immigrants from southern and eastern Europe. To old stock, Protestant Americans, many of whom were caught up in the fervor of the temperance movement, these institutions threatened community order and undermined American capitalism. Increasingly, reformers looked to schools to provide new social centers in the urban areas and to "Americanize" the new immigrants. Schools embraced this role by adding many new features: kindergartens, playgrounds, auditoriums, and health facilities.

The kindergarten movement began in Germany in 1840 when Friedrich Froebel opened the first "garden of chil- **Kindergarten** dren." Young children were allowed to romp in gardens,

gently guided by elders who encouraged social interaction and the cultivation of plants. It was premised on a romantic concept that nature had
the capacity to draw forth children's innately good impulses. Children
required gentle guidance from maternal figures who designed forms of
play permitting the exercise of children's creative impulses. In the United
States, it was only widely implemented after the Civil War as a response to
the perception that city children were stunted in their moral and intellectual development because of their lack of exposure to nature and because
of their mothers' supposed distractions and ignorance. One advocate
explained the compensatory functions of kindergarten in this way:

[T]he great lack of most home life for our little ones is the lack of a proper place
and materials to carry out these creative instincts. Too often the mother, worried
and tried by many cares, has no leisure to devote to "play," and to her the kindergarten offers its fostering influences to her neglected child, where he finds every
means for his complete development. (Pardee 54)

Kindergartens were meant to benefit the children of the urban poor as
well as their families. Initially, kindergartens not only provided structured
play opportunities for children, they provided classes for mothers and

In this Washington, D.C., kindergarten, circa 1899, small children tended a vegetable garden. (Courtesy Library of Congress)

home visits where teachers observed the living conditions of their students. The kindergarten teacher often viewed herself as a missionary, giving lectures on proper food and clothing, cleaning standards, and childrearing methods. Corporal punishment of children was discouraged, while mothers were encouraged to create a neat and orderly environment in order to encourage self-discipline in children (Lazerson, *Urban Reform and the Schools* 122–23).

School playgrounds and libraries were to serve similar functions in urban areas. Both were supported by working-class parents who sought safe public spaces for their children, but the leaders who spearheaded campaigns for playgrounds and libraries tended to have other motivations. The "two-book" system in libraries, for example, was designed to foster what middle-class patrons believed were proper tastes in the working class. Believing fiction to have morally questionable effects upon readers, boards of education often required library patrons to check out a nonfiction book for every work of fiction they checked out (Button and Provenzo 164–65). Similarly, school playgrounds were designed to keep children away from the negative influences of the street. Reformers believed that street children learned to swear, smoke, or behave promiscuously through unsupervised contact with adults on the street. The playgrounds were to discourage juvenile delinquency—petty theft, gambling, drinking—by providing alternative activities. Initially, they were to be monitored so that children would develop good work habits through organized games that fostered a respect for the rules of the game and cooperation (Spring 203).

Playgrounds and Libraries

Public schools expanded their function in many ways; not only did they begin to educate pre–school age children and occupy the after-school hours of children, they also began to instruct the immigrant adults in the neighborhood. Public schools began offering evening classes in English, American history, and government, all necessary information for those wishing to become naturalized citizens. Their auditoriums also housed lectures and plays designed to offer alternatives to the saloon.

Public School Expansion into Family and Community Life

The distinctive cultures and values of new immigrants were little valued in late nineteenth-century America, and schools explicitly embraced their mission of Americanizing immigrants. The immigrant child's first encounter with the teacher often involved Anglicizing his or her name. A Lithuanian named Yekl might become Jake; a Greek girl named Despina might become Debbie. Joel Spring comments:

There is little doubt that most immigrant groups flocked to the schools, but on their arrival there, they often found a great deal of hostility toward their language and customs. Immigrant children found their names being Anglicized and were frequently told not to speak the language of their parents and to forget their native customs. In these situations, Americanization meant cultural imperialism and the building of a national spirit that was suspicious of foreign countries and ways of living. (206)

Feeding this culture of suspicion was the belief that the new immigrants came with values that threatened the stability of American society. Socialism, communism, and Catholicism were believed by some to be antithetical to American liberty and democracy. Consequently, American history books and even the primers children recited from presented a negative view of these beliefs. The Roman Catholic Church was associated with a corrupt, authoritarian hierarchy and a deliberate policy of keeping their congregants ignorant. Socialism and communism were associated with lawlessness and mob rule.

Some cultures responded by rejecting the public schools. In 1887, the Roman Catholic Church instituted a new rule, requiring each parish to house a Catholic elementary school. Even before that, Catholic parishes often erected separate Catholic schools before they had even built their churches. These schools frequently taught children in their parents' language and defended Catholic creeds and practices in the face of significant anti-Catholic feeling in the United States. However, most immigrant groups embraced the public schools, despite the threat they posed to the transmission of old country traditions and beliefs.

RELIGIOUS FREEDOM AND *MCGUFFEY'S READER*

The anti-Catholic and anti-Jewish nature of some pieces from the *McGuffey Reader* provoked criticism from defenders of religious freedom. One such critic, Joseph Brandon, a Jewish immigrant to San Francisco, published an 1875 pamphlet inveighing against the custom of having children recite the Lord's Prayer in school and having them read aloud religiously sectarian pieces. He condemned several entries in the reader, most especially one about the crucifixion of Jesus:

One of these choice extracts is as follows. (A blind preacher is relating the sufferings of Jesus—spoken of, as a matter of course, as "our Savior"): "His enunciation was so deliberate that his voice trembled on every syllable; and every heart in the assembly trembled in unison. His peculiar phrases had that force of description that the original scene appeared to be at that moment acting before our eyes. We saw the very faces of the Jews; the staring, frightful distortion of malice and rage. We saw the buffet. My soul kindled with a flame of indignation, and my hands were involuntarily and convulsively clenched."

It is from McGuffey's Fifth Reader, from which limpid stream of knowledge the gallant and impulsive Christian mariner, who so violently and unprovokedly assaulted the Chatham-street dealer in gentlemen's habiliments, must evidently have "drunk deep."

If deemed necessary to convey such instruction as is contained in the foregoing extract as a fortifier of faith in Christianity, one would think it had better be given in the Sunday or denominational schools, and not in the public ones, which should be the places where our

children should be Americanized, and all old sectarian hate be allayed.
—From "A Protest against Sectarian Texts in California Schools in 1875"

WOMEN'S EDUCATION

Prior to the industrial era in the United States, a range of educational options existed for girls. Most northern and western girls began their schooling alongside boys in the common schools that educated children up until eighth grade. Because there were few public schools in the South, southerners who were wealthy often hired private tutors or sent their children to private boarding schools. The vast majority of girls finished their educations at this point, though some proceeded on to academies or seminaries.

Education for girls gained esteem throughout the nineteenth century. The United States dropped property requirements for male voters early in the century, causing many to fear "mob rule." Education was deemed crucial in training voters without property to subordinate their short-term, individual interests to those of the "permanent classes," property-holders. Women, who themselves could not vote, were charged with the increasingly important task of training young citizens. Teaching in the common schools was considered a direct outgrowth of women's traditional child-care responsibilities. In order to develop a democratic culture, women had to do more than nurture the bodies and spirits of their children; they had to train children to be the enlightened citizens required in a successful democracy.

The ladies' academies that attracted wealthy girls generally taught fine arts and decorative crafts such as the piano, voice, drawing, and penmanship. Founders of the ladies' academies developed a curriculum that would foster gracious hostesses and pleasing wives. **Academies and Seminaries**

To signal a difference from these "finishing schools" for the wealthy, many schools had adopted the title "female seminaries" by the mid-nineteenth century. At female seminaries, women faculty taught girls the English curriculum: history, philosophy, modern languages, and natural sciences. Faculty also taught domestic arts such as sewing, managing the family budget, and caring for the sick (H. L. Horowitz 11).

In the 1820s and 1830s, Zilpah Grant and Mary Lyon developed the model for female seminaries that was followed through the 1870s. They established a system of external and internal discipline that was to create strong, independent women who could resist the lure of marriage in favor of a life of teaching or missionary work in the public sphere. Bells to mark transition periods and constant supervision ordered the students' days. The faculty supplemented these with "section meetings" and periods of private meditation that were to inculcate an internal sense of discipline. At the section meetings, students were required to confess publicly to any infractions such as whispering in class (H. L. Horowitz 15).

Mary Lyon's Mount Holyoke was housed in a single, large building where all classes were held and where students and faculty all lived. In the single building students were constantly monitored; they were required, for example, to leave their bedroom doors open at bedtime and were forbidden from visiting with one another. Every few months students changed roommates so that they would not become overly attached to other students. Instead, they developed intense mother-daughter bonds with their teachers, who directed them toward lives of public leadership as missionaries and teachers (H. L. Horowitz 17).

Mount Holyoke, with its commitment to fostering the development of public women, was organized in a far different way than male colleges and universities. It gave its students far less independence than men's colleges, which expected students to live apart from faculty, move freely between classes, and develop a relatively autonomous student culture. Moreover in curriculum, there were no female seminaries equivalent to the male-only colleges and universities that expected their graduates to become knowledge producers and national leaders. Between the opening of Vassar College in 1865 and Barnard College in 1889, Mount Holyoke's ideal for creating female public leaders would be tested and transformed (H. L. Horowitz 4).

The First Female Colleges and the "New Woman" After the Civil War, visionary founders established the remaining six of the "Seven Sisters" colleges that transformed women's higher education in America. The Seven Sisters included: Mount Holyoke, Vassar College, Wellesley College, Smith College, Radcliffe College, Bryn Mawr University, and Barnard College.

Vassar College pioneered a truly college course of study, dispensing with courses in the domestic arts, hiring male faculty, and requiring female students to meet the same standards that men in college met. Wellesley College rejected Mount Holyoke's architecture, with its provisions for constant supervision. Women had more opportunities to form friendships and a student culture. By the time Smith College opened its doors in 1875, the all-female social life of the other women's colleges had become a source of concern for many. Some believed it caused too much stress for women to study and eat in large groups with little opportunity for more intimate socializing. Moreover, with little chance of seeing men, either in church or in public space, some suggested women were tempted to "vices of body and imagination" (H. L. Horowitz 75). In other words, they turned their passionate feelings toward other women in the absence of men. Moreover, these "unnatural" women developed visions for social action and reform, critics claimed, that unfit them for the domestic sphere. Smith College sought to rectify this by exchanging the single, multipurpose seminary building for an academic building surrounded by smaller residential cottages. Smith had no chapel or library, expecting students to walk to town for Sunday services and books. Bryn Mawr became the first of the women's colleges to be modeled on the university, expecting faculty to do original research and opening graduate programs. To make time for such research, neither male nor female faculty members were expected to monitor students.

These changes made it possible for women to form an autonomous student culture that often challenged the missionary purposes of the original founders. Mount Holyoke, Wellesley, and Smith were explicitly established to spread the evangelical message of the conservative Congregational church. As more wealthy families began sending their daughters to these colleges and as some of the colleges developed differing levels of housing—Bryn Mawr offered suites with fireplaces to those who could pay significantly higher fees—social lives became far more segregated by wealth. At Wellesley, trustees granted exclusive clubs, the precursors of sororities, the right to build their own houses and select residents. In modest dormitories elsewhere on campus, those who could not afford the full residential fees served food and washed dishes to defray expenses.

Stories of female college life at the turn of the century reveal that the ideal college woman was a vigorous, talented, group-spirited leader. This "new woman" excelled in the university's basketball and rugby games, their theatrical productions (in which women frequently dressed as men and played men's roles), their debating clubs, or their literary magazine or newspaper. Female college life inspired erotic attractions among students, many of whom understood this leadership ideal to also be a masculine ideal. Women developed "crushes" on other women and sent them flowers and letters in which they wrote admiringly of the beloved's beauty. Frequently, such crushes involved differences in power; a younger girl would develop a fascination for an older girl she admired and wished to pattern herself after. The desire to be accepted into particular social clubs and thus climb the social ladder likely accentuated a young collegian's feelings (H. L. Horowitz 163–69).

Despite concerns about "unnatural" feelings between women, most late-nineteenth-century Americans understood female affections to be far less sexual than male affections. Female friendships could constitute crushes and love without being homosexual as we understand the term today. Most female professionals believed their careers were incompatible with marriage. Frequently, female professors and social workers developed intense professional and personal partnerships with other women who shared their work. Women formed "Boston marriages" in which they lived together the bulk of their adult lives. Even while the "crush" carried overtones of slavish devotion and immaturity, and college women increasingly condemned such crushes, they generally respected the attachments their female professors had to other women. From the 1870s through the 1920s, 40 to 60 percent of female college graduates did not marry and many of these women became leaders of educational and social reform movements (Smith-Rosenberg, "The New Woman as Androgyne" 253).

In 1870, only 11,000 women attended seminaries or colleges (H. L. Horowitz 56). That changed by 1900 with the growth of these competitive female colleges and with the growing opportunities for women in the prestigious male colleges. Cornell admitted women and Harvard and Columbia both opened female annexes by 1889. Radcliffe, Harvard's female annex, and Barnard, Columbia's female annex, offered courses enrolling only women but taught by the Harvard and Columbia faculty and using the same exams. By 1900 the Seven Sisters colleges all enrolled hundreds each fall, and many more state universities and private colleges began to admit women. By 1910, women comprised 40 percent of undergraduates in the United States (Cott, *Grounding* 40). This is particularly striking given how few Americans had the privilege of attending college; fewer than 4 percent of those aged 18–21 were enrolled in 1900 (40). These "new women" formed the core of the twentieth-century public health movement, which reduced the incidence of infectious diseases in the United States and established worker safety regulations.

MEDICAL CARE: INDUSTRIAL ERA THREATS TO HEALTH

The primary threats to human health in the industrial era were from infectious diseases, especially pneumonia, influenza, tuberculoses, and gastroenteritis (Grob 192). Children were the primary victims of infectious disease because they were more susceptible to the bacteria in contaminated milk and water supplies and because they faced dreaded childhood illnesses such as measles, scarlet fever, diphtheria, and whooping cough. In 1900, 19 percent of Massachusetts's infants died before their first birthday (192). Those who survived childhood were generally people who had successfully weathered and developed immunities to these common infections.

Pulmonary disorders, especially tuberculosis, were the largest single killer of adults in the era (Grob 114). Historian Gerald Grob attributes the high level of pulmonary disorders to harmful dusts in mines, factories, and workshops (165). Miners, textile operatives, packinghouse workers, metal workers, hat makers, wallpaper manufacturers—in all about 10 percent of workers were exposed to harmful levels of metallic, mineral, or organic dust (165). Lead, mercury, and arsenic—which were used in the manufacture of hats, paint and wallpaper—sickened and killed many. The extraordinarily high rates of black lung disease among miners and tuberculosis among textile workers were the result of high levels of dust in the atmosphere of their working environments.

Other workplace sources of injury and fatality included industrial accidents. Mine collapses, violent furnace blasts in steel plants, and lost digits or infected cuts in packinghouses all led to increased rates of workplace injury. Between 1870 and 1910, the number of people employed in mining and manufacturing, the most hazardous job environments, had quadrupled, rising from 2,930,000 to 11,580,000 (Grob 172). In the absence of safety and health regulations or legal precedents for suing employers, manufacturers did little to protect the well-being of their employees. Gerald Grob notes:

It is ironic that the material progress characteristic of nineteenth-century America failed to translate into better health.... The concurrence of increasing prosperity and declining health poses a fascinating problem, for it runs counter to the intuitive and widely held belief that a rising standard of living leads to the improvement of health. (122)

To account for that irony, we have to consider the changes in living and working patterns as well as a culture that, at times, discouraged even those habits widely regarded as healthful.

INFECTIOUS DISEASES AND THE SANITARY MOVEMENT

As this volume's chapter on the city shows, the increased concentration of people in urban areas led to sanitation problems that created ideal circumstances for the spread of disease. Crowded tenements with poor ventilation proved to be fertile ground for contagious illnesses, especially the childhood diseases and influenza mentioned above. Moreover, polluted wells, located alongside outdoor privies, caused gastrointestinal diseases like diarrhea, typhoid fever, and cholera. It was only with the concerted efforts of sanitation reformers that cities undertook the large-scale engineering projects necessary for protecting the health of urban dwellers.

Ironically, before the 1880s, sanitation reformers believed dirt or even foul odors caused disease and their efforts were directed toward minimizing these (Rosen 222; Melosi 12). The effect was that cities invested in a number of crucial reforms that improved urban health without quite understanding how these reforms worked. For example, cities invested in street cleaning, which had a minimal effect on health, as well as a clean, centralized water supply, which saved the lives of many. Prior to the discovery of bacteria as the root source of many deadly diseases, the sanitation movement initiated widespread reforms in urban infrastructure and in living habits that improved the health of many.

Cities established public health departments and charged departments of education with the task of improving the health of cities. City health departments inspected private properties to make sure they were complying with sanitation guidelines, and toured streets, making sure nuisances like dead horses, horse dung, and garbage were removed. They also provided free smallpox vaccines, the first vaccine to become widely available, to recent immigrants and school children (Cassedy 110). Medical inspections of school children were systematically introduced in Boston in 1894, initially to control an outbreak of diphtheria, and made permanent to combat malnutrition and a host of communicable illnesses such as measles, scarlet fever, skin diseases, and eye diseases. By 1897, Philadelphia, Chicago, and New York had also established such inspections (Rosen 342–43).

MEDICAL ADVICE LITERATURE AND THE GROWTH OF THE AMERICAN MEDICAL ASSOCIATION

Until the last few years of the nineteenth century, physicians could actually do very little to cure illness. Antibiotics did not yet exist and surgical techniques were as yet relatively primitive. At worst, physicians prescribed highly addictive medications to relieve pain and discomfort, treatments that often proved worse than the symptoms they were meant to alleviate. At best, they could advise individuals on how to prevent disease or injury, and in this field they were challenged by the extensive advice literature of the period.

One health advisor of the era declared the impotence of doctors and medicines in this way, "There is no curative "virtue" in medicines, nor in anything outside of the vital organism.... Health is found only in obedience to the laws of the vital organism. Disease is the result of disobedience" (Russel T. Trall qtd. in Fellman and Fellman 26). In other words, only by living a healthful life could one hope to recover from disease; many believed the intervention of medicine or doctors was useless.

Another advisor, J.R. Black, devised this list of "The Ten Laws of Health," clearly modeled on the Ten Commandments (39):

I.   Breathing a pure air.
II.   Adequate and wholesome food and drink.
III.   Adequate out-door exercise.
IV.   Adequate and unconstraining covering for the body.
V.   The exercise of the sexual function only for, and no interferences with, the natural course of reproduction.
VI.   A Habitation in the climate for which the constitution of the body is adapted.
VII.   Pursuits which do not cramp or overstrain any part of the body, or subject it to irritating and poisonous substances.
VIII.   Personal cleanliness.
IX.   Tranquil state of the mind, and adequate rest and sleep.
X.   No intermarriage of blood relations.

These laws were specifically directed at what many authors of medical advise literature saw as dangerous practices. The fifth "law," for example, reflected the fear that native-born, white women were avoiding pregnancy and thus undermining the dominance of white Protestants in the nation. This fear led to passage of the Comstock law in 1873 forbidding the dissemination of birth control information via the mail. It also contributed to the anti-abortion movement between 1860 and 1880. The American Medical Association, along with the Roman Catholic Church and individual Protestant clergymen, successfully lobbied for criminalizing abortion in the first four months of pregnancy (Smith-Rosenberg, "The Abortion Movement" 218). One might similarly read the sixth law as a warning against the immigration of people from warmer climates, notably southern Europeans and African Americans from the South, to the temperate states in the northeast and upper Midwest.

The American Medical Association was formed in response to several factors, including this perception that physicians' interventions were costly and often ineffectual. Leading physicians formed the American Medical Association in order to more tightly regulate the education and licensing of doctors, to combat competition from "irregulars" like midwives and homeopathic physicians, and to enhance the prestige of the field (Cassedy 90; Smith-Rosenberg 232–33). While it included only 8,000 members by 1900, its leaders successfully initiated medical school reforms and it was poised to become a very powerful organization in the coming decades.

PUBLIC HEALTH AND MOTHERS

In the absence of effective treatments for the cure of infectious disease, public health campaigns focused on containing infectious diseases, especially with the cooperation of mothers. Because young children were especially vulnerable to infectious disease, protecting their food and drink, as well as their immediate environment, became a top priority for public health campaigns.

Many believed that the protection of children began with the protection of the future mother's body prior to pregnancy. Dress reform, as well as the diatribes leveled at women's education, were both aimed at improving maternal health. A belief that "brain work" would deprive the uterus of needed blood and energy, led many to recommend a less intellectually demanding course of study for women.

Dress Reform

Female leaders, however, often looked elsewhere to explain women's complaints. They blamed women's poor health on the deforming and restrictive dress fashions of the era. Tightly laced corsets simultaneously pushed the breasts up, cinched the waist, and compressed the reproductive organs. Bustles, attached to the waistband of a dress, gave the illusion of wide hips, suggesting fertility. Heavy skirt hoops, made of wood, metal, or bone, along with several layers of petticoats, pushed the woman's skirts

By compressing the waist, corsets pushed down on a woman's reproductive organs, causing injuries, and they prohibited exercise because women could not take deep breaths. (Courtesy Library of Congress)

outward. The effect was to give the illusion of ample hips and breasts, good for bearing and feeding a child. The reality was that the style caused physical distortions and damaged a woman's general health, ironically undermining her ability to bear children (Green 122–23).

Dress reformers advocated shorter skirts as well as the elimination of corsets for easier mobility. Catherine Beecher, in her frequently republished 1869 guide, *The American Woman's Home,* commented:

This pressure of the upper interior organs upon the lower ones, by tight dress, is increased by the weight of clothing resting on the hips and abdomen. Corsets, as usually worn, have no support from the shoulders, and consequently all the weight of the dress resting upon or above them presses upon the hips and abdomen, and this in such a way as to throw out of use and thus weaken the most important supporting muscles of the abdomen, and impede abdominal breathing. (161)

The corset could cause a prolapsed uterus, a uterus that had been pushed down into the vagina, causing discomfort and menstrual difficulties. To combat this, women sometimes wore pessaries, devices inserted into the vagina to hold up the uterus. These were made out of a range of materials, including rubber, ivory, wood, or steel. Pessaries that were left for long periods in the body or were seldom cleaned often caused internal infections.

Gastrointestinal diseases were the number one cause of death among infants aged under one year, accounting for 25 percent of infant deaths even as late as 1900 (Grob 193). The reason for this was that infants who were not breast-fed lived on cow's milk that was often contaminated.

Responses to Contaminated Milk

Cows could transmit infectious diseases to infants. Stored in unsterilized bottles, milk quickly turned sour en route to market where unscrupulous grocers disguised it with chemicals. Poor families seldom had refrigeration and may have found milk so expensive that they diluted it down with water from contaminated wells. One expert commented, "A city's milk supply is so often richer in bacteria than its sewage" (qtd. in Golden 132).

Because of the connection between bottle-feeding and very high rates of infant mortality, mothers were heavily encouraged to breastfeed. Sometimes, however, mothers could not or would not nurse their infants. Doctors and advice columnists often railed against the society matron who didn't want to be restricted by a demanding infant or who believed nursing would damage her figure. Other babies were born to women who soon died or who were too sick to nurse. These children, if they were born to wealthy families, might be protected if the family could hire a wet nurse, a mother who was lactating and could breastfeed the family's baby. Studies indicate the majority of wet nurses were poor women who were either single mothers, deserted, or widowed (Golden 106–7). Often they were recruited from infant asylums and lying-in hospitals catering to "fallen women." In these institutions, single mothers and impoverished women who could not afford home care were given free or subsidized care. They could pay for their care by hiring out as a wet nurse, but because most families wanted women to come without their own infants, they had to leave their babies, generally to be bottle-fed. One physician lamented that "by the sacrifice of the infant of the poor woman, the off-spring of the wealthy will be preserved" (Charles West qtd. in Golden 97).

To reduce infant mortality, the newly created New York City Health Department issued a leaflet on infant care and distributed it door to door in 1874 (Rosen 223). Visiting nurses in major cities spoke to families in their homes or children in school about cleanliness and hygiene, and they also urged breastfeeding (Cassedy 111). Because of contamination, cities increasingly took responsibility for regulating milk supplies. New York City was a leader; philanthropist Nathan Strauss established milk stations in 1893 that provided pasteurized milk, modified for young infants and sold at a discount in nursing bottles. The city of Rochester, New York, was the first city to provide milk stations as a public service and other cities soon followed. Nursing stations became places where experts gave mothers advice about caring for infants and where infants were regularly weighed to monitor their health (Rosen 331). With these efforts to make cow's milk safer and with significant public disapproval of wet-nursing, the number of wet nurses quickly dwindled throughout the period and by 1897 there were only a handful of advertisements in major Boston and Philadelphia newspapers for wet-nursing positions (Golden 68–69).

INSTITUTIONAL HEALTH CARE

General hospitals were relatively rare in 1870, when there were slightly over 100, but by 1920 there were over 6,000 general and specialty hospitals (Cassedy 73). One reason for the tremendous growth of hospitals was their growing acceptance by the middle class, especially middle-class women, who by the end of the industrial era began to give birth in hospitals. Initially, the growth in hospitals stemmed from the transformation of almshouses into hospitals serving the poor whose contagious illnesses posed a serious hazard to densely populated cities. But at the beginning of the period, physicians' ignorance of germ theory proved deadly to patients who frequently succumbed to infections contracted in the hospital. Middle-class patients began seeing physicians in hospitals when improved antiseptic procedures made hospitals safer. By the end of the century, physicians began washing their hands and sterilizing their instruments before surgery (92). The development of anesthesia, x-rays, and laboratory diagnostics made diagnoses more reliable and surgery less frightening (93).

While general hospitals mushroomed, much of the new building occurred through private investment, churches, and philanthropists (Cassedy 74). According to Gerald Grob, the largest _public_ social welfare investment of the nineteenth century was in mental hospitals (Lightner 149). A champion of the mentally ill, Dorothea Dix campaigned for state investments in mental asylums where patients would be humanely treated rather than restrained and isolated. Because many associated mental illness with "over-civilization," it was considered a by-product of industrialization and a public responsibility. Dix traveled through prisons, identifying the mentally ill and arguing for their transfer to mental asylums.

CONCLUSION

Increased respect for specialized experts and greater investment in public institutions dramatically changed and centralized the fields of education and health care. Teachers and doctors had to meet standardized training requirements, assuring a more consistent standard of education and health care. Public institutions that had at one time been shunned by the middle class were now embraced.

While many historians have argued that public schools, mental asylums, and lying-in hospitals for new mothers were used as instruments of social control, they were also empowering. Public schools "Americanized" immigrants, but they also offered important skills for success in the large, impersonal urban workforce. Public schools taught the working class to respect authority, but the best also gave them the skills to read widely and think critically about labor unions and monopoly capitalism. Lying-in hospitals often coerced women to nurse infants who were not theirs in order to make the money to support their own infants, but at the same time they cared for women who often had nowhere else to turn during their convalescence. Mental hospitals often isolated the homeless or those deemed sexual deviants, but at the same time they offered treatment to those who were languishing in prisons. Many were protected and even empowered by these burgeoning, centralized social institutions.

9

Religious and Civic Life

INTRODUCTION

Both religious and civic life during the industrial era involved people coming together in groups to address issues, whether social or theological, which were understood to be of more than just personal concern. In fact, there were often close connections of religion, ethnicity, and work that drew people together or set them against one another. A vibrant religious and civic culture had long been a hallmark of American life, as was noted by Alexis de Tocqueville in *Democracy in America*:

The Americans make associations to give entertainments, to found seminaries, to build inns, to construct churches, to diffuse books, to send missionaries to the antipodes; in this manner they found hospitals, prisons, and schools...Wherever at the head of some new undertaking you see the government in France, or a man of rank in England, in the United States you will be sure to find an association. (106)

However, the United States in the industrial era had changed in some important ways since the 1830s, when de Tocqueville toured the nation. For example, governments played a more prominent role in large-scale undertakings, particularly in urban areas, and religious and civic organizations differed in their capacity to adapt to the waves of immigrants who brought new beliefs and traditions with them. But, in a general sense, de Tocqueville's earlier observations could be applied to much of American life from 1870 to 1900, as a strong sense of community still informed much of everyday experience.

RELIGION IN THE INDUSTRIAL ERA

Leading Protestant denominations entered the industrial era already deeply divided by the Civil War and prewar controversies over slavery and theology. Baptists and Methodists had split into Northern and Southern branches in 1845, and two separate groups of Presbyterians also divided sectionally in the years before the war. However, though religious life in America may have seemed divisive in the aftermath of the Civil War, it was relatively unified compared to the transformation of the country's religious life by the turn of the twentieth century. Rising immigration and urbanization during the industrial era created a more diverse religious landscape. The Roman Catholicism and Judaism practiced by many immigrants challenged many Americans' definition of the United States as a "Protestant nation." Many Catholics and Jews struggled between desires to maintain their religious practices and aspirations to become "Americanized." One of the historical ironies of this period is that the rise of competing religious traditions had the effect of minimizing sectarian differences among many Protestants. As the population of U.S. Catholics grew rapidly, many Protestants felt that Catholic religious practices threatened fundamental American institutions such as public schools (Christiano 140; Williams 286).

THE LARGEST RELIGIOUS DENOMINATIONS IN 1895

The U.S. census first took note of religious membership in 1890. Though exact statistics may be elusive (for example, membership was defined differently in different denominations), H.K. Carroll built upon the census data to establish the following snapshot of religious participation in the United States in 1895.

Denomination	Membership
1. Catholic	8,014,911
2. Methodist	5,452,654
3. Baptist	4,068,539
4. Presbyterian	1,458,999
5. Lutheran	1,390,775
6. Disciples of Christ	923,663
7. Episcopalian	626,290
8. Congregationalist	600,000
9. Reformed	343,981
10. United Brethren	262,950
11. Latter-Day Saints	234,000
12. Evangelical	145,904
13. Jewish	139,500
14. Friends	114,771

(rpt. in Gaustad 91–92)

Across denominational lines, many Americans applied their religious beliefs to the households they formed. As Colleen McDannell argues, "The belief that the home served as the nursery of the nation and the God-given foundation of society was held in common by Protestants and Catholics, clergy and laity" (72). Religious principles impacted daily decisions made by many Americans and shaped household experience. Despite many shared concerns, however, religious life during the industrial era was characterized by greater diversity than had ever been seen in the United States.

PROTESTANTISM

By the beginning of the industrial era, the rigid Calvinism associated with Puritan settlers as well as with eighteenth century theologians such as Jonathan Edwards no longer defined American Protestantism. As Ann Douglas notes, "By 1875, American Protestants were much more likely to define their faith in terms of family morals, civic responsibility, and above all, in terms of the social function of churchgoing. Their actual creed was usually a liberal, even a sentimental one for which Edwards and his contemporaries would have felt scorn and horror" (7). Under what was termed "liberal theology," the world was seen as a fundamentally good

An 1878 lithograph of church members attending a Watch meeting in winter. (Courtesy Library of Congress)

and benevolent place, not as a battleground between good and evil. Over time, this orientation led to the development of the early twentieth century movement termed the Social Gospel that called on followers to improve social conditions on the basis of religious principles. However, the emergence of Protestant Fundamentalism in the industrial era was in many ways a response to and repudiation of liberal theology.

Home and Family Worship   For many Protestants, the industrial era was marked by a privatization of religion. The home became a central site of religious worship, and decisions about running a household took on an increasingly theological bent. As McDannell writes, "By linking morality and religion with the purchase and maintenance of a Christian home, the Victorians legitimized acquisition and display of domestic goods" (49). Decorating decisions took on much greater importance when they were seen to reflect one's religious beliefs and principles.

Within this new religious context, women assumed a central role. Not only was the decoration and upkeep of the home understood to be primarily their responsibility, but so too was the religious upbringing of children. A "proper" home was understood to operate as a positive influence, particularly on children. Of course, judging a person's devotion on the basis of her or his household had a tendency to make distinctions of social class loom large, and made it easy for poverty to be judged not as simply a lack of material goods but as a reflection of one's moral and religious state (McDannell 51).

It was common for middle-class Protestant families to conduct some kind of daily or twice-daily family worship, though evidence would indicate that the actual practice of this worship often varied from its ideal. In the ideal setting, family worship operated as a continuation of the church. At a set time (usually after a meal) the family would gather for prayer, hymn singing, and a scriptural reading, led by the father of the household reading from a family Bible. Bibles were accorded a place of prestige within the household. In practice, family worship varied widely in formality and frequency. Writers advised against long-winded sermons from fathers and warned against holding services near the bedtime of small children, which suggests that both may have been regular occurrences (McDannell 79–83).

The contrast between the ideal role played by the father in daily worship and the centrality of the mother in religious matters is indicative of larger contradictions over religion and gender in the industrial era. While women had gained more control over religious life, religion shrank in overall importance in the culture at large, leading to a series of concerns that were played out in the foundation of Protestant Fundamentalism.

Fundamentalism   Fundamentalism began as a middle-class Protestant movement. Though in some ways a continuation of evangelical beliefs, it countered the dominant liberal theology, by insisting on the "inerrancy" of the Bible in all matters including those of science and history. Despite its doctrinal rigidity, fundamentalism was an interdenominational movement, bringing together a range of groups (though primarily Baptists and Presbyterians) to events like the annual Niagara Bible Conference, which began in 1876 (Williams 274–76).

Historians have also argued that fundamentalism was a response to the increasing prominence of women in mainstream Protestant denominations and the disruption of traditional gender roles under industrialism. Betty A. DeBerg claims that while fundamentalist leaders still "championed the home as the bastion of true religion," they also "waged a passionate battle for control of the church against both modernists and women and promoted a manly Christianity to replace the practices of feminized evangelical Christianity" (97). Fundamentalist clergy were to be models of traditional masculinity, and the position of women within these denominations was much more limited than in mainstream Protestant churches (86).

ROMAN CATHOLICISM

Catholics in America during the industrial era were the most ethnically diverse religious group, consisting of large populations of ethnic Germans, Irish, Italians, and Poles. Though Germans had been the main Catholic ethnic group early in the nineteenth century (and Southern and Eastern Europeans made up the majority of Catholic immigrants at the end of the century), the unprecedented wave of Irish immigration during and after the great potato famine made the Irish the dominant ethnic group within American Catholicism. By 1886, one-half of U.S. Catholic bishops were of Irish ancestry, though they led an increasingly diverse denomination (McDannell xvi, 15; Williams 293).

Unlike Protestant denominations that were usually linked by geographical or linguistic similarities (most Episcopalians were ethnically British; most Lutherans could trace their ancestry to German-speaking regions), and without a Jewish sense of a shared history experience, there was little to intrinsically unify Catholics in America. Though the Catholic hierarchy in Rome aimed to serve as a centralizing force, the animosity directed toward Catholics in a country dominated by evangelical Protestants did more than anything else to develop a shared Catholic culture (Williams 292).

Serving largely poor, immigrant communities, the parish emerged as the central institution, particularly for Irish Catholics. Parishes played a variety of social roles, serving not only as a religious center, but also as marker of an ethnic community's establishment (hence the naming of many parishes after ethnically identified saints, such as St. Patrick, St. Anthony, and St. Stanislaus). In an era prior to the creation of a welfare state, parishes also became vital social service organizations, meeting

Catholic priest at confirmation or girls' first communion. (Courtesy Library of Congress)

material needs of their parishioners. The parish played a crucial role both in integrating immigrants into the mainstream of American life and in providing a space apart from that mainstream where ethnic traditions could be maintained (McDannell 65).

The parish assumed an even more prominent position in the daily life of American Catholics following the 1884 decision by American Catholic Bishops to require all parishes to run their own parochial elementary school, superceding even the construction of churches. This decision led to a tripling of Catholic school enrollment between 1880 and 1910. It was not uncommon during this time for priests to have to say mass in school auditoriums or gymnasiums that had been completed before churches had actually been built (McDannell 15, 75).

Though the parish superceded the house as a religious site for most Catholics, the same sensibility that led many Protestants to consciously try to create a "Christian home" had a Catholic equivalent. Small altars and holy water fonts became part of some homes (and wealthy Catholics even built their own in-house chapels). Religious engravings and lithographs also proved popular, and it was not uncommon to see pictures of saints or clergy decorating the parlor of a Catholic family's home. Family worship, which was common in many Protestant homes, was less typical in Catholic households. Morning and evening prayers were considered an individual undertaking, and Bible reading played less of a role (McDannell 67–68, 86–89).

PROTESTANT-CATHOLIC CONFLICT

The last decades of the 1800s saw a number of fierce controversies between Protestants and Catholics and the rise of an anti-Catholic nativist movement. Though some of the disputes echoed theological debates that had been going on since the Protestant Reformation, others spoke to the increasing prominence of Catholics in American life and the change that represented for many Protestants. At times religious questions became tangled up with ethnic- and class-related disputes. For example, in Boston the rise of the anti-Catholic organization, the American Protective Association (APA), coincided with the first success of Irish Catholic politicians in city elections. Protestant clergy led the APA, and they feared that the influence of Catholics would undermine American institutions. When Catholics began to form their own parochial school system, one minister declared "Rome was out to destroy the public schools" and the APA sought unsuccessfully to establish a state inspection system for Catholic schools (qtd. in Kennedy 60). A later controversy over how the Protestant Reformation was taught in public schools added fuel to this fire, and the two sides came to blows during an Independence Day riot in 1895. The riot was precipitated by the city's refusal to allow the APA to join the annual Independence Day parade with a little red schoolhouse float (the group's well-known symbol). The APA and other nativist organizations proceeded to hold an alternate parade. Few were surprised when a riot broke out between Protestants and Catholics resulting in one death (Kennedy 57, 74).

Catholic-Protestant conflicts in Boston and in other metropolitan areas drew the attention of many commentators who took the opportunity to both reassert prior positions and rethink questions of religion, ethnicity, and education. Charles C. Starbuck surveyed the controversy in *New Englander and Yale Review* and concluded, "the basis of our school system ought to be Protestantism. We are in fact, and ought to be by legal decision, a Protestant Christian country. We do not want schools in which we have to mention the Lord Christ with bated breath" (352). However, Gail Hamilton, writing in *The North American Review,* called for removing religious history from the curriculum, stating "The differences between Protestants and Catholics are not to be fought out in the public school. There are times, seasons, fields for this fight; but the public school is not one of them" (578). Catholic-Protestant conflicts continued into the twentieth century, particularly when they corresponded with ethnic rivalries and shifting political fortunes.

JUDAISM

The decade of the 1880s was crucial for American Judaism. Prior to this period there had been a small American Jewish population that was mostly of German descent. However, that changed when Russian Jews became scapegoats following the assassination of Czar Alexander II in 1881. A series of devastating pogroms caused the unprecedented immigration of Jews from Russia and other areas under Russian control, such as Poland. In total, over five million Jews immigrated to the United States between 1881 and 1890 (making up 19 percent of all U.S. immigrants during that decade). Although even more Jews would come to the U.S. during the first decade of the twentieth century, clear patterns of Jewish immigration were established during the 1880s (Karpf 33).

German Jews in New York City set up organizations to assist new Jewish immigrants, but there were huge cultural differences between the English-speaking, largely assimilated, German Jews and the newly arrived Yiddish-speakers. Many new immigrants were uninterested in giving up their language and traditions in the name of "Americanization." This animosity only increased when some new immigrants found themselves working in sweatshop conditions for fellow Jews. Some prominent German American Jews publicly called on Russian and Polish Jews to stay put (Karpf 37; Williams 309).

Jewish immigrants, particularly those uprooted by Russian pogroms, were among the poorest of the poor. However, many had been trained as artisans and brought with them a range of skills. As one 1890 newspaper article noted, "They were the tailors, shoemakers, butchers, bakers, carpenters, and what not of the great empire, and, coming here, each man went to the trade he had learned" (Levy 37). Many quickly achieved some measure of financial security and found themselves with both the means and freedom to fully participate in religious life. Substantial Jewish communities were established in major cities such as New York, Philadelphia, and Chicago. Concentrated Jewish populations allowed for the creation of institutions ranging from colleges to Hebrew schools to kosher food industries (Karp 128).

By 1890 the major branches of Judaism in the United States—Reform, Conservative, and Orthodox—had been established. However, the theological positions each branch stood for did not neatly conform to ethnic divisions nor did they explain individual stands on the overarching issue of "Americanization." Some Jews, of all branches, believed that the maintenance of Jewish traditions and religious practices was vital to Jewish identity, and they felt threatened by American standards set by the Protestant majority. Others believed Jewish traditions could be maintained separately while assimilating into most other aspects of American life. Still others defined themselves in secular terms and recognized a shared Jewish history more than a set of religious practices (Karpf 42–47; Williams 310).

NEW DENOMINATIONS AND SECTS

Religious changes in the industrial era were by no means limited to the dominant denominations. As Peter W. Williams notes, "particularly intensive periods of [social] change have been fertile incubators for religious excitement and innovation...The simultaneous exhilaration and insecurity generated by these wide-ranging changes affecting such large numbers of Americans led to the generation of new, experientially oriented and doctrinally innovative movements" (269). New religions, denominations, and sects (as well as established religions newly arrived in the United States) arose in the industrialized North, in the recovering South (particularly among African American communities establishing their own churches for the first time), in rapidly growing urban centers, and in rural communities. Even the territory of Alaska, which had been acquired from Russia in 1867, added to religious diversity as one-sixth of its population was Russian Orthodox. Many of the groups established during this period have grown and remain active today (Gaustad 81).

One of the most unique denominations to emerge in the industrial era was the Salvation Army, founded in America in 1880 by English immigrants led by George Scott Railton. Though most familiar for their military-style uniforms and organization, the Salvation Army truly stood apart from **The Salvation Army** other denominations for its focus on the poor and for its refusal to recognize traditional distinctions between public and private space.

Parishioners outside an African American church in Atlanta in 1899 or 1900. (Courtesy Library of Congress)

Declaring that those distracted by physical needs would not be open to religious messages, the Salvation Army set up a series of soup kitchens, homeless shelters, and social service centers designed to meet the material needs of the poor while openly criticizing the economic system that created such needs. As Frederick Booth-Tucker wrote, "Churchlessness was with these classes the natural outcome of homelessness, worklessness and worthlessness. To combat the evil, its causes must be radically dealt with" (182). Frank Smith, head of the Army from 1884 to 1887, was an avowed socialist, and many in the Army went on to be supporters of the Socialist labor leader, Eugene Debs (Winston 370–71; Williams 261).

The early Salvation Army hoped to draw the attention of the urban poor, and they employed sensational tactics to do so. They rented rooms in saloons for services, marched in the streets with brass bands, and held open-air services in city squares. They did not present themselves as an alternative to the consumer culture of the city; rather, they used the very methods of consumer culture to attract followers. Their insistence on "sacralizing" the common space of everyday life went against the general trend toward privatized religion among Protestant denominations. Many of the innovations they developed during this period, such as clothing salvage stores and the Christmas kettle collection, are still part of the Salvation Army's operations today (Winston 374–83).

The central beliefs of Christian Science, more formally known as the Church of Christ (Scientist), can be found in Mary Baker Eddy's 1875 book, *Science and Health with Key to Scriptures.* In that work, Eddy laid out a theology that claimed that the material world (including physical bodies) was an illusion and that all that was real was Spirit. Most notably, Christian Science followers rejected traditional medical care and developed a model of healing based on prayer (its ministers went by the title of "practitioner"). According to Ann Braude, Christian Science "provided consolation for the bereaved by denying the reality of death, hope for the sick by denying the reality of disease, and support for the irrelevance of Calvinism by denying the reality of evil" (184). Christian Science proved controversial, famously drawing a book-length attack by author Mark Twain entitled *Christian Science.* He found claims of faith healing preposterous and said of the church that "It is a despotism (on this democratic soil); a sovereignty more absolute than the Roman Papacy, more absolute than the Russian Czarship" (Twain, *Christian* 251). Twain's criticism notwithstanding, Christian Science grew rapidly under Eddy's tight leadership and by 1906 was estimated to have 85,000 members. The church had a particular appeal for middle- and upper-class women, and, though it was smaller than many mainstream denominations, Christian Science quickly grew to have the wealthiest membership per capita in the United States (Williams 334–37).

Christian Science

CIVIC LIFE IN THE INDUSTRIAL ERA

A common historical narrative marks the years from 1870–1900 as a time of rapid economic and technological advances, which consequently had a devastating impact on American civic institutions; the Progressive Era that follows (approximately 1900–1915) then gets credit for creating new civic institutions that revitalized American society. There is some truth to that narrative: urban metropolises grew with little forethought as to the new services industrial cities would require, and many of the institutions of small town life did not survive the rise of corporations that centralized both wealth and power in the hands of a few industrialists. Similarly, the power of corporate monopolies (often called "trusts") went unchallenged at the federal level of government until the presidency of Theodore Roosevelt, which began in 1901; and the decade within which the most civic organizations (citizen associations created independent of government control) were created in American history was the 1910s. Nevertheless, this familiar story glosses over much of what was notable and significant about civic life from 1870–1900 (Putnam 388).

The late nineteenth century remains the period during which voter participation reached its highest rates in United States history. And, though the number of civic organizations created in the industrial era did not equal that of the early twentieth century, those that were created represented the greatest expansion of American civic life to date. While immigrants were often accused of representing the greatest threat to the nation's social fabric during this time, they, in fact, were among the most likely to engage in civic involvement, particularly as many were taken aback by the differences between tight-knit rural life in Europe and the anonymity produced by the seemingly endless expanses of American cities.

Civic Involvement After the Civil War an increasing number of Americans joined together in a proliferation of organizations dedicated to improving social conditions. As Robert Putnam notes, "Beginning in the 1870s and extending into the 1910s, new types of associations multiplied, chapters of preexisting associations proliferated, and associations increasingly federated into state and national organizations...Americans organized clubs and churches and lodges and veterans groups" (383). Not only was there a flurry of organizational activity at this time, but associations formed during the industrial era also proved to be among the longest lasting in the history of the United States. Even a cursory glance at a list of civic and professional organizations formed during this period will reveal many names familiar today. These associations were part of what Robert Wiebe termed "the Search for Order," an attempt to create institutions and groups that could better manage the vast transformations of the industrial era. As importantly, civic organizations were a primary means through which women, unable to vote in most states, found a voice in public debate.

COME TOGETHER

This partial list shows notable civic associations, professional organizations, and labor groups founded between 1869 and 1900.

Civic Associations

American Bowling Congress (1895)
Fraternal Order of Eagles (1898)
General Federation of Women's Clubs (1890)
Knights of Columbus (1882)
Loyal Order of Moose (1888)
National Civic League (1894)
National Consumers League (1899)
National Rifle Association (1871)
Parent-Teacher Association (PTA) (1897)
Red Cross (volunteers) (1881)
Shriners (1872)
Sierra Club (1892)
Veterans of Foreign Wars (1899)
Volunteers of America (1896)
Women's Christian Temperance Union (1874)

Professional Organizations

American Association of University Women (1881)
American Bar Association (1878)
American Institute of Certified Public Accountants (1887)
American Nurses Association (1896)
American Society of Mechanical Engineers (1880)
American Institute of Electrical Engineers (1884)

Labor Groups

American Federation of Labor (1886)
International Association of Machinists (1888)
International Brotherhood of Electrical Workers (1891)
International Ladies Garment Workers Union (1900)
International Longshoremen's Association (1892)
Knights of Labor (1869)
United Mine Workers (1890)

—From Robert D. Putnam, *Bowling Alone*, 386–87, 438–39

Fraternal Organizations

Industrial era fraternal associations, like the Ancient Order of Hibernians, the Fraternal Order of Eagles, and the Independent Order of Odd Fellows, had a range of purposes and functions. Some operated as social clubs, some focused on community service, others were mutual aid or insurance societies, and still others were a means of establishing business connections. Most were organized via a system of democratically governed local lodges with a specific set of secret rituals (hence many were called "secret societies"). Robert Putnam argues that the rapid growth of fraternal organizations "represented a reaction against the individualism and anomie of this era of rapid social change, asylum from a disordered and uncertain world" (389). In the industrial era, these groups played a vital role by offering a social safety net to many individuals (Beito 183).

Many fraternal orders offered members sickness and life insurance that they would have otherwise been unable to afford. Odd Fellows members (there were 456,000 in 1877; 810,000 in 1897) paid a premium that gave them a right to guaranteed benefits if they were to fall ill. The Ancient Order of United Workmen offered a thousand dollar guaranteed death benefit for a one dollar per capita member assessment. It attracted 361,000 members by 1897. In fact, by 1895, fully one-half of all life insurance policies in the United States were held through fraternal organizations (Beito 191–95; Harwood 620).

"THE GOLDEN AGE OF FRATERNITY"

In an 1897 article in *The North American Review,* W.S. Harwood tabulated the total U.S. membership in fraternal organizations and estimated how much money they paid out to members in sickness, death, and other insurance benefits over the course of 1896. Though suspicious of the secrecy surrounding membership in various orders, Harwood nonetheless declared that, "these closing years of the century might well be called the Golden Age of fraternity" (623).

The following list, adapted from Harwood, only shows select organizations, but the complete record details 52 groups with a total 5,454,329 members and benefit dispersals amounting to $649,082,471.

Name of Order	Membership	Estimated yearly benefits paid to members
Ancient Order of Hibernians	98,000	$681,928
Ancient Order of United Workmen	361,301	$71,729,180
B'nai B'rith Independent	34,925	$43,175,000
Improved Order Red Men	165,000	$14,200,000
Knights of Honor	118,287	$62,009,200
Knights of the Maccabees	244,704	$7,233,930
Knights of Pythius	475,000	$10,362,000
Masons	750,000	$90,000,000
Modern Woodmen of America	204,332	$7,229,985
Odd Fellows	810,000	$74,600,000
United Order of Odd Fellows (African American)	130,350	$238,783
(Harwood 620)		

The concept of mutual aid proved a popular one. Individuals who feared a change of fortune might one day make them a recipient of aid were likely to become donors to these groups. Such aid was not thought of as charity but rather as a benefit for which a member had paid. While fraternal organizations looked after their members, they were restrictive in terms of who could join. These groups were usually segregated along race and gender lines. Joining a fraternal lodge was unlikely to take one out of an ethnic or geographical community; instead, lodge affiliation usually reinforced one's ethnic or religious identity (as would be the case if one joined the Sons of Italy or the Women's Christian Temperance Union). However, American fraternal groups were distinctive in that they did tend to attract members from across economic classes (Beito 190–91).

Professional Organizations   Professional organizations, such as the American Bar Association, the American Medical Association, and the American Nurses Association, served a range of purposes. In addition to providing a venue through which people in similar jobs could address issues of professional concern, these organizations also served to police the boundaries of new professions by establishing rules for inclusion and guidelines for conduct. As Robert H.

Wiebe writes, "The so-called professions meant little as long as anyone with a bag of pills and a bottle of syrup could pass for a doctor, a few books and a corrupt judge made a man a lawyer, and an unemployed literate qualified as a teacher" (13–14). By joining together in professional associations, members built respect for their work and gained a measure of control over its practice.

Among the foremost members of professional organizations were members of the new middle class (also now commonly referred to as the professional-managerial class). These were not the traditional shopkeepers and local businessmen of small town America whose prominence had been eclipsed by urban expansion and corporate consolidation; rather, the new middle class consisted of professionals and managers often working for large institutions. Professional organizations (which were more segregated by class than fraternal organizations) became an important tool of class formation; they were a means through which the professional-managerial class came to think of itself as a class. Once professionals could see that like-minded and similarly situated people shared their concerns and beliefs, they sought to establish greater credibility for those positions through myriad projects of reform (Ohmann 220).

Women were eager participants in many civic organizations. By the end of the nineteenth century, as many as two million women participated in clubs. Legally barred from voting and restricted by custom from many forms of **Women's Clubs** employment and education, many women poured their energies into associations. Those associations subsequently became involved in any number of social activities and concerns. As Richard Ohmann writes, "The 1870s and 1880s brought an explosion of women's clubs, many devoted to self-improvement—reading clubs, literary societies, cultural groups—along with sewing circles and purely social clubs. In the 1890s, women's clubs dedicated themselves to community improvement, park development, recreational reform, the quality of schools, and so on" (155). Women club members faced a complex situation. Efforts toward self-improvement and education by women were often criticized as selfish and at odds with the "selfless" ideal for feminine behavior. Therefore, women's clubs often spoke of their goals under the guise of providing public services. While the aims of women's clubs could be narrow, clubs also extended themselves into political and social realms where women's voices were rarely heard. When confronting a dilemma like poverty or girls' education, women's clubs often became political by addressing the social causes of a problem, as in the case of the Working Girls' Clubs (Gere 5, 10).

Working Girls' Clubs appeared in many cities beginning in the 1880s. These clubs catered to the many young, unmarried, working-class women who increasingly found employment outside of the home (often as department store clerks) but lived with their families. These girls had little physical space of their own, and they rarely had enough spending money to frequent commercial amusements in cities. Clubs offered these girls a parentally approved place to meet friends. In addition to providing a chance to socialize, Working Girls' Clubs initially offered classes, brought lecturers to speak, and maintained lending libraries. While the clubs charged a nominal membership fee, a wealthy, female patron typically funded them. Under the influence of patrons during their early years, these clubs tended to focus on the "problem" of working girls and how they could maintain their virtue and dignity while working in the new urban environment. However, as members themselves gained more control over club operations, the clubs became simultaneously more involved in social activities, such as dances, and increasingly concerned with labor reform issues. By the turn of the twentieth century, many of these Working Girls' clubs were in decline; politically attuned women began joining labor organizations and the growing commercial amusement industry in cities led many others to seek entertainment elsewhere (Murolo 24, 145–47; Peiss 168–78).

Labor Organizations   The most prominent labor organization of the industrial era was the Knights of Labor. Founded in Philadelphia in 1869 as a secret society (originally it did not even allow its name to be made public), it soon grew into a mass movement. At its peak in 1886, it had as many as 729,000 members organized into local assemblies across the country. Approximately 70,000 of the Knights were female and 60,000 were African American. The Knights of Labor was a unique organization, part trade union, part fraternal organization, and part political group. Their aims were ambitious. The Knights aimed not just to improve employment conditions but also to restructure American society along a more cooperative model. Unlike many other unions, the Knights of Labor attempted to organize all workers within a given industry, regardless of skill level. This gave them the ability to launch successful limited strikes (most spectacularly against the Southwest Railway in 1885) as well as boycotts of specific employers. However, being such a broad based organization also made it rather unwieldy to manage. Internal conflicts as well as a hostile political atmosphere following the Haymarket Affair led to the group's gradual decline (P. Foner, *First* 22; McMath 63; Murolo 14; Putnam 392; Weir 78).

The American Federation of Labor (AFL) was founded in 1886, and in many ways it became the successor organization to the Knights of Labor. The aims of the AFL were narrower than the Knights—the AFL organized by craft or trade, focusing on highly skilled workers—but it proved more successful in achieving its goals. The AFL developed more slowly than the Knights of Labor had in their heyday. From 1886 to 1892 it grew from 13 to 40 national unions including the 57,000-member United Brotherhood of Carpenters and Joiners and the 27,000-strong Cigar Makers' Union. Membership in AFL affiliated unions was restricted to wage earners, unlike the more broadly defined Knights of Labor. Under the leadership of Samuel

Gompers, the AFL remained hostile to cooperative enterprises and schemes, concentrating instead on winning improvements in labor conditions for its members (P. Foner, *History* 171, 176).

A higher percentage of Americans voted in elections during the industrial era than at any other time in U.S. history **Voting and** (American women did not achieve the right to vote nation- **Political** wide until 1920). From 1876 to 1900, 77 percent of eligible **Participation** voters took part in Presidential elections, with participation levels as high as 85 percent in northern states. As a point of comparison, consider that only 51 percent of eligible voters cast ballots in the 2000 presidential election. Industrial era elections were partisan events that were hotly contested, even if the issues under dispute were not necessarily divisive. As Robert Wiebe notes, "America in the late nineteenth century was a nation of intense partisanship and massive political indifference" (27). During this time, elections involved much more than just casting a ballot. Election campaigns were high profile, public events that were often coordinated on a local level and involved an unprecedented level of voter participation (McGerr 5, 7).

In the years following the Civil War, it was standard practice for men to join local marching companies affiliated with a political party. During election campaigns, these marching companies would be outfitted in military style uniforms and then would participate in huge, public parades on behalf of candidates and political parties. It was not uncommon in urban areas for thousands of men to take up torches (the parades were often at night) and march alongside bands and floats before gathering to hear candidates and other party orators rally the faithful. In New York City, as many as 50,000 marchers typically participated in political parades. Spectators would gather along parade routes and some would signal their support for (or opposition to) the parading party by turning on (or off) all the lights in a house. During some elections there were so many marchers that they had to be divided into "battalions" and "brigades" under the order of "generals." Michael McGerr estimates that in the North, perhaps one-fifth of all voters played an active role in campaigning (26–27).

Political parades encouraged people to vote the party rather than the candidate, and they energized the party faithful. As McGerr writes, "Mid-nineteenth-century partisanship was aggressive, demonstrative, contentious, and often vicious. Party membership was a part of men's identity; as such, their partisanship had to be paraded and asserted in public" (13–14). Party affiliation was seen as more than a choice; it was both a personal and political statement. That said, in a highly charged partisan atmosphere, political parades did little to appeal to undecided voters or "ticket splitters" who tended to vote for candidates of different parties. Gradually, spectacular campaigns began to fall out of favor, and they came to be replaced by the "campaign of education," first run on the presiden-

An 1888 engraving from *Frank Leslie's Illustrated Newspaper* showing a New York City political parade during the presidential campaign. (Courtesy Library of Congress)

tial level by the unsuccessful 1876 Democratic Presidential candidate, Samuel J. Tilden. This approach involved a more centralized campaign focused on issues and the distribution of literature to voters (and later involved substantial advertising). The "campaign of education" was seen to better appeal to undecided voters, and by the turn of the century it came to dominate politics. However, it did so at the cost of lessening the average citizen's role in political campaigns. Not surprisingly, voter participation levels have never reached the level they achieved during the industrial era (McGerr 70–77).

The most successful third-party movement in U.S. history was that of the Populists, officially known as the People's Party. Founded in 1892, the People's Party capitalized on anger in rural areas of the country by running on a platform calling for an end to the gold standard, government control of railroads, and an income tax on the wealthy. The party's 1892 presidential candidate, James Weaver, carried five Midwestern and Western states and received 8.5 percent of the popular vote. Populist-affiliated candidates took two governor's offices and a number of other local and statewide offices as well. In 1896, the Populists ran a "fusion" ticket, endorsing the Democratic nominee, William Jennings Bryan, but running their own candidates as well. Though the party won unprecedented victories, electing 7 senators and 30 congressmen to office, fusion proved a short-lived tactic. Most populists served only one term of office. Nevertheless, many of the issues first raised by the Populists were later addressed in the twentieth century by Progressive and New Deal politicians (McMath 177, 204).

Populism and the People's Party

The Populist movement built upon the economic and civic cooperation begun in the 1880s by the Farmers' Alliance, a loose knit group of agrarian activists. Among the projects taken on by the Farmers' Alliance were cooperatives designed to pool the resources of individual farmers to achieve better prices for the goods they bought and sold. These cooperative ventures included "trade agreements with local merchants, establishment of joint-stock stores (which sold goods to members at an immediate discount), and formation of...purchasing and marketing cooperatives" in addition to cooperatively owned grain elevators and lumberyards (McMath 73). The success of these local projects relied upon the civic culture of rural America, but the obstacles they faced politicized many farmers and paved the way for the People's Party.

CIVIC CONFLICT AND THE FOURTH OF JULY

Civic organizations represented the concerns and aspirations of their members, and those values could often prove controversial, as in the case of Fourth of July celebrations in Worcester, Massachusetts during this period. As Roy Rosenzweig charts in his insightful study, *Eight hours for what we will: Workers and leisure in an industrial city, 1870–1920*, the Fourth of July proved to be a flash point for class conflict. It was the only warm-weather holiday most workers received, and it became a central celebration in working-class culture. At the same time, as middle-class workers increasingly began to take vacations in the summer, the Fourth became a less valued, and even private, holiday for them. Independence Day celebrations tended to highlight and exacerbate this divide.

In Worcester in the 1880s, the Ancient Order of Hibernians or AOH (an Irish American civic group) organized annual Fourth of July celebrations. Like European feast days, these tended to be boisterous public celebrations that on occasion would dissolve into fighting and drunken displays. They sharply contrasted with more restrained middle-class celebrations of the time held by civic groups such as the Loyal Women of American Liberty.

[T]he 1893 picnic of the Loyal Women of American Liberty held at a private home featured a sit-down meal, a poetry reading, and formal speeches…The Loyal Women closed their picnic with thanks to their hostess and the singing of "God Be With You Until We Meet Again"; the AOH ended its 1886 picnic with the chasing of a greased pig. (75–76)

The contrast in celebration styles became a center of controversy. Over time police attempted to restrain illegal alcohol sales and newspapers editorialized against "liquid patriotism." Irish American temperance groups even began to organize alternative Independence Day picnics, though boisterous Fourth of July celebrations continued into the twentieth century.

The increasing prominence of civic organizations was a hallmark of life in the industrial era. In fact, differences in religion, ethnicity, class, and culture often were expressed through civic organizations. When these groups came into conflict, their disputes reflected central divisions within late-nineteenth-century America.

Conclusion: Not the Gilded Age

Early on in the process of writing this book, we made a conscious decision not to use the common term "the Gilded Age" to refer to the period from 1870 to 1900 in the United States, opting instead for the heading "the industrial era." Though "the Gilded Age" is an accurate label in some ways, it is a pejorative term that casts a negative light on the period. It is like calling the time of the French Revolution, "the era of beheadings," or classifying America in the 1950s as "the age of suburban sprawl."

The Gilded Age originally was the title of a satiric novel cowritten by Mark Twain and Charles Dudley Warner that was published in 1873. It follows a group of greedy characters seeking to strike it rich through shady land deals and corrupt railroad schemes. When the years following the publication of the novel brought about, in fact, shady land deals and corrupt railroad schemes, Twain and Warner's novel became a ready shorthand by which to refer to and make sense of these developments.

However, the term "the Gilded Age" has had the unintentional effect of diminishing elements of this period that do not fit into a narrative of corruption and greed. Furthermore, it implicitly attributes to the progressive era (approximately from 1900 to 1915) most political and social reforms between the Civil War and World War I. However, several important reforms began prior to 1900. For example, Jane Addams's pioneering work in Hull-House started in 1889, and federal efforts to regulate railroads found success as early as 1887. Of course, "the industrial era" has its own limitations as a definition. The time period from 1870–1900 was not the only moment in U.S. history during which factories and manufacturing were prominent, nor were all regions of the country industrialized at this time. Nevertheless, "the industrial era" does capture, using a non-judgmental classification, the dominant role played by emergent industrialism in shaping the experiences of many Americans at the end of the nineteenth century.

The legacy of the industrial era was to set in motion a series of economic and social developments from which there would be no turning back. The nature of industrialism might change, but the United States would not become a rural nation again. Cities would vary in their relative social and political importance, but small-town life would not dominate public concerns as it once had. Trends and fads would come and go in consumer culture, but mass consumption remained central to the economy. Periodically there would be crises over the state of education or concerning the proper role for women, but there was no return to the status quo of pre-Civil War America.

In casting a backward glance toward the industrial era, one can find many similarities between prominent concerns now—near the turn of the twenty-first century—and at the turn of the twentieth century. Major issues, then and now, included transformations in the relationship between labor and capital, growing concerns about the concentration of wealth, and the development of new forms of mass culture, as well as disputes over immigration, the purpose of government, and religion's place in public life. In those broad terms, the turn of the twentieth century shared much with the situation at the turn of the twenty-first century.

That is not to say that little has been learned from the experiences of the industrial era. In writing this book, we have rarely found ourselves becoming nostalgic. Life was not simpler "way back then," particularly not for the vast majority of Americans who struggled to make a living and support families without any of the social safety nets that are so easily taken for granted today. That said, it is hard not to admire the many women and men who joined together to improve their lives and the lives of others. Though the industrial era was a time of hardship for many, it was a time of cynicism for relatively few. Problems were seen as difficult to solve but not intractable. Many of the major reforms both of the industrial era and of the subsequent progressive era came about because individuals believed that there were solutions to be found. If there is an overriding lesson to be taken from the experiences of those in the industrial era, it is a belief in possibilities.

Glossary

Central Business District—A downtown section of a city zoned largely for commercial and industrial use.

Conspicuous consumption—Making expensive purchases in order to flaunt one's wealth. This concept was first introduced by Thorstein Veblin in his classic study, *The Theory of the Leisure Class* (1899).

The Great Potato Famine—From 1845–50, a potato blight in Ireland caused a series of unsuccessful potato harvests leading to the death of more than a million Irish of disease or starvation. With only limited action being taken by the British government to address the famine, many Irish immigrated to the United States.

The Haymarket Affair—To support a series of coordinated strikes on behalf of an eight-hour workday, an outdoor meeting and rally was held in Chicago's Haymarket Square on the evening of May 4, 1886. When police attempted to disperse what had been a peaceful assembly, an unknown person threw a bomb into the police line, causing the police to open fire. Many prominent Chicago anarchists and labor leaders were arrested, and, though no evidence could connect any to the unknown bomber, some were sentenced to death and executed. In 1893, the remaining Haymarket defendants were pardoned, but the eight-hour movement was dealt a devastating blow.

Manifest Destiny—A common nineteenth-century belief that the United States was destined, and even had a "mission," to expand its territory across the continent to the Pacific Ocean.

The Mason-Dixon line—A boundary first surveyed in the 1760s that runs along the southern edge of Pennsylvania and the western edge of Delaware. It is commonly used to distinguish northern and southern states.

McKay stitcher—A machine that fastened the sole of a shoe to the upper. With its dissemination during the late 1860s, the boot and shoe industry was transformed from a system dependent on outwork to a factory system.

Nativism—An anti-immigrant movement in the nineteenth century that particularly was concerned with the impact of Catholic immigrants on American life.

Neoclassical—In architecture, designs aimed to imitate the look of the temples and buildings of ancient Greece and Rome.

Nuclear family—A family that consists of parents and children. The nuclear family is often contrasted with the extended family, in which many generations and different types of relatives live together in the same household.

Outwork system—A form of industrial organization and employment in which employees are given raw materials to take home and return to the work site in finished condition. Typically, the outwork system pays by the quantity of finished material and not by the amount of time worked.

Panic of 1873—A financial crisis set into motion by the bankruptcy of the investment banking firm, Jay Cooke and Company, which had over-extended itself in railroad speculation. The ensuing depression led to business failures, labor unrest, and the end of the railroad construction boom. The depression did not end until 1879.

Pogroms—A Russian word for the organized persecution of an ethnic group, particularly Jews. A pogrom against Russian Jews following the assassination of Alexander II in 1881 led to the mass migration of Jews, many of whom came to the United States.

Power loom—A machine that weaves yarn into textiles.

Professional-managerial class—A term used to describe a class of skilled workers who worked for salaries often in large corporations. The professional-managerial class began to be considered as a distinct group in the United States in the late 1800s, and they can be contrasted to traditional middle-class professionals who ran their own businesses and earned profits rather than a salary.

Protestant work ethic—A belief that God favors those who achieve success through hard work and self-discipline.

Segregation—A policy of separation of the races. In the United States, this policy often denied African Americans full civil rights and access to public services.

Social Darwinism—A belief that Charles Darwin's theory of evolution could be applied to the workings of society. This belief tended to endorse the status quo, as it could be used to argue that those with the most power simply adapted best via what was called the "survival of the fittest."

Tenement—Initially a term that simply referred to an apartment building, it came to describe a low-cost, multiple-dwelling structure often found in slums.

Works Cited

Adams, Bluford. *E Pluribus Barnum: The Great Showman and the Making of U.S. Popular Culture*. Minneapolis: University of Minnesota Press, 1997.

Addams, Jane. *Twenty Years at Hull-House*. 1938. New York: Signet, 1961.

Alcott, Louisa May. "How I Went Out to Service." *Alternative Alcott*. Ed. Elaine Showalter. New Brunswick: Rutgers University Press, 1988.

Ambrose, Stephen E. *Nothing Like It in the World: The Men Who Built the Transcontinental Railroad, 1863–1869*. New York: Simon & Schuster, 2000.

"American and European Railways." *Scribner's Monthly* 3.4 (February 1872): 490–91.

Ames, Kenneth L. *Death in the Dining Room and Other Tales of Victorian Culture*. Philadelphia: Temple University Press, 1992.

"Andrew Carnegie." *The American Experience*. Prod. Austin Hoyt. PBS. 20 June 2003 <http://www.pbs.org>.

Aron, Cindy S. *Working at Play: A History of Vacations in the United States*. New York: Oxford University Press, 1999.

Barnes, Joseph W. "Katharine B. Davis and the Workingman's Model Home of 1893." *Rochester History* 43.1 Jan. 1981: 1–20.

Barrett, James R. *Work and Community in the Jungle: Chicago's Packinghouse Workers, 1894–1922*. Urbana: University of Illinois Press, 1987.

Battan, Jesse F. "The 'Rights' of Husbands and the 'Duties' of Wives: Power and Desire in the American Bedroom, 1850–1910." *Journal of Family History* 24.2 (Apr. 1999): 165–86.

Beecher, Catherine, and Harriet Beecher Stowe. *The American Woman's Home*. 1869. Hartford: The Stowe-Day Foundation, 1987.

Beecher, Mrs. H. W. *All Around the House; or, How to Make a Home Happy*. New York: D. Appleton and Co., 1878. Provided courtesy of the Harriet Beecher Stowe Center, Hartford, CT.

Beito, David. T. " 'This Enormous Army': The Mutual Aid Tradition of American Fraternal Societies before the Twentieth Century." *The Voluntary City: Choice, Community, and Civil Society.* Ed. David T. Beito, Peter Gordon, and Alexander Tabarrok. Ann Arbor: University of Michigan Press, 2002. 182–203.

Bellamy, Edward. *Looking Backward: 2000–1887.* 1888. New York: Penguin Classics, 1987.

Beveridge, Albert J. "March of the Flag." *Major Problems in American Diplomatic History: Documents and Readings.* Vol. 2 287–91.

Bianculli, Anthony J. *Trains and Technology: The American Railroad in the Nineteenth Century.* Vol. 1. Newark: University of Delaware Press, 2001.

Biggs, Lindy. *The Rational Factory: Architecture, Technology, and Work in America's Age of Mass Production.* Baltimore: The Johns Hopkins University Press, 1996.

Bigott, Joseph C. *From Cottage to Bungalow: Houses and the Working Class in Metropolitan Chicago, 1869–1929.* Chicago: University of Chicago Press, 2001.

Birdoff, Harry. *The World's Greatest Hit.* New York: S. F. Vanni, 1947.

Blewett, Mary H. *Constant Turmoil: The Politics of Industrial Life in Nineteenth-Century New England.* Amherst: University of Massachusetts Press, 2000.

Booth-Tucker, Frederick. "Social Salvation." 1900. *A Documentary History of Religion in America Since 1865.* Ed. Edwin S. Gaustad. Grand Rapids: William B. Eerdmans Publishing Company, 1983. 181–83.

Borchert, James. "Urban Neighborhood and Community: Informal Group Life, 1850–1970." *Journal of Interdisciplinary History* 11.4 (Spring 1981): 607–31.

Borus, Daniel H. *Writing Realism: Howells, James, and Norris in the Mass Market.* Chapel Hill: University of North Carolina Press, 1989.

Bowers, Brian. *Lengthening the Day: A History of Lighting Technology.* Oxford: Oxford University Press, 1998.

Bowlby, Rachel. *Just Looking: Consumer Culture in Dreiser, Gissing and Zola.* New York: Methuen, 1985.

Boydston, Jeanne. *Home and Work: Housework, Wages, and the Ideology of Labor in the Early Republic.* Oxford: Oxford University Press, 1990.

Braden, Donna R. *Leisure and Entertainment in America.* Detroit: Wayne State University Press, 1988.

Brandon, Joseph R. "A Protest Against Sectarian Texts in California Schools in 1875." *Western States Jewish History* 20.3 (1988): 234.

Braude, Ann. *Radical Spirits: Spiritualism and Women's Rights in Nineteenth-Century America.* Boston: Beacon Press, 1989.

Brenzel, Barbara M. *Daughters of the State: A Social Portrait of the First Reform School for Girls in North America, 1856–1905.* Cambridge: The MIT Press, 1983.

Brewer, Priscilla. *The Queen of Inventions: Sewing Machines in American Homes and Factories 1850–1920.* Pawtucket, RI: Slater Mill Historic Site, 1986.

Brown, Bill, ed. *Reading the West: An Anthology of Dime Westerns.* New York: Bedford, 1997.

Brownson, Orestes. "The Laboring Classes." *Boston Quarterly Review* 3.11 (July 1840): 358–95.

Buenker, John D. *The Income Tax and the Progressive Era.* New York: Garland Publishing, 1985.

Bunner, H. C. "Shantytown." *Scribners Monthly* 20.6 Oct. 1880: 855–69.

Button, H. Warren, and Eugene F. Provenzo, Jr. *History of Education and Culture in America*. Englewood Cliffs, NJ: Prentice Hall, 1989.

Cahan, Abraham. *Yekl and The Imported Bridegroom and Other Stories of Yiddish New York*, 1896. New York: Dover Publications, 1970.

Calvert, Karin. *Children in the House: The Material Culture of Early Childhood, 1600–1900*. Boston: Northeastern University Press, 1992.

Cameron, Ardis. *Radicals of the Worst Sort: Laboring Women in Lawrence, Massachusetts, 1860–1912*. Urbana: University of Illinois Press, 1993.

Carl, Conrad. "Testimony of Conrad Carl" Garraty 20–22.

Cassedy, James H. *Medicine in America: A Short History*. Baltimore: The Johns Hopkins University Press, 1991.

Cavallo, Dominick. *Muscles and Morals: Organized Playgrounds and Urban Reform, 1880–1920*. Philadelphia: University of Pennsylvania Press, 1981.

Chesnutt, Charles W. *The Marrow of Tradition*. 1901. New York: Penguin, 1993.

Chindahl, George L. *A History of the Circus in America*. Caldwell, ID: The Caxton Printers, Ltd., 1959.

Chopin, Kate. *The Awakening*. 2nd ed. Ed. Nancy A. Walker. Boston: Bedford/St. Martin's, 2000.

Christiano, Kevin J. *Religious Diversity and Social Change*. Cambridge: Cambridge University Press, 1987.

Christiansen, Jens, and Peter Philips. "The Transition from Outwork to Factory Production in the Boot and Shoe Industry, 1830–1880." *Masters to Managers: Historical and Comparative Perspectives on American Employers*. Ed. Sanford M. Jacoby. New York: Columbia University Press, 1991.

Conant, Helen S. "A Ramble in Central Park." *Harper's New Monthly Magazine* 59.353 Oct. 1879: 689–701.

Cook, Ann, Marilyn Gittell, and Herb Mack, eds. *City Life, 1865–1900: Views of Urban America*. New York: Praeger Publishers, 1973.

Cott, Nancy F. *Public Vows: A History of Marriage and the Nation*. Cambridge: Harvard University Press, 2000.

Crane, Stephen. *Maggie: A Girl of the Streets*. 1893. New York: Signet Classic, 1991.

Culley, Margo, ed. *A Day at a Time: The Diary Literature of American Women from 1764 to the Present*. New York: The Feminist Press at the City University of New York, 1985.

Cumbler, John T. *Working-Class Community in Industrial America: Work, Leisure, and Struggle in Two Industrial Cities, 1880–1930*. Westport, CT: Greenwood Press, 1979.

Daniels, Rudolph. *Trains Across the Continent: North American Railroad History*. 2nd edition. Bloomington: Indiana University Press, 2000.

Davis, J. Frank. "Tom Shows." *Scribner's* 77 (1925): 350–60.

de Tocqueville, Alexis. *Democracy in America*. Vol. 2. Ed. Phillips Bradley. New York: Vintage Classics, 1990.

DeBerg, Betty A. *Ungodly Women: Gender and the First Wave of American Fundamentalism*. 2nd ed. Macon, GA: Mercer University Press, 2000.

Deconde, Alexander. *A History of American Foreign Policy*. Vol. 1. 3rd ed. New York: Charles Scribner's Sons, 1978.

Denning, Michael. *Mechanic Accents: Dime Novels and Working-Class Culture in America*. New York: Verso, 1987.

Dewey, Davis Rich. *National Problems: 1885–1897*. New York: Harper & Brothers, 1907.

Diner, Hasia R. *Erin's Daughters in America: Irish Immigrant Women in the Nineteenth Century*. Baltimore: The Johns Hopkins University Press, 1983.

———. *Hungering for America: Italian, Irish, and Jewish Foodways in the Age of Migration*. Cambridge: Harvard University Press, 2001.

Diner, Steven J. *A Very Different Age: Americans of the Progressive Era*. New York: Hill and Wang, 1998.

Dodge, Pryor. *The Bicycle*. Paris: Flammarion, 1996.

Douglas, Ann. *The Feminization of American Culture*. New York: Doubleday, 1977.

Dreiser, Theodore. *Sister Carrie*. 2nd ed. 1900. New York: W. W. Norton, 1991.

Dudden, Faye E. *Serving Women: Household Service in Nineteenth-Century America*. Middletown, CT: Wesleyan University Press, 1983.

Easthope, Antony. *Literary Into Cultural Studies*. New York: Routledge Press, 1991.

Eaton, Virgil G. "Increase in Opium Use." *Drugs and Drug Policy in America: A Documentary History*. Ed. Steven R. Belenko. Westport, CT: Greenwood Press, 2000. 10–12.

Edson, Cyrus. "Do We Live Too Fast?" *The North American Review* 154.424 Mar. 1892: 281–86.

Eggert, Gerald G. *Steelmasters and Labor Reform, 1886–1923*. Pittsburgh: University of Pittsburgh Press, 1981.

Farr, Finis. *Chicago: A Personal History of America's Most American City*. New Rochelle, NY: Arlington House, 1973.

Fellman, Anita Clair, and Michael Fellman. *Making Sense of Self: Medical Advice Literature in Late Nineteenth-Century America*. Philadelphia: University of Pennsylvania Press, 1981.

Ferry, John William. *A History of the Department Store*. New York: The Macmillan Co., 1960.

Fischer, Gayle V. *Pantaloons & Power: A Nineteenth-Century Dress Reform in the United States*. Kent, Ohio: Kent State University Press, 2001.

Foner, Eric, and John A. Garraty, eds. *The Reader's Companion to American History*. New York: Houghton Mifflin Company, 1991.

Foner, Philip S. *First Facts of American Labor*. New York: Holmes & Meier, 1984.

———. *The Great Labor Uprising of 1877*. New York: Monad Press, 1977.

———. *History of the Labor Movement in the United States*. Vol. 2. New York: International Publishers, 1955.

———, ed. *American Labor Songs of the Nineteenth Century*. Urbana: University of Illinois Press, 1975.

Formanek-Brunell, Miriam. "The Politics of Doll Play in Nineteenth-Century America." *Small Worlds: Children & Adolescents in America, 1850–1950*. Ed. Elliott West & Paula Petrik. Lawrence: University Press of Kansas, 1992. 107–24.

"'From the Stockyards': Letter from a Worker Who Was Displaced by a Child." *German Workers in Chicago*. 74–76.

Garraty, John, ed. *Labor and Capital in the Gilded Age: Testimony Taken by the Senate Committee upon the Relations between Labor and Capital-1883*. Boston: Little Brown and Company, 1968.

Gaustad, Edwin S., ed. *A Documentary History of Religion in America Since 1865*. Grand Rapids: William B. Eerdmans Publishing Company, 1983.

Gere, Anne Ruggles. *Intimate Practices: Literacy and Cultural Work in U. S. Women's Clubs, 1880–1920*. Urbana: University of Illinois Press, 1997.

Gerhard, William Paul. "Domestic Sanitary Appliances. IV. Comforts of a Bathroom: Its Sanitary Construction and Arrangement." *Good Housekeeping* 5 Sept. 1885: 1–4. Provided courtesy of the Harriet Beecher Stowe Center, Hartford, CT.

German Workers in Chicago: A Documentary History of Working-Class Culture from 1850 to World War I. Ed. Hartmut Keil and John B. Jentz. Urbana: University of Illinois Press, 1988.

Giamo, Benedict. *On the Bowery: Confronting Homelessness in American Society*. Iowa City: University of Iowa Press, 1989.

Golden, Janet. *A Social History of Wet Nursing in America: From Breast to Bottle*. New York: Cambridge University Press, 1996.

Goldstein, Warren. *Playing for Keeps: A History of Early Baseball*. Ithaca: Cornell University Press, 1989.

Gompers, Samuel. "Testimony of Samuel Gompers." *Garraty* 7–18.

Goodwin, Lorine Swainston. *The Pure Food, Drink, and Drug Crusaders, 1879–1914*. Jefferson, NC: McFarland & Co., 1999.

Gordon, Sarah H. *Passage to Union: How the Railroads Transformed American Life, 1829–1929*. Chicago: Ivan R. Dee, 1996.

Gossett, Thomas F. *Uncle Tom's Cabin and American Culture*. Dallas: Southern Methodist University Press, 1985.

Gould, Joseph E. *The Chautauqua Movement: An Episode in the Continuing American Revolution*. New York: State University of New York Press, 1961.

Grant, H. Roger, and Charles W. Bohi. *The Country Railroad Station in America*. Boulder, CO: Pruett Publishing Co., 1978.

Green, Harvey. *The Light of the Home: An Intimate View of the Lives of Women in Victorian America*. New York: Pantheon Books, 1983.

Greene, J.L. et al. "For Manual Training: Courses Recommended in the Public Schools." *Hartford Courant* 28 January 1896: 10. Courtesy of the Harriet Beecher Stowe House.

Griffith, Ernest S. *A History of American City Government: The Conspicuous Failure, 1870–1900*. New York: Praeger, 1972.

Grob, Gerald N. *The Deadly Truth: A History of Disease in America*. Cambridge: Harvard University Press, 2002.

Gunton, George. *The Economic and Social Importance of the Eight-Hour Movement*. 2nd ed. 1889. Rpt. in *American Labor: From Conspiracy to Collective Bargaining*. Ed. Leon Stein and Philip Taft. New York: Arno, 1969.

Gutman, Herbert G. and Ira Berlin. "Class Composition and the Development of the American Working Class, 1840–1890." *Power and Culture: Essays on the American Working Class*. New York: Pantheon Books, 1987.

Gutman, Herbert G, et al. *Who Built America?: Working People and the Nation's Economy, Politics, Culture and Society*. Vol. 1. New York: Pantheon, 1989.

Habenstein, Robert W., and William M. Lamers. "The Patterns of Late Nineteenth-Century Funerals." *Passing: The Vision of Death in America*. Ed. Charles O. Jackson. Westport, CT: Greenwood Press, 1977.

Hall, H.N. from "The Art of the Pullman Porter." 1931. *Workin' on the Railroad: Reminiscences from the Age of Steam*. Ed. Richard Reinhardt. Palo Alto, CA: American West Publishing Co., 1970. 299–305.

Halpern, Rick. *Down on the Killing Floor: Black and White Workers in Chicago's Pack-inghouses, 1904–1954.* Urbana: University of Illinois Press, 1997.

Hamblen, Herbert E. "The General Manager's Story." 1898. *Workin' on the Railroad: Reminiscences from the Age of Steam.* Ed. Richard Reinhardt. Palo Alto, CA: American West Publishing Co., 1970. 84–88.

Hamilton, Gail. "Catholicism and Public Schools." *The North American Review* 147.384 Nov. 1888: 572–80.

Harris, Neil. "The Cemetery Beautiful." *Passing: The Vision of Death in America.* Ed. Charles O. Jackson. Westport, CT: Greenwood Press, 1977.

Hart, James D. *The Popular Book: A History of America's Literary Taste.* New York: Oxford University Press, 1950.

Harwood, W. S. "Secret Societies in America." *North American Review* 164.485 (April 1897): 617–25.

Hazard, Blanche Evans. *The Organization of the Boot and Shoe Industry in Massachu-setts Before 1875.* Cambridge: Harvard University Press, 1921.

Heininger, Mary Lynn Stevens, et al. *A Century of Childhood, 1820–1920.* Rochester, NY: The Margaret Woodbury Strong Museum, 1984.

Historical Statistics of the United States: Colonial Times to 1970. Part 1. Washington, D.C.: Government Printing Office, 1975.

Hochman, Barbara. *Getting at the Author: Reimagining Books and Reading in the Age of American Realism.* Amherst: University of Massachusetts Press, 2001.

Hogan, William T. *Economic History of the Iron and Steel Industry in the United States.* Vol. 1. Lexington, MA: Lexington Books, 1971.

"The Homestead Act." *National Park Service.* 29 July 2003 <http://www.nps.gov/home/homesteadact.html>.

Hooker, Richard J. *Food and Drink in America, A History.* Indianapolis: The Bobbs-Merrill Co., 1981.

Hoover, Dwight W. "Roller-skating toward Industrialism." *Hard at Play: Leisure in America, 1840–1890.* Ed. Kathryn Grover. Amherst: University of Massachu-setts Press, 1992. 61–76.

Horowitz, Daniel. *The Morality of Spending: Attitudes toward the Consumer Society in America, 1875–1940.* Baltimore: The Johns Hopkins University Press, 1985.

Horowitz, Helen Lefkowitz. *Alma Mater: Design and Experience in the Women's Col-leges from Their Nineteenth-Century Beginnings to the 1930's.* New York: Alfred A. Knopf, 1984.

Howard, Robert S. "Testimony of Robert S. Howard" Garraty 22–26.

Hull-House Maps and Papers. New York: Thomas Y. Crowell & Co., 1895.

Hunter, Robert. "Tenement Conditions in Chicago." *City Life, 1865–1900: Views of Urban America.* Ed. Ann Cook, Marilyn Gittell, and Herb Mack. New York: Praeger Publishers, 1973. 127.

Jones, Evan. *American Food: The Gastronomic Story,* 2nd ed. New York: Vintage, 1981.

Joselit, Jenna Weissman. *A Perfect Fit: Clothes, Character, and the Promise of America.* New York: Metropolitan Books, 2001.

Joseph, Morris. "The Modern Significance of Passover." *The Passover Anthology.* 1903. Ed. Philip Goodman. Philadelphia: Jewish Publication Society of America, 1961. 189–90.

Kaestle, Carl F. "The Public Schools and the Public Mood." *American Heritage* 41.1 (February 1990): 66–81.

Kasson, Joy S. *Buffalo Bill's Wild West: Celebrity, Memory, and Popular History.* New York: Hill and Wang, 2000.

Karcher, Carolyn. *The First Woman in the Republic: A Cultural Biography of Lydia Maria Child.* Durham: Duke University Press, 1994.

Karp, Abraham J. *Haven and Home: A History of the Jews in America.* New York: Schocken Books, 1985.

Karpf, Maurice J. *Jewish Community Organization in the United States.* New York: Bloch Publishing Company, 1983.

Katz, Michael B. "The Origins of Public Education: A Reassessment." *The Social History of American Education.* B. Edward McClellan and William J. Reese, eds. Urbana: University of Illinois Press, 1988.

Kelly, John R. *Leisure.* 3rd ed. Boston: Allyn and Bacon, 1996.

Kennedy, Lawrence W. "Pulpits and Politics: Anti-Catholicism in Boston in the 1880's and 1890's." *Historical Journal of Massachusetts* 28.1 (Winter 2000): 56–75.

Kristof, Nicholas D. "At This Rate, We'll be Global in Another Hundred Years." *New York Times* 23 May 1999: 5.

Kunstler, James Howard. *The Geography of Nowhere.* New York: Touchstone, 1993.

Larrabee, Lisa. "Women and Cycling: The Early Years." *How I Learned to Ride the Bicycle: Reflections of an Influential 19th Century Woman.* Ed. Carol O'Hare. Sunnyvale, CA: Fair Oaks Publishing, 1991. 81–98.

Lazerson, Marvin. *Origins of the Urban School: Public Education in Massachusetts, 1870–1915.* Cambridge: Harvard University Press, 1971.

———. "Urban Reform and the Schools: Kindergartens in Massachusetts, 1870–1915." *History of Education Quarterly* 11.2 (Summer 1971): 115–42.

Leavitt, Judith Walzer. " 'Science' Enters the Birthing Room: Obstetrics in America since the Eighteenth Century." *Women's Bodies: Health and Childbirth.* Munich: K. G. Saur, 1993. Vol. 11 of History of Women in the United States. Ed. Nancy F. Cott. 20 vols. 1993. 324–47.

———. "Under the Shadow of Maternity: American Women's Responses to Death and Debility Fears in Nineteenth-Century Childbirth." *Women's Bodies: Health and Childbirth.* Munich: K.G. Saur, 1993. Vol. 11 of History of Women in the United States. Ed. Nancy F. Cott. 20 vols. 1993. 252–77.

Lemay, Philippe. *Interview with Louis Pare.* 1938–39. New Hampshire Federal Writers' Project. American Life Histories: Manuscripts from the Federal Writers' Project, 1936–1940. *American Memory.* 19 June 2003 <http://memory.loc.gov>.

Levenstein, Harvey A. *Revolution at the Table: The Transformation of the American Diet.* New York: Oxford University Press, 1988.

Levine, Lawrence. *Highbrow/Lowbrow: The Emergence of Cultural Hierarchy in America.* Cambridge: Harvard University Press, 1988.

Levy, Louis Edward. "Jewish Immigrant Life in Philadelphia." 1890. *American Jewish Archives* 9.1 (1957): 32–42.

Ley, Sandra. *Fashion for Everyone: The Story of Ready-to-Wear, 1870's–1970's.* New York: Scribner, 1975.

Lichtenstein, Nelson, et al. *Who Built America?* Vol. 2. New York: American Social History Productions, Inc., 2000.

"The Life Story of a Greek Peddler." *The Life Stories of Undistinguished Americans, As Told by Themselves.* 63–79.

"The Life Story of a Lithuanian." *The Life Stories of Undistinguished Americans, As Told by Themselves.* 9–33.

The Life Stories of Undistinguished Americans: As Told by Themselves. Ed. Hamilton Holt. New York: James Pott & Company, 1906.

Lightner, David L. "Managing Madness." *Canadian Review of American Studies* 26.1 (Winter 1996): 147–58.

Livesay, Harold C. *Andrew Carnegie and the Rise of Big Business.* Ed. Oscar Handlin. New York: Longman, 2000.

Major Problems in American Diplomatic History: Documents and Readings, Vol. 2. Ed. Daniel M. Smith. Boston: D.C. Heath and Co., 1964.

Malloy, Jerry. *Introduction. Sol White's History of Colored Base Ball, with Other Documents of the Early Black Game, 1886–1936.* Lincoln: University of Nebraska Press, 1995. xiii–lxiv.

McBee, Randy D. *Dance Hall Days: Intimacy and Leisure Among Working-Class Immigrants in the United States.* New York: New York University Press, 2000.

McDannell, Colleen. *The Christian Home in Victorian America, 1840–1900.* Bloomington: Indiana University Press, 1986.

McGerr, Michael E. *The Decline of Popular Politics: The American North, 1865–1928.* New York: Oxford University Press, 1986.

McGuffey, William Holmes. *The Annotated McGuffey Reader.* Ed. Stanley W. Lindberg. New York: Van Nostrand Reinhold, 1976.

McIntosh, Elaine N. *American Food Habits in Historical Perspective.* Westport, CT: Praeger, 1995.

McMath Jr., Robert C. *American Populism: A Social History, 1877–1898.* New York: Hill and Wang, 1993.

McPherson, James Alan, and Miller Williams, eds. *Railroad: Trains and Train People in American Culture.* New York: Random House, 1976.

Melosi, Martin V. *The Sanitary City: Urban Infrastructure in America from Colonial Times to the Present.* Baltimore & London: The Johns Hopkins University Press, 2000.

Meyers, Marvin, et al. *Sources of the American Republic: A Documentary History of Politics, Society, and Thought.* Vol. 2. Chicago: Scott, Foresman and Company, 1961.

Miller, Donald L. *City of the Century: The Epic of Chicago and the Making of America.* New York: Simon & Schuster, 1996.

Misa, Thomas J. *A Nation of Steel: The Making of Modern America: 1865–1925.* Baltimore: The Johns Hopkins University Press, 1995.

Mohl, Raymond A. *The New City: Urban America in the Industrial Age, 1860–1920.* Harlan Davidson, Inc., Arlington Heights, IL, 1985.

Montgomery, Maureen E. "Female Rituals and the Politics of the New York Marriage Market in the Late Nineteenth Century." *Journal of Family History* 23.1 Jan. 1998. *Expanded Academic ASAP Plus.* University of Northern Iowa. 1 April 2003 <http://0-infotrac.galegroup.com.unistar.uni.edu/itw/infomark>.

Moore, Clement Clarke. "The Night Before Christmas." 8 December 2003 <http://www.blackdog.net/holiday/christmas/twas.html>.

Moran, William. *The Belles of New England: The Women of the Textile Mills and the Families Whose Wealth They Wove.* New York: St. Martin's Press, 2002.

Murolo, Priscilla. *The Common Ground of Womanhood: Class, Gender, and Working Girls' Clubs, 1884–1928.* Urbana: University of Illinois Press, 1997.

Nasaw, David. *Children of the City: At Work and At Play.* Garden City, NY: Anchor Press/Doubleday, 1985.

———. *Going Out: The Rise and Fall of Public Amusements.* New York: Basic Books, 1993.

Norris, James D. *Advertising and the Transformation of American Society, 1865–1920.* New York: Greenwood Press, 1990.

Nugent, Walter. *Crossings: The Great Transatlantic Migrations, 1870–1914.* Bloomington: Indiana University Press, 1992.

O'Dea, William T. *The Social History of Lighting.* New York: Macmillan, 1958.

O'Donnell, Thomas. "Testimony of Thomas O'Donnell." Garraty 33–36.

Ogle, Maureen. *All the Modern Conveniences: American Household Plumbing, 1840–1890.* Baltimore: The Johns Hopkins University Press, 1996.

Ohmann, Richard. *Selling Culture: Magazines, Markets and Class at the Turn of the Century.* New York: Verso, 1996.

Okihiro, Gary Y. *The Columbia Guide to Asian American History.* New York: Columbia University Press, 2001.

Oliver, F. E. "Why People Used Opium." *Drugs and Drug Policy in America: A Documentary History.* Ed. Steven R. Belenko. Westport, CT: Greenwood Press, 2000. 5–6.

Olmsted, Frederick Law. "Public Parks and the Enlargement of Towns." *Civilizing American Cities: A Selection of Frederick Law Olmsted's Writings on City Landscapes.* Ed. S. B. Sutton. Cambridge: The MIT Press, 1971.

O'Loughlin, Jim. *Literature without Guarantees: American Fiction in the Public Sphere.* Diss. State University of New York at Buffalo, 1998.

O'Neill, Eugene. *A Long Day's Journey into Night.* 1956. 2nd Ed. New Haven: Yale University Press, 2002.

P. T. Q. "Home and Society." *Scribners Monthly* 12.1 (May 1876) 127–30.

Pardee, Fanny C. "The Kindergarten as Related to Motherhood." *The Christian Register.* 24 January 1895: 54. Courtesy of the Harriet Beecher Stowe Center.

Pawa, Jay M. "Workingmen and Free Schools in the Nineteenth Century: A Comment on the Labor-Education Thesis." *History of Education Quarterly* 11.3 (Fall 1971): 287–302.

Peiss, Kathy. *Cheap Amusements: Working Women and Leisure in Turn-of-the-Century New York.* Philadelphia: Temple University Press, 1986.

Plante, Ellen M. *The American Kitchen, 1700 to the Present.* New York: Facts on File, Inc., 1995.

Pleck, Elizabeth H. *Celebrating the Family: Ethnicity, Consumer Culture, and Family Rituals.* Cambridge: Harvard University Press, 2000.

Putnam, Robert D. *Bowling Alone: The Collapse and Revival of American Community.* New York: Simon and Schuster, 2000.

Ralph, Julian. "Capitals of the Northwest." *City Life, 1865–1900: Views of Urban America.* Ed. Ann Cook, Marilyn Gittell, and Herb Mack. New York: Praeger, 1973. 61.

Ramirez, Bruno. *On the Move: French-Canadian and Italian Migrants in the North Atlantic Economy, 1860–1914.* Toronto: McClelland & Stewart, 1991.

Reddin, Paul. *Wild West Shows.* Urbana: University of Illinois Press, 1999.

Reinhardt, Richard, ed. *Workin' on the Railroad: Reminiscences from the Age of Steam.* Palo Alto, CA: American West Publishing Co., 1970.

Restad, Penne L. *Christmas in America: A History.* New York: Oxford University Press, 1996.

Riis, Jacob A. *How the Other Half Lives: Studies Among the Tenements of New York.* New York: Dover Publications, 1971.

Roediger, David R., and Philip S. Foner. *Our Own Time: A History of American Labor and the Working Day.* Westport, CT: Greenwood Press, 1989.

Rorabaugh, W. J. "Beer, Lemonade, and Propriety in the Gilded Age." *Dining in America 1850–1900.* Ed. Kathryn Grover. Rochester, NY: Strong Museum, 1987.

Rosen, George. *A History of Public Health.* Expanded ed. Baltimore: The Johns Hopkins University Press, 1993.

Rosenblatt, W. M. "The Jewish Dietary System." *The Galaxy* 18.5 (Nov. 1874): 673–78. Nineteenth Century in Print. *American Memory.* 10 Feb. 2003 <http://cdl.library.cornell.edu>.

Rosenzweig, Roy. *Eight Hours for What We Will: Workers and Leisure in the Industrial City, 1870–1920.* Cambridge: Cambridge University Press, 1983.

Rothman, Ellen K. *Hands and Hearts: A History of Courtship in America.* New York: Basic Books, Inc., 1984.

Rudolph, Richard, and Scott Ridley. *Power Struggle: The Hundred-Year War over Electricity.* New York: Harper & Row, 1986.

Ryan, David. *US Foreign Policy in World History.* London: Routledge Press, 2000.

Rydell, Robert W. *All the World's a Fair: Visions of Empire at American International Expositions, 1876–1916.* Chicago: University of Chicago Press, 1984.

Sanchez-Eppler, Karen. "Playing at Class." *English Literary History* 67 (2000): 819–42.

Sanger, Margaret. *An Autobiography.* New York: W. W. Norton & Co., 1938.

Schroeder, Fred E. H. "Feminine Hygiene, Fashion, and the Emancipation of American Women." *Women's Bodies: Health and Childbirth.* Munich: K.G. Saur, 1993. Vol. 11 of History of Women in the United States. Ed. Nancy F. Cott. 20 vols. 1993. 348–57.

Schultz, James R. *The Romance of Small-Town Chautauquas.* Columbia: University of Missouri Press, 2002.

Sinclair, Upton. *The Jungle.* 1906. New York: Signet Classic, 1990.

Smith, Robert A. *A Social History of the Bicycle: Its Early Life and Times in America.* New York: American Heritage Press, 1972.

Smith-Rosenberg, Carroll. "The Abortion Movement and the AMA, 1850–1880." *Disorderly Conduct: Visions of Gender in Victorian America.* Oxford: Oxford University Press, 1985.

———. "The New Woman as Androgyne." *Disorderly Conduct: Visions of Gender in Victorian America.* Oxford: Oxford University Press, 1985.

Spack, Ruth. *America's Second Tongue: American Indian Education and the Ownership of English, 1860–1900.* Lincoln: University of Nebraska Press, 2002.

Spain, Daphne. *How Women Saved the City.* Minneapolis: University of Minnesota Press, 2001.

Spencer, Herbert. *On Social Evolution: Selected Writings.* J.D.Y. Peel, ed. Chicago: University of Chicago Press, 1972.

Spillane, Joseph. "Cocaine in Soft Drinks." *Drugs and Drug Policy in America: A Documentary History.* Ed. Steven R. Belenko. Westport, CT: Greenwood Press, 2000. 20–21.

Spring, Joel. *The American School: 1642–1996.* 4th ed. New York: McGraw-Hill Co., Inc., 1997.

Starbuck, Charles C. "Considerations Touching the School Question." *New Englander and Yale Review* 51.236 Nov. 1889: 331–52.

"State-Specific Maternal Mortality Among Black and White Women-United States, 1987–1996." *The MMWR Weekly.* 48.23 18 June 1999: 492–96. 28 Apr. 2003 <http://www.cdc.gov/epo/mmwr>.

Stover, John F. *American Railroads.* 2nd ed. Chicago: University of Chicago Press, 1997.

Stowell, David O. *Streets, Railroads, and the Great Strike of 1887.* Chicago: University of Chicago Press, 1999.

Strasser, Susan. *Never Done: A History of American Housework.* New York: Pantheon Books, 1982.

———. *Satisfaction Guaranteed: The Making of the American Mass Market.* New York: Pantheon Books, 1989.

Strickland, Charles. "The Rise of Public Schooling and the Attitude of Parents: The Case of Atlanta, 1872–1897." *Schools in Cities: Consensus and Conflict in American Educational History.* Ronald K. Goodenow and Diane Ravitch, eds. New York: Holmes & Meier, 1983.

Stromquist, Shelton. *A Generation of Boomers: The Pattern of Railroad Labor Conflict in Nineteenth-Century America.* Urbana: University of Illinois Press, 1987.

Strong, George Templeton. *The Diary of George Templeton Strong: Post-War Years 1865–1875.* Ed. Allan Nevins and Milton Halsey Thomas. New York: The Macmillan Company, 1952.

"A Study of Death." *The Atlantic Monthly.* 76.458 Dec. 1895: 844–848. Nineteenth Century in Print. *American Memory.* 10 Feb. 2003 <http://cdl.library.cornell.edu>.

Sumner, William Graham. "The Absurd Effort to Make the World Over." 1893. *War and Other Essays.* Ed. Albert Galloway Keller. New Haven: Yale University Press, 1911. 195–211.

Sutherland, Daniel E. *The Expansion of Everyday Life, 1860–1876.* New York: Harper & Row, 1989.

Tarr, Joel Arthur. "From City to Suburb: The 'Moral' Influence of Transportation Technology." *American Urban History* 2nd ed. Ed. Alexander B. Callow, Jr. New York: Oxford University Press, 1973. 202–12.

"The Teaching of Death." *Harper's New Monthly Magazine.* 19.113 Oct. 1859: 652–53. Nineteenth Century in Print. *American Memory.* 10 Feb. 2003 <http://cdl.library.cornell.edu>.

Teaford, Jon C. *The Unheralded Triumph: City Government in America, 1870–1900.* Baltimore: The Johns Hopkins University Press, 1984.

Temin, Peter. *Iron and Steel in Nineteenth-Century America: An Economic Inquiry.* Cambridge: The MIT Press, 1964.

Thernstrom, Stephan. "Urbanization, Migration, and Social Mobility in Late Nineteenth-Century America." *American Urban History* 2nd ed. Ed. Alexander B. Callow, Jr. New York: Oxford University Press, 1973. 399–409.

"Three Cases of Families Receiving Aid from the German Society in Chicago." *German Workers in Chicago* 119–25.

Tice, Patricia M. *Altered States: Alcohol and Other Drugs in America.* Rochester, NY: Strong Museum, 1992.

Tindall, George Brown. *America: A Narrative History.* W. W. Norton. 9 June 2004 <http://www.wwnorton.com/tindall/ch21/resources/documents/ sumner.htm>.

Trachtenberg, Alan. *The Incorporation of America: Culture and Society in the Gilded Age.* New York: Hill and Wang, 1982.

Trattner, Walter I. *Crusade for the Children: A History of the National Child Labor Committee and Child Labor Reform in America.* Chicago: Quadrangle Books, 1970.

Twain, Mark. *Adventures of Huckleberry Finn, Tom Sawyer's Comrade.* 1884. Berkeley: University of California Press, 1985.

———. *Christian Science.* Rev. ed. 1899. New York: Harpers & Brothers, 1907.

Uminowicz, Glenn. "Recreation in Christian America: Ocean Grove and Asbury Park, New Jersey, 1869–1914." *Hard at Play: Leisure in America, 1840–1890.* Ed. Kathryn Grover. Amherst: University of Massachusetts Press, 1992. 8–38.

United States. Bureau of the Census. *Historical Statistics of the United States, Colonial Times to 1970.* 2 vols. U.S. Dept. of Commerce: Washington, D.C., 1975.

Veblin, Thorstein. *The Theory of the Leisure Class.* 1899. New York: Dover Publications, 1994.

Vreeland, H. H. "The Street Railways of America." *City Life, 1865–1900: Views of Urban America.* Ed. Ann Cook, Marilyn Gittell, and Herb Mack. New York: Praeger, 1973. 47–49.

Walker, Robert H. *Everyday Life in Victorian America, 1865–1900.* 2nd ed. Malabar, FL: Krieger, 1994.

Ward, David. *Poverty, Ethnicity, and the American City, 1840–1925: Changing Conceptions of the Slum and the Ghetto.* Cambridge: Cambridge University Press, 1989.

Ward, Geoffrey C. *Baseball: An Illustrated History.* New York: Alfred A. Knopf, 1994.

Warner, Charles Dudley. "Studies of the Great West: III—Chicago." *Harper's New Monthly Magazine.* 76.456 May 1888: 869–79.

Watkins, William H. *The White Architects of Black Education: Ideology and Power in America, 1865–1954.* New York: Teachers College Press, 2001.

Weber, Adna Ferrin. *The Growth of Cities in the Nineteenth Century: A Study in Statistics.* 1899. Ithaca: Cornell University Press, 1963.

Weir, Robert E. *Knights Unhorsed: Internal Conflict in a Gilded Age Social Movement.* Detroit: Wayne State University Press, 2000.

Wiebe, Robert. *The Search for Order: 1877–1920.* New York: Hill and Wang, 1967.

Wilder, Laura Ingalls. *The Long Winter.* 1940. New York: Harper & Row, 1968.

Willard, Francis. *How I Learned to Ride the Bicycle: Reflections of an Influential 19th Century Woman.* Ed. Carol O'Hare. 1895. Sunnyvale, CA: Fair Oaks Publishing, 1991.

Williams, Peter W. *America's Religions: From Their Origins to the Twenty-first Century.* Urbana: University of Illinois Press, 2002.

Wilson, Christopher P. *The Labor of Words: Literary Professionalism in the Progressive Era.* Athens: University of Georgia Press, 1985.

Winston, Diane. "'The Cathedral of Open Air': The Salvation Army's Sacralization of Secular Space, New York City, 1880–1910." *Gods of the City: Religion and the American Urban Landscape.* Ed. Robert A. Orsi. Bloomington: Indiana University Press, 1999. 367–92.

Wisan, Joseph E. "The Cuban Crisis." *Major Problems in American Diplomatic History: Documents and Readings.* Vol. 2. 297–308.

"Woman's Relation to the State." *The Household* Vol. 2 (1869): 79–80.

Women's Christian Temperance Union, 20 June 2002 <http://www.wctu.com/early history.html>.

Wormser, Richard. *The Iron Horse: How Railroads Changed America.* New York: Walker & Co., 1993.

Index

Abortion, 144–45, 217
Addams, Jane, 25–26, 40–43, 182, 243
Addiction, 162–63. *See also* Alcohol;
    Drugs
Adorno, Theodor, 175
Adventures of Huckleberry Finn (Twain),
    200
Advertising, 170–71
African-Americans, 18, 64, 98, 186–87,
    204–5
Agrarian economy, 10. *See also* Farmers; Homesteading
Albany, New York, 58
Albert, Prince of England,
    142
Alcohol, 158–62
Alcott, Louisa May, 117–18
Alexander II, Czar of Russia, 7, 136,
    230
Amalgamated Association of Iron and
    Steel Workers, 90
Ambrose, Stephen E., 49
American exceptionalism, 132
American Federation of Labor, 11, 179,
    238–39

Americanization, 209–10, 221, 224,
    230–31
The American Kitchen (Plante), 157
American Medical Association, 201,
    216–17
American Protective Association
    (APA), 229–30
American Settlement movement, 41.
    See also Hull House; Settlement
    houses
American Woman's Home (Beecher and
    Stowe), 101, 115, 156, 218
Ames, Kenneth L., 104
Ancient Order of Hibernians (AOH),
    242
Anson, Cap, 186
Anthony, Susan B., 102, 185
Argentina, 6
Armour Meat company, 93
Armstrong, Samuel, 204
Artisans, 1
Asia, trade with, 48. *See also* China
Associations, 234–38. *See also* specific
    associations
The Awakening (Chopin), 140

"Ballad of the Heathen Chinee"
    (Harte), 10
Baptists, 224
Barnard College, 212, 214
Barnum, P. T., 192
Barret, James R., 97
Baseball, 185–87
Battle of San Juan Hill, 4
Beecher, Catherine, 117–18, 124; *American Woman's Home,* 101, 115, 156, 218
Beecher, Henry Ward, 171
Bellamy, Edward, 152, 174–76
Bernhardt, Sarah, 171
Bessemer converters, 73, 86–88
Beveridge, Albert J., 4
Bible, 226–27
Bicycling, 183–85
Bigott, Joseph, 29
Birth control, 143–45. *See also* Comstock Law
Black, J. R., 216
Black lung disease, 214
Blanchard, J. G., 178
Bohi, Charles W., 58
Booth-Tucker, Frederick, 232
Borchert, James, 32
Boston marriages, 213
Bottle feeding of infants, 123, 219–20
Bowlby, Rachel, 169
Boxer Rebellion, 194
Boydston, Jeanne, 102
Brace, Charles Loring, 127
Braden, Donna R., 195
Brandon, Joseph, 210
Brands, 153–54
Braude, Ann, 233
Breaker boys, 128
Breastfeeding, 123, 219–20
Breen, John, 84
Brenzel, Barbara, 131
British immigrants, 6–8, 10, 12
Broadway, 174
Brooklyn Bridge, 34
Brooklyn Dodgers, 23–24
Brownie camera, 190
Brownson, Orestes, 118
Brunner, Arnold, 41

Brush, Charles, 34
Bryan, William Jennings, 241
Bryn Mawr College, 213
B. T. Babbitt's soap, 171
Bunner, H. C., 32
Burnham, Daniel, 41
Bushnell, Horace, 133

Cable cars, 23
Cahan, Abraham, 25
California Gold Rush, 172
Calling cards, 140–41
Calvinism, 121, 225
Canada, 3
Carnegie, Andrew, 13–14, 88–90, 97, 205
Carnegie Steel, 88
Carroll, H. K., 224
Castello, Dan, 192
Cast-iron stoves, 108–9
Cather, Willa, 197
Catholicism. *See* Roman Catholic Church
Cattle Butchers' Union, 95
Cavallo, Dominick, 26
Cemeteries, 148
Central Pacific Railroad, 48, 54
Central Park (New York), 26–27
Chase, Andrew, 90
Chautaquas, 191, 196
Chesbrough, Ellis, 40
Chesnutt, Charles, 65
Chicago, 1, 20, 22, 37–45, 95; Great Fire of, 38–39; growth of, 37, 44–45; Hull-House and, 25–26, 40–43; meatpacking and, 90, 91; World's Fair in, 40–42, 114, 191, 193. *See also* Packingtown
Chicago and Northwestern line, 53
Chicago, Burlington & Quincy Railroad, 59
Child, Lydia Maria, 102
Child labor, 43, 75, 79, 98, 126–29
Children, 112–13, 122–27; bottlefeeding of, 123, 219–20; childbirth and, 122–23; death of, 146–47, 214, 220; play of, 124–26; social control and, 129–31
China, 194

Chinese Exclusion Act (1882), 5, 11, 62
Chinese immigrants, 5–6, 10–11, 61–62, 68, 164–65
Christian Science, 233
Christkindel, 133, 136
Christmas, 132–36
"A Christmas Visit" (Moore), 133–34
Cincinnati, Ohio, 91
Circuses, 191–93
Cities, 19–45; Chicago and, 38–39, 44–45; government of, 32–37; housing and, 28–32; parks and, 26–28; population growth and, 19–21; railroads and, 56–58; settlement houses and, 40–43; structure of, 22–25. *See also* specific cities
City Beautiful movement, 41
Civic life, 223, 233–34, 233–38; conflict in, 241–42; political participation and, 239–41
Civil War, 16, 131–32
Class: alcohol and, 158–62; child care and, 123–24; children and, 126–31; courtship and, 139–42; drugs and, 163–67; eating and, 155–59; houses and, 104–6; leisure and, 180–82; professional-managerial, 89, 97, 105, 180; working class, 105–6, 126–29, 158
Cleveland, Ohio, 34
Clothing, 171–74; corsets, 217–19; jeans, 172; sewing machines, 74–75, 106, 172
Coca-Cola, 162–63
Cocaine, 162–63
Cody, William "Buffalo Bill," 193
Colonialism, 3–5
Communism, 210
Compulsory school attendance laws, 202, 205
Comstock Law (1873), 144–45, 217
Conant, Helen S., 27
Confederacy, 3
Consumers, 151–52, 168–73; alcohol and, 158–62; drugs and, 163–67; eating and, 156–59; factories and, 97; food and, 152–55; *Looking Backward* and, 152, 174–76
Contract labor, 62

Cook County, Illinois, 39
Copyright, 197
Corsets, 217–19
Cotton textile industry, 9, 16
Courtship, 138–42
Craft shops, 73
Crane, Stephen, 99, 161
Cuba, war in, 3–4

Daguerrotype, 147
Daniels, Rudolph, 48, 56, 61
Darwin, Charles, 12–13, 146
Davis, Katherine, 114
Deadwood Dick (cowboy character), 199
DeBerg, Betty A., 227
Debs, Eugene, 232
Democracy in America (Tocqueville), 223
Democratic Party, 17
Denning, Michael, 56, 199–200
Department of Justice, 91
Department stores, 167–69
Depression of 1873–1877, 17, 47, 56, 89. *See also* Great Uprising of 1877
Depression of 1893–1897, 17, 47, 56
De Smet, South Dakota, 60
Detroit, Michigan, 20
Dewey, John, 207
Dickson, William, 97
Dime novels, 199–200
Disease, 214, 215–16, 219; germ theory and, 36, 40, 108, 220. *See also* Health care
Dix, Dorothea, 220–21
Dolls and gender, 125–26
Domestic servants, 116–18
Dominican Republic, 3
Dorr, Rheta Childe, 103
"Double Mammouth" shows, 196
Douglas, Ann, 100–101, 225
Dreiser, Theodore, *Sister Carrie,* 169, 173–74
Drugs, 158, 162–67
Dudden, Faye, 116
Duluth, Minnesota, 57
Du Maurier, George, 197

Eastern European immigrants, 6–9, 136–38

Easthope, Anthony, 175

Eastman, George, 190

Eating, 155–59. *See also* Food

Economic policy, 14–17

Eddy, Mary Baker, 233

Edison, Thomas, 34, 189–90

Edson, Cyrus, 181

Education, 201–14; immigrants and, 207–10; manual training and, 205–6; reform schools, 129–31; religious freedom and, 210–11; rote learning, 206–7; women and, 203, 211–14

Edwards, Jonathan, 225

Eighteenth Amendment (Prohibition), 162

Eight-Hour movement, 178–79

"Eight Hours" (Blanchard and Jones), 178–79

Eight hours for what we will: Workers and leisure in an industrial city, 1870–1920 (Rosenzweig), 241–42

Electricity, 2, 34–35

Embalming, 147. *See also* Funerals

Entertainment, 177–96; baseball, 185–87; bicycling, 183–85; circuses, 191–93; leisure, 177–82; movies, 189–90; peep shows, 189; penny arcades, 190; recreation, 181–82; saloons, 158, 161, 188; theatres, 188; traveling shows, 191–95; *Uncle Tom's Cabin* shows, 191, 195–96; vaudeville, 189; Wild West shows, 177, 191, 193–95. *See also* specific shows

Ethnicity, 22. *See also* specific ethnic group

Ethnic organizations, 95–96

Evans, Chris, 55

Factories, 71–98; meatpacking industry and, 90–93; organized labor and, 81–85; Packingtown and, 94–98; steel industry and, 72–73, 86–90; textile industry and, 75–80, 86

Fall River, Massachusetts, 76, 80–83

Farmers, railroads and, 59–61

Farmer's Alliance, 241

Fashion, 171–74

Feminine disestablishment, 100. *See also* Women

Finishing schools, 211

Fistulas, 122

Foner, Philip, 67

Food, 51–52, 152–56; adulteration of, 154–55, 166; canned goods, 155; home preparation of, 112–13; meat consumption, 153; milk contamination, 219–20; pressure cookers, 152; recipes for, 157–58

Formanek-Brunell, Miriam, 126

Fourth of July conflicts, 241–43

France, 1871 civil war in, 9–10

Frankfurt School, 175

Fraternal organizations, 235–36

Fred Harvey restaurants, 52

Frick Coke Company, 89

Froebel, Friedrich, 207

Fundamentalism, 226–27

Funerals, 145–48

Gardening, 114

Gender, 83, 125–26

General Time Convention, 66

German immigrants, 6, 8–9

German Society, 96

Germ theory, 36, 40, 108, 220

Geronimo, 194

Gilded Age, 16, 243–44

The Gilded Age (Twain), 243

Globe Theater (Boston), 188

Going Out (Nasaw), 179

Gompers, Samuel, 11, 239. *See also* American Federation of Labor

Good Housekeeping (magazine), 107

Gordon, Sarah, 53, 58

Gould, Jay, 12

Government reform of industry, 81

The Grange, 60

Granite Mill fire, 80

Grant, Frank, 186

Grant, H. Roger, 58

Grant, Zilpah, 211

Great Britain, 3

Great Chicago Fire, 38–39

The Great Train Robbery (film), 189

Great Uprising of 1877, 16, 47, 56,
  66–69, 98
Greeley, Horace, 84
Griffith, Ernest S., 33, 47
Grob, Gerald, 214–15, 220
Gum, 162
Gunton, George, 179

Haiti, 3
Hale, Sarah Joseph, 131
Hall, H. N., 64
Halsted Street (Chicago), 25
Hamblen, Herbert E., 63
Hamilton, Gail, 230
Hampton Institute, 204–5
Hancock, Winfield, 156
Hart, James D., 199, 200
Harte, Bret, 10
Harvey Houses, 52
Harwood, W. S., 235–36
Hawaii, annexation of, 5
Hayes, Rutherford B., 67
Haymarket riot, 98, 238
Health care, 115, 214–21; hospitals,
  220–21; patent medicines,
  162–64, 166; public, 214, 215–16,
  217–20
Hearst, William Randolph, 3
Heininger, Mary Lynn Stevens, 124
*A History of American City Government:
  The Conspicuous Failure, 1870–1900*
  (Griffith), 33
Hobos, 55–56
Hobsbawn, Eric, 56
Holidays: Christmas and, 132–36;
  Passover and, 136–39; Thanksgiv-
  ing and, 131–32
Homestead Act of 1862, 14–15
Homesteading, 9, 60
Homestead Strike, 90, 98
Hooker, Richard J., 152
Hospitals, 220–21
The Household (magazine), 101
The House of Mirth (Wharton), 197
Housework, 99, 102–19; cooking and
  baking, 112–13; domestic servants
  and, 116–18; ironing, 112; laundry,
  110–12; technology and, 106–10;
  women and, 111–15

Housing, 28–32, 104–6; back alley, 32;
  balloon frame, 28–29; boarding
  houses, 29; row, 29–30;
  shantytowns, 32; tenements, 29–32
Howard, Robert, 82–83
Howells, William Dean, 200
How the Other Half Lives (Riis), 29–30,
  165
Hull-House, 25–26, 40–43, 243. *See also*
  Jane Addams
Hull-House Maps and Papers (Addams),
  43
Hunt, Mary, 166
Huntington, Samuel, 54–55

Ice boxes, 152. *See also* Refrigeration
If Christ Came to Chicago (Stead), 23, 43
Immigrants, 5–9, 20, 132; education
  and, 207–10; meatpacking and, 94;
  railroads and, 52–53; unions and,
  83; workforce and, 76–77. *See also*
  specific groups
Imperialism, 3–5, 194, 195
Income tax, 17
Independent Order of Odd Fellows,
  235
Indian removal policies, 194. *See also*
  Native Americans
Individualism, 37
Industrial accidents, 215
Industry, government reform of, 81.
  See also Factories; specific industries
Infants: bottle feeding of, 123, 219–20;
  mortality in, 214, 220. *See also* Chil-
  dren
Ingalls, Charles, 60–61
International Copyright Act, 197
Interstate Commerce Act (1887), 60
Irish immigrants, 6–8, 10, 12, 77, 227
Italian immigrants, 6, 9
Ivory Soap, 170

James, Henry, 127
James, Jesse, 56
Jay Cooke and Company, 54
Jeans, 172
Jefferson, Thomas (President of the
  United States), 10
Jewish Daily Forward (newspaper), 25

Jewish immigrants, 7, 136–39. *See also* Judaism

Johnson, David N., 74

Jones, Jesse H., 178

Jordan Marsh department store, 168

Joselit, Jenna Weissman, 172–73

Joseph, Morris, 137

Judaism, 136–39, 224, 230–31

Julian West *(Looking Backward)*, 174–76

The Jungle (Sinclair), 71–72, 155

Keith, Benjamin Franklin, 189

Kellogg's cereal, 154

Kelly, Florence, 43

Kelly, Michael, 177

Kindergarten movement, 207–9

Kinetoscope, 189

Kinship networks, 138

Knights of Labor, 82, 238

Kodak, 190

Kriss Kingle, 133. *See also* Christmas

Labor, 1, 9–14, 81–85; child, 43, 75, 79, 98, 126–29; division of, 74; organizations for, 238–39. *See also* Immigrants; Unions; specific industries

Lake Michigan, 40

Lancashire, England, 82–83, 86

Lancaster, Massachusetts, 129–31

Lawrence, Massachusetts, 82–84

Lee, Joseph, 182

Leisure, 177–82

Levenstein, Harvey, 152, 156

Levine, Lawrence, 188–89

Levi Strauss, 172

Libraries, 209

Lincoln, Abraham, 131–32, 147

Linotype, 196

Lithuanian famine, 136

"Little House on the Prairie" books, 60

London, Jack, 197

Long Day's Journey into Night (O'Neill), 164

"Long Haul–Short Haul" controversy, 60

The Long Winter (Wilder), 60

Looking Backward: 2000–1887 (Bellamy), 152, 174–76

Los Angeles, California, 20

Lowell, Francis Cabot, 75–76

Lower East Side (New York), 127–28, 145. *See also How the Other Half Lives;* Jacob Riis; Tenements

Loyal Women of American Liberty, 242

Lydia Pinkam's Tonic, 164

Lynn, Massachusetts, 74–75

Lyons, Mary, 211–12

Macy's department store, 168, 170

Magazines, 180–81

Maggie: Girl of the Streets (Crane), 161

Mail order catalogs, 53–54, 167, 169–70

Manifest Destiny, 3–5

Mann, Horace, 202

Manual training, 204–6

"Marble Palace," 167

Marriage, 138–42; sexuality and, 143–45

The Marrow of Tradition (Chesnutt), 65

Marshall Fields department store, 168

Martin, William, 184

Mason jars, 152

McDannell, Colleen, 225, 226

McGerr, Michael, 239

McGuffey's Reader, 206–7, 210–11

Machine politics, 32, 34, 37

McKinley, William (President of the United States), 3

McMath, Robert C., Jr., 60

McPherson, James Alan, 64

Meat consumption, 153

Meatpacking industry, 71–73, 90–93, 155; Packingtown and, 94–98

Mechanization, 1

Medical advice literature, 216–17

Melosi, Martin V., 35

Mental hospitals, 220–21

Methodists, 224

Midwives, 122

Milk contamination, 219–20

Miller, Donald L., 43–44

Milwaukee, Wisconsin, 20

Minneapolis, Minnesota, 20, 23

Minstrel shows, 196

Mohl, Raymond, 37, 57
Molly Maquires, 199
Montgomery, Maureen, 141
Montgomery Ward's department store, 170
Moore, Clement Clarke, 133–34
Mount Holyoke College, 212–13
Mourning, 145, 148
Movies, 189–90
Mrs. Winslow's Soothing Syrup, 163–64
Mule spinners, 80
Mussel Slough, California, 55

Narcotics, 162–67, 166
Nasaw, David, 179, 187–88
Nast, Thomas, 134–35
National Consumers League, 129
Native Americans, 3–4, 15, 132, 194–95, 204
Negro Leagues (baseball), 187
Neighborhoods, 22
Newark, New Jersey, 22
New Deal, 241
Newsboy's Lodging Houses, 127, 129
"New woman" movement, 213
New York City, New York, 19
New York City Health Department, 220
New York Evening Sun (newspaper), 30
New York Morning Journal (newspaper), 3
New York Stock Exchange, 54
New York Tribune (newspaper), 30
Niagara Bible Conference, 227
Nicholas, saint, 133, 136
Nickelodeons, 190
"The Night Before Christmas" (Moore), 133–34
Normal Schools, 202
Norris, Frank, 197; *The Octopus*, 55
Northern Pacific Railroad, 52, 54, 57
Nothing Like It in the World (Ambrose), 49
Novels, 196–200
Nugent, Walter, 7
Nutrition, 152

The Octopus (Norris), 55
Ogle, Maureen, 108
Ohmann, Richard, 151, 170, 180, 237
Olmsted, Frederick Law, 26–28, 41
O'Neill, Eugene, 164
Opium dens, 164–66
Organizations, 234–38. *See also* Labor; Unions
Outwork system, 73–74

Pacific Main Mill (Lawrence, Massachusetts), 83–84
Packingtown (Chicago), 71, 94–98
Pale of Settlement, 7, 136
Panic of 1873, 54, 57, 67. *See also* Depression of 1873–77
Parks, 26–28
Parochial schools, 229
Party affiliation, 239, 241
Passover, 136–39
Patent medicines, 162–64, 166
Peep shows, 189
Pemberton, John, 162. *See also* Coca-Cola
Pennsylvania Railroad, 67–68
Pennsylvania Station (New York City), 58
Penny arcades, 190
People's Party, 241
Philadelphia, Pennsylvania, 23
Philippines, 3
Photography, 147, 190
The Pit (Norris), 197
Plante, Ellen, 157
Play, 124–27
Playgrounds, 209
Pleck, Elizabeth H., 102
Plessy vs. Ferguson (1898), 65
Plumbing, 107–8. *See also* Sanitation
Political machines, 32, 34, 37
Political participation, 239–41
Pontellier, Edna *(The Awakening)*, 140–41
Popular novels, 198
Populists, 241
Potato blight of 1845–50 (Ireland), 8
Poverty, 2
Presbyterians, 224

Presidential elections, 239
Price fixing, 91
Primghar, Iowa, 59
Professional-managerial class, 89, 97, 105, 180
Professional organizations, 236–37
Progressive Era, 30, 233, 241
Prohibition (18th Amendment), 162
Promontory, Utah, 48
Protestantism, 225–27, 229–30
Public education, 201–4
Public health, 214, 215–16, 217–20
Public water, 36, 108, 215
Pulitzer, Joseph, 3
Pullman, George, 64
Pullman cars, 50–52
Pullman porters, 64
Pullman strike, 98
Pulmonary disorders, 214
Pure Food, Drink, and Drug Act (1906), 155, 166
Putnam, Robert, 234–35

Radcliffe College, 214
Railroads, 47–69, 243; brakemen, 63–64; building of, 53–55, 61–62; cities and, 56–58; conductors, 63; construction of, 5; engineers, 62; farmers and, 59–61; federal policy and, 14–17; firemen, 62–63; food on, 51–52; Great Uprising of 1877 and, 66–69; hobos, 55–56; segregation and, 64–65; transcontinental, 48–50, 53, 61, 62; work on, 62–64
Railroad time, 65–66
Railton, George Scott, 231
Ralph, Julian, 23
Ramirez, Bruno, 9
Ready-to-wear clothing, 172–73. *See also* Clothing
Realist novels, 198
Rebecca of Sunnybrook Farm (Wiggins), 197
Reconstruction, 3, 15–17, 53
Recreation, 181–82
Reform schools, 129–31
Refrigerated rail car, 54, 90–91, 153
Refrigeration, 97, 152
Religious freedom, 210–11

Restad, Penne, 134
Rice, Joseph Mayer, 206, 207
Riis, Jacob, 29–30, 31, 165, 182, 203
Rituals, 149. *See also* specific holidays; specific rituals
Robber barons, 47
Robinson, Charles Mulford, 41
Robinson, Jackie, 187
Roller skating, 182
Roman Catholic Church, 159, 210, 217, 224, 227–30; labor and, 83, 96
Roosevelt, Theodore, 233
Rosenzweig, Ray, 241
Rote learning, 206–7
Rothman, Ellen, 143
Rough Riders, 194
Rudkus, Jurgis *(The Jungle)*, 161
Ryan, David, 4
Rydell, Robert, 191

Safety Appliance Act (1893), 64
Saloons, 158, 161, 188
Salvation Army, 231–33
Sanchez-Eppler, Karen, 127
San Francisco, California, 23
Sanger, Margaret, 144–45
Sanitation, 25, 35–36, 40; food and, 154–56; indoor plumbing, 107–8
Sanitation movement, 201, 215–16
San Joaquin Valley, California, 55
Santa Claus, 133–36
Schools. *See* Education
Science and Health with Key to Scriptures (Eddy), 233
Scientific sanitarians, 108
Sears, Joseph, 54
Sears & Roebuck Company, 54, 170
Segregation, 187
Seminaries, 211–12
"Separate but equal," 65
Servants, domestic, 116–18
Settlement houses, 25–26. *See also* Hull House
"Seven Sisters" colleges, 212–14
Sewage systems, 36, 40
Seward, William, 3
Sewing machines, 74–75, 106, 172
Sewing patterns, 172
Sexuality, 143–45. *See also* Marriage

Shakespeare plays, 188
Sharecroppers, 18
Shoe industry, 73–74
Sinclair, Upton, 92, 99, 156; *The Jungle,* 71–72, 155, 162
Singer sewing machines, 106
Sioux tribe, 15
Sister Carrie (Dreiser), 169, 173–74
Sitting Bull, 194
Smith, Frank, 232
Smith, Henry Nash, 197
Smith College, 212–13
Soap advertising, 170–71
Social class. *See* Class; specific class
Social Darwinism, 13, 100, 181, 193
Social Gospel, 226
Socialism, 210, 232
Socialist Wheelmen's Club, 183
Social service organizations, 227
Social services, 36–37
Solidarity, 83
Sontag, George, 55
Southern Pacific Railroad, 54–55
South Side Gas Works, 38
Southwest Railway, 238
Spanish-American War, 3–5, 190, 194
Spencer, Herbert, 100, 181. *See also* Social Darwinism
Spiritual health, 100–101
Spring, Joel, 209
Stanford, Leland, 48
Stanton, Elizabeth Cady, 102
Starbuck, Charles C., 230
State Industrial School for Girls (Lancaster, Massachusetts), 129
Stead, William, 23, 43, 44
Steam Era, 61. *See also* Railroads
Steel industry, 72–73, 86–90
Stewart, A. T., 167
Stover, John H., 55, 60
Stowe, Harriet Beecher, 99; *American Woman's Home,* 101, 115, 156, 218; *Uncle Tom's Cabin,* 101, 191, 195–96
Stowell, David O., 67
Strasser, Susan, 110
Strauss, Nathan, 220
Street children, 130
Street life, 25
Street peddlers, 127

Strikes, 90, 98
Strong, George Templeton, 10
Strong, William L., 36
Subways, 23
Sumner, Charles, 3
Sumner, William Graham, 13
Sun time, 65–66
Supreme Court, 65
Sweat shops, 43
Swift, Gustavus, 90, 153

Tammany Hall, 34
Tariffs, 16–17
Tax policy, 16–17, 160
"The Teaching of Death" (Victorian poem), 146–47
Teaford, John C., 33
Technology, 2. *See also* specific inventions
Tenement House Commission (1884), 30
Tenements, 29–32
Ten hour work day, 84–85
"The Ten Laws of Health" (Black), 216
Textile industry, 72–73, 75–80; unions and, 81–83, 85–86; wages and, 84
Thanksgiving, invention of, 131–32
Theaters, 188, 189–90
The Theory of the Leisure Class (Veblin), 182
Thernstrom, Stephen, 21
Tice, Patricia, 162
Tilden, Samuel J., 241
Tocqueville, Alexis de, 223
"Tom troupes," 196
Toynbee Hall settlement house, 41
Trachtenberg, Alan, 169
Train robbers, 55–56
Transcontinental railroad, 48–50, 53, 61, 62
Transportation, 22–24. *See also* Railroads
Traveling shows, 191–95
Trilby (Du Maurier), 197
Trolleys, 23–24
Tuberculosis, 214
Turner, Frederick Jackson, 21
Tuskegee Institute, 204–5

Twain, Mark, 99, 195, 199–200, 233, 243
Tweed, William "Boss," 34
Twenty Years at Hull-House (Addams), 26
"Two-book" system, 209

Uncle Tom's Cabin shows, 191, 195–96
Uncle Tom's Cabin (Stowe), 101
Unheralded Triumph: City Government in America, 1870–1900, The (Teaford), 33
Union Pacific Railroad, 48, 52
Unions, 238–39; education and, 202; meatpacking and, 92; steel industry and, 86–90; strikes and, 52; textile industry and, 81–83, 85–86
Union Station (Chicago), 94
Union Stockyards (Chicago), 95
University of Chicago laboratory school, 207
Urban government, 32–37
Urban planning, 25. *See also* Cities
U.S. Steel trust, 90

Vanderbilt, Cornelius, 14
Vanderbilt, William, 47
Vassar College, 212
Vaudeville, 189
Veblin, Thorstein, 182
Victoria, Queen of England, 142
Victorian houses, 28
Vincent, John Heyl, 195
Virgin Islands, 3
Vitascope, 190
Voting rights for women, 103, 143

Wage reductions, 84
Waring, George E., Jr., 36
Warner, Charles Dudley, 44, 243
Warner, Susan, 99
Washington, Booker T., 205
Waste materials, 73–74
Water supply, 36, 98, 215
Weaver, James, 241
Weddings, 142. *See also* Marriage

Wellesley College, 212–13
Wharton, Edith, 99, 197
Wheeler, Edward L., 199
"The White City," 41, 191
White collar. *See* Professional-managerial class
Wiebe, Robert, 234, 237, 239
Wiggins, Kate, 197
Wilder, Laura Ingalls, 60
Wild West shows, 177, 191, 193–95
Willard, Frances, 166, 185
Williams, Peter W., 231
Williams' Shaving Soap, 171
Wilson-Gorman Tariff of 1894, 17
Women, 110–15; education and, 203, 211–14; fashion and, 172–74; labor and, 83–84; marriage and, 138–42; mothering and, 217–19; organizations for, 237–38; roles of, 99–104; textile industry and, 76, 79; voting rights for, 103, 143. *See also* Housework
Women's Christian Temperance Union (WCTU), 161–62, 166, 185, 236
Woodward, Mary Dodge, 112
Woolworth's Store, 167
Worcester, Massachusetts, 241–42
Work day: eight hour, 178–79; ten hour, 84–85
Working class, 105–6, 158; children of, 126–29. *See also* Unions
Working Girl's Clubs, 237–38
Workingman's Party, 68
Working outside the home, 116–18
World affairs, 2–5
World's Columbian Exposition (1893), 40–42, 114, 191, 193
World's Fairs, 191
The World (newspaper), 3
Wright, Carroll D., 158

Yekl (Cahan), 25
Yellowstone National Park, 50
Younger, Thomas, 56

About the Authors

JULIE HUSBAND is Assistant Professor of English at the University of Northern Iowa, Cedar Falls.

JIM O'LOUGHLIN is Assistant Professor of English at the University of Northern Iowa, Cedar Falls.